THE YOUTH GROUP HOW-TO BOOK

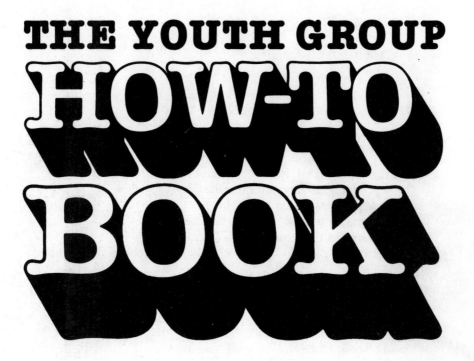

THE YOUTH GROUP HOW-TO BOOK

Copyright © 1981 Thom Schultz Publications, Inc.

Fourth Printing

Library of Congress Catalog No. 81-81966

ISBN 0936-664-03-7

CREDITS

Art
Rand Kruback: 12, 20, 35, 55, 113, 168
Laurel Watson: cover, 98, 99, 127

Photography
Bob Combs: 66, 97
Paul Conklin: 28, 43, 213
Lois Duncan: 96
Fellowship of Christian Athletes: 85, 86
Berne Greene Ltd.: 60
Rick Kotter: 76
Robert Maust: 58
Richard Nowitz: 135
John Paul: 144, 146, 147
Charles Quinlan: 196
Rising Hope: 36, 39, 42, 82, 214, 222
Schwinn: 192, 194
Thom Schultz: 23, 24, 25, 26, 27, 58, 61, 63, 76, 91, 111, 115, 116,
120, 123, 125, 128, 131, 132, 134, 140, 148, 150, 151, 160, 170, 171,
172, 178, 197, 198, 199, 200, 202
Ben Smith: 50, 75
Lee Sparks: 43, 89, 187, 216
David Strickler: 15, 16, 19, 46, 47, 49, 52, 73, 78, 110, 111, 112,
152, 153, 167, 185
Leo Symmank: 172
Bob Taylor: 34, 44, 72, 92, 188
UPI: 58, 59
Jim Whitmer: 10, 69, 81, 96, 137, 207, 221
World Vision: 102, 107, 109

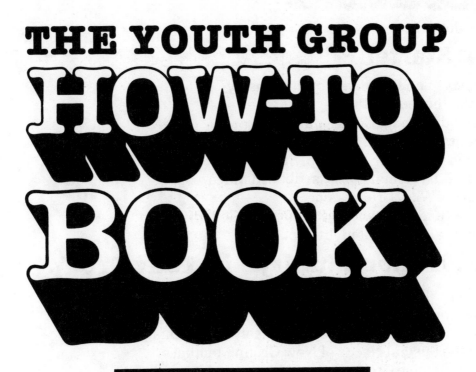

THE YOUTH GROUP HOW-TO BOOK

66 Practical Projects and
Programs To Help You Build
A Better Youth Group

Edited by Lee Sparks
Designed by Laurel Watson

group BOOKS

P.O. Box 481
Loveland, Colorado 80537

Contents

Dare to be Creative— How to Use the Arts

Thinking Big—
How to Use Publicity and Plan Big Projects

Hitting the Road—
How to Take a Group Trip

Fine Tuning for Experienced Leaders

Introduction

Here is a treasure of 66 "nuts and bolts" ideas and guidelines for your local youth ministry's programs, activities and projects.

The Youth Group How-to Book is a thoughtful collection of goodies from seven years of GROUP, the interdenominational magazine for Christian youth groups. The various authors of these "how-to" ideas represent the combined "field" experience of decades. The volume's purpose is to help both professional and volunteer youth leaders with their ongoing planning for youth ministry. These "how-to" suggestions are designed to be easily plugged-in to local youth groups. Feel free to adapt, change and add to these ideas to make them tailor-fit your group.

These 66 chapters are grouped into eight progressive sections. The initial sections deal with the more basic aspects of youth ministry. Succeeding sections describe more challenging (and fruitful) opportunites for young people and leaders. Here are some details about each section:

"How do we get started?"
The first section offers basic guidelines of youth ministry, such as crowd breakers, leadership models, sponsors, games and attendance builders. These activities build interest and enthusiasm in new programs or rekindle older ones.

"After the fun stuff gets the kids to the meeting, how do we mold the group into a Christian community?"
Section two includes several ideas to move your group beyond surface relationships to agape fellowship. Here you'll get lots of suggestions on how to build group trust, unity, acceptance, communication and values. Also, we'll offer three program ideas to help your youth experience cults, old-age and group potential.

"We would like to go on a retreat. How do we plan and do it?"
Retreats provide excellent opportunities for intensive community-building among your group. Jesus and his disciples often went away from the crowds into the wilderness for special times of fellowship and learning. Section three begins with a general article on how to plan retreats, including ten examples. A variety of specific retreats ranging from self-identity to fishin' should help your group get some ideas for its future retreat adventures.

"Our group has a lot of fun and has come closer together. But we would like to start doing things for others. Any ideas?"
More successful youth programs balance three important dimensions of the Christian life: fun, fellowship, mission. The fourth section offers some tips for your group's mission to show the love of Christ to others. The first three articles deal with service through worship. The remaining ones show your group ways to serve others, ranging from workcamps to Christmas season activities. We think your group, through giving itself to others, will experience a special kind of joy.

"Our group activities are always the same. How can we be more creative?"

Section five challenges your group to free its God-given talent of imagination. Here are ideas on how to use both the more common media (banners, puppets, mime) and the more exotic media (radio, cassettes, clowns, even filming your own candid camera shows). These chapters should help to release your group's creativity.

"Our group would like to try some big projects, but we don't even know how to begin. How do we publicize our stuff? How do we launch big projects?"

The bigger you think, the better for your group. Section six shows your group how to use publicity, newsletters and the mail. It also has big ideas for fund raising, bus recycling and promoting Christian concerts.

"We'd like to take a trip this summer. How can we make it all that it should be?"

The group trip is indeed a powerful youth ministry tool. Often a group grows very close, both to God and to each other. Section seven shows you how to plan and take an adventure, how to save travel money, various kinds of adventures and how to put together a multimedia presentation of your trek.

"After giving and giving of myself and time, I'm ready to raise the white flag. Problems always come, some of the kids irk me and I'm exhausted. I'm burned out. How can I get fired up again?"

The high turnover rate among youth leaders (most last only about 18 months) in part reveals the burn-out most of them suffer. Some youth leaders, however, seem to experience burn-out less than others. Section eight is specifically for youth leaders. It gives helpful advice for solving problems, dealing with cliques, loving obnoxious kids, managing time and avoiding burn-out.

The Youth Group How-to Book is not the final word on the "how-to's" of youth ministry. Rather, it is a collection of some of the better articles from GROUP. They were written by folks actively engaged in youth work. They themselves have asked, "How do I. . .?" These chapters are reflections of the ways they answered the question and tested the answers with youth. It is our hope that these 66 fragments of the endless "how-to's" in youth ministry will prove as helpful to you as other youth leaders have found them.

So, here are some "how-to's." The "do's" are now up to you.

How to Get Started

Basic Aspects of Youth Ministry

Five Basics of an Effective Youth Ministry

by Lee Sparks

The first question after saying "yes" to a call of youth leadership in your congregation is "now what?" Before jumping into the water and flapping around without direction, it is better to think out some of the basics of youth ministry. Roland Martinson, dean of students at Luther-Northwest Seminaries, suggests five basics of your ministry to youth: mission, kids in their culture, leadership, frameworks and processes.

The question of mission in youth ministry is basically, "Why do youth ministry at all?" Related to that question is, "What are the goals of youth ministry?" Martinson offered some guidelines for answering questions of mission. One, believe that young people are not the church of *tomorrow*; they are to be treated as equals among the *present* body. Another is to see youth ministry as larger than programs. Youth ministry is person-centered—not only to those kids who regularly attend meetings, but also to the kids on the church's periphery.

The second basic of youth ministry is the need to learn about kids in their culture. A researcher of **Five Cries of Youth**, Martinson said a good many youth experience self-hatred, wishing they were someone else. Many youth are psychological orphans, searching for a "home" (peer groups, etc.) if the real home is broken. Most youth are idealists, seeking truth, justice and fairness. Youth want to "fit in" to the establishment, as indicated by the revival of campus Greek organizations and competition for grades and jobs. And youth seek a meaningful religious experience, searching for it in spectator sports and huge rock concerts if failing to find it in the church.

The third basic, leadership, covers all facets of this crucial need in youth ministry. The first facet encompasses the "identifiable symbols" of leadership—youth pastors, professional youth workers and volunteer adult sponsors. The second facet of leadership is the group of adults which responds to the governing body of the church. Sometimes the group is called a "youth committee" or a "youth board." This leadership group is essential for the ongoing ministry of the church to youth, since it assists the youth pastor, answers to and secures funds from the board of trustees and provides stability in shaky situations. The third facet of leadership is the group which keeps the ministry going from day to day: adults who eat in the school cafeteria, coaches, teachers and others who have almost daily contact with kids.

Frameworks for youth ministry, the fourth of Martinson's basics, refers to the places where the church should minister to kids. In worship, young people should regularly be included in music, ushering, speaking and all other lay duties. A youth group is essential to provide a community where kids can find ways of relating to one another, other than those they experience in the world. Schools, families and the streets are other frameworks for youth ministry.

The fifth basic of youth ministry is process. One process is developing and maintaining conversation with the people who are in any way involved in youth ministry, such as the senior pastor, the governing board, parents and sponsors. Another process is planning programs with the kids. Informing the congregation of current events and needs of the youth ministry is another process. Finally, an evaluative process is needed for growth and change in the church's youth ministry.

CHAPTER

2

"Breaking the Ice" at the Beginning

by John Bushman

Toni arrives at 7:20 for the evening youth get-together. She's puzzled, but no one is really doing anything. No one seems to be in charge. Instead, everyone just seems to be standing around. "I really don't know anyone in the room," she thinks. "Do I really want to stay?"

These thoughts are commonly expressed—verbally and nonverbally—by many people as they attend a beginning session.

It isn't just the first meeting of a particular group that is cause for concern. Even when almost everyone knows each other, many gatherings have problems getting started. There seems to be a definite need for some structure to get any group underway. This structure enables the group to function as a group, removing the emphasis on individual acts that tend to take away from the positive group dynamics.

What is important, then, is for the group or the group leader to structure an activity at the beginning of any meeting. These "ice breakers," as they are most commonly called, provide a structure as the beginning of an event but also help correct the uneasiness that is often found at the time a group begins its sessions.

It's important that these ice-breaking experiences create a positive atmosphere. There is a tendency to plan activities for fun and excitement, but this often happens at the expense of an individual's feelings. I have been in activities that degrade the humanness of each individual. While these activities may be fun and while there is no harm intended, I believe that they will not be a constructive influence on the group as a whole. Activities such as hitting each other with rolled-up newspapers and squirting water at each other may, indeed, break the ice of the group; they may, too, break the individual spirit of each person. It is very difficult to know the impact of such activities on young people over a long period of time.

The following activities are structured so that group members can participate to the fullest extent without experiencing the negative feelings mentioned earlier.

And, many activities can start as the group gathers, thus alleviating the problem of waiting until all are present. Some are intended to help groups get better acquainted. Others are designed simply to get the group started.

"Name Tags"

Create name tags using biblical or secular names. As participants arrive for the group activity, attach a name tag on the back of each individual's clothing. Each person is to seek his/her identity by asking others

"Breaking the Ice" CONT.

questions which can be answered with a yes or no. Each person can ask three questions of any one person. As the identities are established, participants may be seated until all have finished.

Possible biblical names: Adam, Eve, Mary, Joseph, Jesus, Thomas, Ruth, Matthew, Mark, Luke, John, Paul, John the Baptist, and Esther.

Possible contemporary names: Johnny Carson, Bob Hope, Robert Redford, Lassie, Mickey Mouse, Babe Ruth, Howard Cosell, Pete Rose, Mary Tyler Moore, Phyllis Diller, Dan Rather, Batman, Superman, Walter Matthau and George Burns.

"Names in a Hat"

This activity helps to get the members of a group at ease with one another as well as enable the members to begin learning each other's names. Participants write their names on three slips of paper and place all three in a hat. They then draw out three names (not their own) and attempt to find the people whose names they have drawn. After finding the appropriate people, participants find out three things about each of them and share this information with the entire group.

"How Are We Alike?"

This activity has as its major purpose to break the ice of the group. It is fun and certainly helps to reduce the inhibitions that frequently occur as groups get together. It is assumed that by this point the group leader knows the group and the members know each other as well. In addition, the activity serves to provide a structure for interaction among the group. Participants will need to talk to one another.

As the group assembles, the leader places members in a subgroup according to one of the following criteria:
• shoes that people are wearing—types, colors, ages, etc.
• number of letters in first name, last name
• sibling information: oldest child, youngest child, middle child, only child

You may use other sub-groupings, too.

After the subgroups are together, members discuss within each group to determine what the central mystery element is that is shared by each of them. The activity is non-threatening; participants simply have an open, free discussion in which they seek the thread that holds them together.

"25 Questions"

The following can be quite useful in getting members of a group to loosen up and feel comfortable with each other. Participants seek signatures from persons who meet the descriptions given on hand-out sheets. These statements/questions are usually quite general and can serve any group. The directions state that no more than two signatures are accepted from any one person. Possible statements include the following:
• A person who has a gold filling

• A person who has given a sermon
• A person who can recite the Twenty-Third Psalm
• A person who subscribes to GROUP
• A person who sings in the church choir
• A person who wants to teach English
• A person who lives in a split-level house
• A person who has had his/her appendix removed
• A person who has served on a policy-making board of a church
• A person who enjoys acting
• A person who has lived in a foreign country
• A person who has attended the National Christian Youth Congress
• A person who likes licorice
• A person who has been on TV
• A person who has a Snoopy bath towel
• A person who has the same number of letters in his/her name as you do
• A person who vacations out of the country
• A person who is a member of a Scout troop
• A person who has taught Sunday school
• A person who has a cocker spaniel
• A person who is reading a best seller
• A person who wants to attend a Big 8 school
• A person who likes to scuba dive
• The point of this activity is to get participants up and moving about. After the signatures have been secured, try a general discussion of the activity. Did everyone get around to ask everyone else a question? Did the group respond freely and grow a little as a group?

"Do You Know the Question to This Answer?"

This activity can be used effectively after group members are acquainted. It serves as a beginning activity—to get the group functioning as a group.

The group leader reads several *answers* and asks that members write them down on a sheet of paper. Possible answers:
• To love
• Revenge
• Anger
• A smile

The leader then asks the group to list possible questions that could go with the answers that they have written before them
Possible questions:
• What is the most important teaching of Jesus?
• What do I feel when someone hurts me?
• What do I feel when someone abuses an animal?
• What should you give a sad person?

To begin the sharing, the leader reads an answer and the group members share their questions that they have written down. A discussion of the responses follows.

These are but a few of the many activities that can help groups break the ice. They are fun and positive. They help to loosen up the group but still offer structure to get things started. Use them and have fun.

Finding and Keeping Good Adult Sponsors

by Lee Sparks

WANTED: People in the congregation who will not take the "job" of adult sponsor, but rather the opportunity of making a difference in young persons' lives, a difference for Christ.

This brief essay will cover the characteristics of good adult sponsors, how to recruit them, how to train them, identifying their responsibilities and supporting them.

Finding and Keeping Good Adult Sponsors CONT.

Characteristics

Dying are the days when the "ideal" youth minister is a bright, fair-haired young man fresh out of seminary, armed with flashy ideas. All kinds of people are going into youth ministry. The same is true about volunteer sponsors. Any beliefs about the "perfect" sponsor are also dying. Youth ministry needs many kinds of sponsors.

Larry Richards, noted youth ministry expert, was interviewed by GROUP about the character traits needed for a good youth sponsor. Here are some ideas.

First, a sponsor should have a solid faith in Christ. This may seem more than obvious. But a faith that is solid is mature. Youth sponsors must have a mature faith, not to act as a bastion from which to instruct the kids, but to act as a foundation and a context. A sponsor should have a solid commitment to the church as well. He or she should not see youth work as the most important part of the church's ministry, but rather in the context of the whole church. No service function of the church should take precedence over the total mission of the church. Youth sponsors should see their work in light of the total mission.

Part of a sponsor's commitment of faith is his or her willingness to grow spiritually. A good sponsor is always developing and learning new wonders of the Christian faith. Other adults in group Bible studies, adult fellowships, etc., are needed to keep a balanced faith. A stagnant person can be sensed in a moment by young people.

A second characteristic of a good sponsor is a willingness to develop significant relationships with young people, both as a group and individually with as many as possible. A youth sponsor should be a friend. This does not mean a sponsor should be just another pal or chum of a kid. A sponsor's relationship with a youth group should not snap on 20 minutes before a group meeting and then off 20 minutes after it ends. Sponsors need to develop friendships outside of formal meetings. But there is no guarantee for success in friendship relationships, so don't force them. As with any relationship, becoming a friend to youth takes some time. The willingness, however, should be there all the time.

Among the congregation is often the mindset that youth sponsors need to be young—typically a good-looking married couple in their twenties. In many ways, congregations look almost naturally to these external circumstances and try to shop around for adult sponsors as they would for watermelons. The problem is that prospective youth sponsors cannot be thumped or squeezed or judged by how ripe they are. Perhaps that 60-year-old widow may be more effective in enabling young people to grow spiritually and developing friendships than Punch and Judy Young Married Couple, who look "beautiful" and full of energy.

Recruitment

Recruiting good adult sponsors is a tricky matter. Opinions differ on the bureaucratic techniques to get them. Some congregations use the church board to select them. In other churches the decision is purely the pastor's. Regardless of the techniques, the church should be careful not to institutionalize the role of an adult sponsor. It should not be viewed as a job that needs to be done in a one- or two-year term of office.

Youth pastors usually have a good "feel" about persons in the congregation who might be good sponsors. Usually a good process is to actively seek out those who might be good. Sometimes adults will volunteer. But not all volunteers are fit to serve.

Informal interviews might be arranged with prospective sponsors. It will be during this time that the youth pastor will check out the hopeful sponsors to see if they are spiritually growing and willing to develop friendship relationships with kids. Search out hidden agendas at this time. Do they want to work with youth or do they need to be pastored themselves? Are they willing to devote sufficient time and energy to the church's ministry with youth?

Also check out the feelings of your youth group about the prospective helper. If your members don't want him or her you might be in for unneeded trouble. You may want to bring the adult before the group for an interview. You might bring the adult to a group meeting and explain to the group that he or she is thinking about becoming a sponsor and would like to check out the scene first. Give both the youth and the prospective sponsor a chance to get to know each other before making a decision.

Obviously, the best training is experience. The sponsors should constantly be evaluating themselves.

Responsibilities

The most important responsibility of the youth sponsor is to be there for the young people. This means being at every meeting and every special event, such as fund raisers, camps, etc. Building relationships is crucial. To do this, sponsors must take time and be there for everything, not simply as a representative stuck in the role of a youth sponsor.

Support of the youth program is another responsibility. The sponsors should identify their goals with the group's goals. They should act as a bridge of communication to members in the church who may misunderstand what the group is doing.

Never take sides in conflicts. Sponsors should act as a "middleman" between the young person and his parents, between the youth pastor and other church staff, between the church and the youth of the church. A youth sponsor should support the group, but never take up arms and damage relationships within the body of Christ.

Try not to set limits on their term of service. Youth sponsors should see their position as something they are, not what they do, nor what their role is. "The base question is, 'Am I a person interested in kids?' If you are, you don't sign up to be interested for a year. It's being who you are," said Richards.

Support

It is no secret that youth sponsors do not serve very long. Of course there are the obvious reasons for dropping out: The young married couple suddenly becomes a young family; the corporation transfers the sponsor; the adult sponsor finds he or she isn't cut out for youth work.

What about those ex-sponsors whose families remain stable, who aren't transferred by the corporation, who love youth work, but leave anyway? The cause often can be directly related to the church's leadership. Hoards of sponsors leave youth work for reasons of lack of support from the youth minister, the senior pastor, the church board, or the "shakers and movers" of the congregation. Sometimes there is even a coalition of all or some of the above, either actively "doing in" a sponsor or failing to support him or her.

As youth ministers or lay youth leaders, it is in everybody's best interests for you to support, encourage and even defend your sponsors. Keep lines of communication open. When a problem comes up, deal with it with courage. Do not sacrifice sponsors for political ends.

The key in all of this is to be friends to your sponsors as well as to your kids. Develop personal friendships with the sponsors. Have them over for dinner. Enjoy entertainment activities together. The more you share with the sponsors, the more they'll give to the youth program.

Training

Richards says the training of a sponsor often results in learning how to play a role, which is damaging to relationships with kids. "I would rather have a lot of simple friendship relationships between adults and kids than sometimes what happens with the sponsor structure," he said. Many of these relationship-destroying roles are working presently within youth groups. For example, there is the "control" role. "If you say to your sponsors, 'Okay, it's your job to get kids out to meetings, organize the programs, etc.,' you're programming the sponsors to be responsible for the behavior of the young people," he said. "When you do that you force the adult into an authority role which is very destructive to relationships." A friend does not control another. Rather, he tries to be helpful and to care. A sponsor must earn respect, not demand it, from the kids.

Another example is the "pal" role. The sponsor is forced into a smiling "good ol' buddy." This is destructive to relationships because an adult is not a peer. To be a pal is to try the impossible game of being just like the kids.

In training, then, encourage the sponsors to be themselves. Allow plenty of meetings where the new sponsor gets to know the kids and vice versa. Ease them into the group. Don't splash.

Some denominations have resources and materials available from district and national offices for training youth sponsors. You might want to check these out. Encourage your sponsors to attend youth leadership workshops and seminars.

Six Leadership Models for Groups

by Thom Schultz

Good youth groups have good leadership. But there's no single master leadership plan that works for all groups.

Every group is different—and that means different styles of leadership will be needed. Even within the same group, different leadership structures may be needed as the group itself evolves and matures.

All of the leadership models on these pages are intended for groups where the adult sponsors are willing to allow the youth themselves to make important decisions affecting the group.

These leadership models are certainly not the only ways to structure a group. Look through these ideas—choose, throw out, and combine them to build the best kind of structure for your group.

PRES.—V.P.—SEC.—TREAS.

This is the traditional structure for a countless variety of clubs, as well as for youth groups. The group as a whole nominates and then elects a president (in charge of coordinating all group matters), a vice president (helps president and fills in when the president is away), secretary (takes care of correspondence and record-keeping), and treasurer (cares for group's money and fund raising). Adult sponsors work closely with the four elected officers, and particularly with the president.

ADVANTAGES: This is a well known system, easily understood by all members. There are clear lines of authority; everyone knows who to contact concerning various youth group business.

DISADVANTAGES: Many members may see this system too much like other school clubs—perhaps a popularity contest. This structure is dependent upon the president to share responsibilities. If he is too strong or too weak, this greatly affects the rest of the group.

ONE LEADER [DEMOCRATIC]

Democracy is the focal point of this structure. One leader is elected by the entire group. This leader then serves the group by presenting it with all decision choices. The leader has no more decision-making power than any other member. All decisions are discussed in the total group, then voted upon by the total group. All group projects are carried out by the whole group. In this system, adult sponsors would offer support and guidance to the total group.

ADVANTAGES: A good system for groups of 20 or fewer. This structure works well for groups with a clearly defined, mostly unified, set of values. It offers a high level of involvement by the members. Freedom of expression is encouraged.

DISADVANTAGES: A true democracy often discourages the minority voice. If the majority always gets its way, those in the minority opinion may drop out due to frustration. This system is very inefficient for large groups. The discussions necessary for even small decisions may go on forever.

ONE LEADER [REPUBLICAN]

One well-accepted member is elected by the group to do almost all decision-making and delegating of duties. The leader or president hears the opinions of the group, but may make decisions that are contrary to the will of the majority of the group. The group at large looks to the adult sponsors to work closely with the single leader and "keep him in line" if necessary.

ADVANTAGES: This system is designed for large groups where individual involvement from every member is not possible. This plan offers the opportunity to take into consideration the needs of the minority voice. The single leader can delegate some decisions and authority, which helps to train new leaders.

DISADVANTAGES: Too much dependence and trust is required of the leader. This system is very subject to the leader's strengths and weaknesses.

PRESIDENT WITH COMMITTEES

This features a central leader and an assortment of sub-leaders serving in specific areas of interest or ability. Standing committees handle separate tasks such as fund raising, the group newsletter, worship, refreshments, etc. The president and the chairman of each standing committee are elected by the total group. Members may serve on one or more committees. Adult sponsors work closely with the president and, when necessary, with particular committee heads.

ADVANTAGES: Many, if not all, members become involved under this system. Leadership and responsibility opportunities are spread widely. This structure encourages the use of special talents and abilities. "Popularity contests" are less likely.

DISADVANTAGES: The president must be a skillful organizer of personnel; committees must be coordinated. Committees may become unaware of the total group's needs or wishes.

AD HOC COMMITTEES

This system handles things as they arise. As a need or duty becomes apparent, a committee is formed to accomplish the task. Separate committees may handle a fund raiser, a retreat, a worship service, a series of weekly meetings, etc. Adult sponsors are relied upon to oversee the ongoing, week-to-week operating of the group, and to support and guide the various temporary committees.

ADVANTAGES: The prospect of working with a temporary committee on a particular project is appealing to many members. This allows a member to be involved in a variety of work. Special interests and minority voices can find satisfaction.

DISADVANTAGES: Perhaps no one will get things going. Committee decision-making may be slower than with an individual leader. No youth representatives are a part of the long-range planning for the group.

STEERING COMMITTEE

This is government by coalition. A group of three to nine youth (depending upon the size of the total group) is in charge of leadership for the group—somewhat like a city council or a school board. The steering committee is elected by the total group. No one member of the steering committee has more power than another. The steering committee has the right to make decisions for the group at large. Adult sponsors in this system work with the steering committee, often sharing sensitive problems with these few rather than exposing the problem to the whole group.

ADVANTAGES: The burden of responsibility is not placed on one person, but on several. The talents, abilities and opinions of several members can be brought together as one decision-making unit. This system allows for "brainstorming"—a very creative process.

DISADVANTAGES: The steering committee may become a clique, and may become insensitive to the needs of the group. The total group may feel ineffective in directing the course of the group.

CHAPTER

5 Simulation Games Worship, Study, Fe

by Dennis Benson

Two angry lovers can be seen in the distance. He is waving his arms in exaggerated gestures. She turns her back on him and seems to be weeping. While they are seriously working through some difficulty, from where we stand, it looks like melodrama being performed by two immature people. They are playing what the late psychologist, Eric Berne, has

called emotional "Game."

The young men and women on one side of the line gather in a huddle. Joe draws a play on the ground with his finger. "Annie will run out toward the oak tree and then cut back for the pass." They line up and prepare for the snap of the ball. They are playing a recreational or sports game.

RAND KRUBACK

The teenagers gather in the circle. They take turns finding another person to hook arms and swing around in company to the cadence sung by the leader. There is much laughter as the visitors to the mental institution freely play with the residents in this event. They are participating in a "New Games" non-competitive experience where fellowship and fun are the focus.

It is a heavy afternoon. The small groups of adults and young people have been placed in small plastic bubbles made from construction plastic and supported by fans. They are following the instructions of "Ralph." This voice computer tells them that they are the only living survivors of a nuclear accident. They must create a new world as if the persons in each bubble

Simulation Games CONT.

were the last living people. The last unemotional voice transmission has been the hardest. "I have computed that there is not enough air in your environment for the number of inhabitants in your survival shelter. Someone will have to leave. Decide how you will select this person. Then this person will be released from your shelter to his or her death."

After a few minutes one lady in the shelter volunteers to leave. "You don't know this, but I have cancer and the doctor says that I do not have long to live. I am willing to leave the shelter." There is a moment of stunned silence. Then another lady reaches over and touches her. "I had cancer five years ago. I beat it. I think that you should stay and we will pray for you now." They pray. These folks are playing a simulation game.

There are many games and many ways of combining play with life. We have done it all our lives. Many believe that those days around the old Monopoly board established reality of adulthood. Many youth groups are finding that games add a great deal to the life of their worship, study, fellowship and outreach.

Worship. One group presented its youth service using a simulation about the trial of Jesus as the sermon. The worshippers were asked to be the jury. The cases for and against Jesus were presented. The congregation was encouraged to ask questions of the lawyers. Ballots were then cast.

Study. This is probably the most frequent setting for simulation games. The hunger focus has utilized this kind of game as a learning experience. There have been many variations on the hunger meal where the guests are given portions according to the world distribution of food. Fasting over a 24-48 hour period has been combined with study to help youth get in touch with the realities of this frightening problem.

Fellowship. The recreation life of your group may be one of the most important socializing aspects of your time together. In the past, the free time on retreats and Sunday night programming has been seen as an escape from the "hard" content stuff. Yet, New Games and other approaches suggest that fun and community building are really part of our faith development. For instance, a group in Australia has taken an old army custom called "dead ants" and built a strange, but special game. It seems that during the war when a group of flyers was gathered in a bar, someone would yell, "Dead ants!" and everyone would fall to the floor. The last man down would pay for the refreshments. Grant Nichol and his kids have transformed that game into an important fellowship event. Sometime during the evening Grant will cry out, "Dead ants!" The last couple kids down will wash the dishes. However, it has now become a trademark for the group's unity when they go to conventions and rallies.

Grant will give the call and all of his kids will fall to the floor with their hands and legs in the air.

Outreach. The games of clowning have been some of the most important ways a group of youth can reach out to the world. For instance, Pauline Hubner and her folk have worked in shopping centers during the Christmas holidays. The group of 40 stage an experience of games with the huge crowd and then offer each person a card that simply says, "Keep Hoping." Each card has a bright flower glued to it. They gave away 12,000 cards last year! The responses were amazing. Some folk cried when they were given this simple gift.

It is true that these simple examples cross over from one kind of setting to another. The joy of gaming in all its facets puts us in touch with the childlike quality of life. I know that everyone tells us to grow up. Yet Jesus was serious when he suggested that we must know the childlike qualities in order to enter the Kingdom of God.

There are many books on gaming, kits and other materials to aid your group in using this mode of Christian experience. Yet, I would also encourage you to invent your own games. Everyone reading this chapter has vast experience playing and inventing games. You have suffered through colds or the measles playing imaginary simulations. Every Christmas in your early life presented you with boxed games.

I encourage you to take this vast experience and apply it to the gaming approach the next time you are planning a retreat or a Sunday night program. There are just a couple steps you might take in this process:

1. Use four to eight people in the planning session.
2. Focus on a theme or learning that you want to explore (hunger, forgiveness, loneliness, etc.).
3. Decide how long you have to play the game.
4. Encourage ideas on how you can simulate (make like reality) a situation in which people will have to experience the problems of the theme.
5. Build in enough time for a full debriefing after the experience. This may mean more time than you took to play the game.

There is no magic in creating and playing games. They really come from biblical parable genre. The only difference between the gaming way and reading way of approaching this material is that the gaming way asks you to crawl inside.

I am encouraging you to see this approach to your Christian life together as being very possible and very exciting. Plunge ahead and use the insights and experiences you already have. The nice thing about the gaming approach for Christians is that it forces us to face areas of concern directly. A Christian can never stand back and just think about things. Christ compels us to put on the cares and needs of those around us. The gaming approach helps us become more directly involved. In gaming, *you're it*.

How to Build a Human-size Cardboard Maze

by Thom Schultz

What do you think of when someone mentions a maze? Something to put an educated mouse in? Something you and your pencil would fight your way through while waiting in the dentist's office?

Well, you may still enjoy those little mazes on paper. But wait till you've tried to find your way through a life-size maze! Crawling on hands and knees through total darkness, running into dead ends, bashing into an unseen friend, listening to the terrified screams of another friend in the dark, trying seemingly endless new routes in an attempt to discover the one and only way out—all these crazy experiences and more are yours when your group decides to build a cardboard maze.

This wild project works especially well for special meetings where you hope to attract many new kids.

You'll need to set up a committee of a few maze builders. This group should be kept small because you'll want to keep the design and solution to the maze a secret.

Collect a couple dozen large cardboard boxes. Check with appliance stores for refrigerator, washer and dishwasher boxes.

Select a large room in your church and start designing your maze.

It's best to draw a maze diagram on paper before actually setting up the maze. Design plenty of dead ends, frequent turns, and perhaps a circular detour (some kids will go 'round and 'round, never realizing they're getting no where).

After the design of the maze is decided, put the boxes in place, putting any open ends down so you'll have solid sides and tops.

Next, following your maze diagram, cut the doorways to join boxes. You may wish to make some doorways narrower and lower than others.

Then, punch holes near each doorway. Bind adjoining boxes together by tying twine or strong string through the punched holes. It's necessary to tie the boxes together or else they'll separate while in use and create unwanted openings in your maze.

Now you should be ready. Turn out the lights. It should be totally dark inside the maze. Station a couple of your maze-makers outside the maze to watch for any problems, and to scream and pound on top of the boxes as your terrified members grope around inside in the darkness. Also place one or two maze-makers inside the maze with flashlights to handle unforeseen problems and also to scare visitors. These people may want to wear masks or hairy gloves to add a little fright.

Start members through the maze one at a time. And, do not allow too many people in the maze at once or you'll wind up with a hopeless traffic jam. Have refreshments waiting for those who successfully find their way to the exit.

CHAPTER 7

THUMPER

A Wild, Crazy Game

by Thom Schultz

Everyone sits in a circle. Each person must determine a "sign." The sign can be almost anything. It could be a yawn. It could be a kick. It could be a little dance.

After the signs have been chosen, each person gives a little demonstration of his sign for the rest of the members to see and remember.

You're now ready to commence with Thumper competition.

The game begins with all members slapping their knees gently, alternating left and right slaps. Then a selected leader says, "What's the name of the game?" And all participants say, "Thumper!" The leader then asks, "How do you play?" Everyone says, "Thump!"

Then the leader gives his own sign, then does the sign of someone else in the circle. Now, the person possessing that sign just performed by the leader, must do his own sign—then someone else's. And so on.

You must always first perform your own sign—then immediately perform another person's sign.

Meanwhile the other members continue to "thump" with their hands on their knees.

When someone fails with any phase—he's out of the game. If he fails to see or hear his sign performed— he's out. If someone fails to do his own sign before presenting another person's—he's out. If someone can't remember another person's sign, and does not immediately perform it—he's out.

And it's not as easy as it sounds. A rapid Thumper game can leave your head swimming while signs go flying across the circle with lightning speed.

Whenever anyone messes up and goes out, the leader starts the game anew with the question, "What's the name of the game?"

When a person goes "out," he does not leave the circle—but stays and continues to "thump" with his hands. This adds a bit more complexity to the game, because any participant who now forgets which members are "out" may try to give the "out's" sign. Anyone who gives the sign of a person who is "out," goes out himself.

The game continues until only one or two or three people remain eligible.

After all of your members become experts at Thumper, the game may tend to run a little slowly. You may then wish to switch to the "Revised Standard Version" of Thumper.

Thumper is weird. But it's that quality that makes it so fun. Thumper is a group game that relies on each member's creativity, alertness and personal weirdness. Here's how to play.

In R.S.V. Thumper, you must first perform the sign of the person from whom you received your sign—then do your own sign, and finally do the sign of another person.

The R.S.V. adds a good deal of confusion.

Perhaps the greatest joy of Thumper comes when you play the game in the presence of other people who have no knowledge of this strange game. For a good laugh, take Thumper to your next regional retreat or rally.

Try to imagine what all of this would look like to a newcomer: A group of kids is sitting on chairs arranged in a circle. They all begin batting their knees with their hands. Some guy yells, "What's the name of the game?" The group responds, "Thumper!" The guy yells, "How do you play?" The kids yell, "Thump!"

Then the guy pulls on his ear lobe, then stands up and yawns. A girl on the other side of the circle stands, yawns, and says, "Boop!" Some other guy says, "Boop!" and joins his hands above his head, roars like a lion, and says, "M-G-M presents. . ." A girl does the same thing with her hands and says, "M-G-M presents. . .underarms!" And some guy across the circle laughs, and yells back, "Underarms!" and then grunts, "Taste good," rubbing his stomach. Another guy says, "Taste good," and then does a dandy imitation of a person with a bad case of hiccups. Then a girl begins with the hiccups and lets loose with a Porky Pig imitation, "D-d-d-d-d-dats all folks!" Another girl does the same imitation, then stands and yawns.

To newcomers, the game appears to be sort of organized, despite the outbursts of laughter. Some of the laughter was born out of the strange combinations of signs and various dramatics of the participants. Other laughter comes when participants observe the bewildered looks on the faces of the newcomers.

Then, for added fun, invite the newcomers to join you. They're usually a little hesitant, but coax them into it. They'll say, "But I don't know how to play!" Tell them it doesn't matter. Sit them down, and ask, "What's your sign? Then, whatever they do, take that as their sign. Some may say, "I don't know." You then exclaim, "Good!" and imitate their "I don't know" sign, hamming it up a bit. When you ask another newcomer for his sign he may innocently reply, "Aquarius," or something like that—usually providing a big laugh for all.

If your group has an occasional taste for the weird, you may find Thumper to be very addicting.

Okay, raise your hand if you've ever been kidnapped by a big gorilla. I doubt too many hands just went up. But that's good. That means the stunt I'm going to tell you about is so unusual that it'll be talked about and remembered for years.

Building Attendance w

Imagine this: you're sitting at home watching the Sunday Night Movie. You've just taken off your shoes and socks and you're nibbling on a root beer Popsicle. Behind you, you hear a strange grunt. For a minute you think it's your dad moaning about your failure to use Odor-Eaters. Then, all of a sudden, you're grabbed from behind by a huge, hairy hand. And, before you know it, you're being carried through the house by a big, black, ugly gorilla. You scream for your dad to save you, but he's collapsed on the couch in gales of laughter.

The big ape runs out the door and dumps you in the back of a van, which is full of kids who are laughing loudly. But as soon as they catch their breath, they greet you with warm words and reassuring pats on the back. You're feeling a little better, but a little more confused as the van pulls away from your house.

This experience is called a Gorilla Kidnap. Its purpose? To introduce new kids to your group.

Every group knows of many kids who would really benefit from the group, but who never come—even after repeated invitations, postcards, and phone calls. Well, the Gorilla Kidnap may be just what you need.

Gorilla Kidnapping is so wild and so fun (for everyone involved) that the new kids really forget all the reasons they had for ignoring your group. And, if your regular members show the kidnappees some warmth

26

and Christian love, you stand a good chance of gaining some new members.

Preparation

First, your group must be committed to the idea of reaching out for new members. Make a list of all the kids who you'd like to see become involved in the life of your group.

Decide upon a date for your Gorilla Kidnap.

Check with the nearest costume rental company for availability and rental charge for a full gorilla costume. The outfit usually includes suit, full pullover mask, hands and feet. If your nearest costume house is quite a distance from you, you can usually arrange to have the costume shipped to you by mail or bus.

The parents of those who are to be kidnapped must be notified in advance. Explain the whole caper to them and get their permission to barge into their houses on Kidnap Night. Also, ask them to keep their kids at home that night. But, it's very important that the parents understand this is to be a surprise—they must not give a clue to their kids about what is to take place.

Next, each member in your group should select one kid on the kidnappee list to "adopt." In this way, your members make sure each kidnappee is made to feel welcome. Throughout the Kidnap Night, your "sponsor" members should remain with the kidnap-

h a Kidnapping Gorilla

by Thom Schultz

pees, showing them around, and introducing them.

Select one of your members or leaders to be the gorilla. Pick someone strong.

You'll also need to line up a van (without seats) or a panel truck. These are best because they add to the flavor of a real kidnapping. But, a bus or cars will work also.

Kidnap night

Load all your members into your van or vans and take off to your first victim's house. The gorilla should hide near the door. The sponsor member for this kidnappee should ring the doorbell. If the kidnappee answers the door, the sponsor member should smile, say hello and give a subtle signal to the gorilla to attack.

If someone other than the kidnappee answers the door, your sponsor member should find out where the kidnappee is, then lead the gorilla in for the attack.

The gorilla should grunt and roar and really play it up as he grabs the victim and takes him/her to the van.

Don't be surprised if your victim becomes extremely frantic at the sight of the gorilla. Some victims will try to run and some even lock themselves in the bathroom. Some friendly persuasion from the sponsor member may be necessary in that case.

Once in the van, your sponsor member should introduce the kidnappee.

After all of your victims have been picked up, drive to your church or other meeting place for refreshments and a get-acquainted time. Do some mixers that help everyone learn names and faces. Perhaps you'll want to play a couple of games. Then, be sure to explain to the kidnappees your group's purpose, meeting times and upcoming special activities.

Allow enough time to drive all your victims home again.

Follow-up

A Gorilla Kidnap may be meaningless unless you take the time to carefully follow-up.

Sponsor members, during the following week, should each be sure to call or visit their kidnappees—to show concern and to invite them to your next meeting.

And you, adult leaders should send a personal letter to all kidnappees, thanking them for being good sports and inviting them to future group meetings and activities.

The kidnappees should also be asked to keep quiet about their experience, so their friends can be surprised on a future Kidnap Night. I guess keeping everybody quiet is the hardest part of this prank. I know that the story of our Kidnap Night raced all through our area high schools the following day.

We just denied the story as a malicious rumor.

Fundamentals of an All-night Lock-in

by Rickey Short

For a great change-of-pace, why not try an all-night lock-in? Your young people will get to know each other in ways they never realized.

This dusk-to-dawn extravaganza mixes games, foolishness, Bible study, discussion—well, almost anything you want to plan. If planned well, a lock-in can become a high point of your summer (or fall or winter or spring) youth program. Whether you schedule a mixture of serious and fun times or whether you plan to skate all night, several basic techniques can increase your lock-in's effectiveness.

The *purpose* of your all-night event, the *planning* and the *preparation* will all affect the lock-in's *performance*. An all-night lock-in involves the total person on the physical, mental, emotional, social and spiritual levels. Everything that happens affects someone on one of these levels.

Because the lock-in is a time of total involvement it becomes a time of high risk for failure by the youth group. Stress, fatigue, and social factors affect activities that would be successful in a normal two-day retreat or a daytime mini-retreat. These different factors will not necessarily cause a good program to fail, but they may produce a lack of motivation to get involved in an activity which seems much less exciting at 5 a.m. than at midnight.

Why risk the failure? Because the chance for success is equally high. Fatigue does wonders in lowering a person's personality defenses (not to mention a clique's defense mechanisms). Youth who are just "speaking friends" will build a bond of friendship after 12 hours of shoulder-to-shoulder, eyeball-to-eyeball interaction.

There is an old saying that you should not marry a person until you have seen your prospective spouse with a bad cold or sick with the flu. There is a "knowing" and "being known" that comes out of being bone tired. Discussions and openness take on new dimensions when the makeup begins to wear off and cute interpersonal techniques wear out.

The following tips can help you increase the potential for success.

Fundamentals of an All-night Lock-in CONT.

Tips for planning

Begin planning well in advance of when it seems most likely that you could schedule a lock-in. Two or three months are usually required. You will need to meet with different committees three or four times to check up on how programs and preparations are progressing. The committees must have their different programs clearly in mind by the last planning session. There are no exceptions. Plan well and plan in detail if you want a successful lock-in.

Determine the purpose first

It may not be easy to get the entire youth group to discuss and determine why you want to have a lock-in. Some will want the overnighter because it was done before or because another group in town had one. The "Why are we doing this?" should be clear to everybody before any lock-in plans are made. The time you've spent in answering this question will bear fruit at the lock-in when someone asks, "What are we supposed to be doing here anyway?"

Drafting a statement of purpose may seem unnecessarily time consuming, but it will bring into focus much of what you plan to do and how it is to be done.

If one goal for your lock-in is to attract other teens to your youth group, you will want to advertise like crazy. If you want to experience and develop a small intimate fellowship, do no advertising except to let the parents and church leaders know your plans.

Seven Important Planning Areas

Recreation. Energetic and fast-paced recreation times can provide a positive contribution to your lock-in. Determine who will be in charge of the recreation and sport times. Ask the planning team to develop a program the planning committee can discuss. The key is to have a well-prepared outline of games, skits and strenuous physical sports. Explanations of how to play new games should be thought out and any materials needed for the recreation time should be secured well in advance. Have all the things you need at the lock-in site a day early.

Balance recreation time with worship and spiritual programs. Balance new games with old favorites everybody knows how to play. Balance competitive games with non-competitive games. Balance skill games with non-skill games.

Use physical activity to stimulate and create energy in the early morning hours. Use table games, crafts and fun songs to fill free time or to make transition to other programs on the agenda.

How about free time? It is better not to fill up the final hours of your lock-in with free time. If the group is tired the free time may be seen as a signal that the lock-in is over. Getting a final wrap-up session started may be impossible if kids have been dozing for an hour or more.

Food. Plan food times to follow recreation times or preceding, during and after any film you wish to show. Choose a food committee to prepare, serve and clean up after snack times. Be sure that whatever you plan to serve can be prepared in large quantities with the available facilities. A household oven will keep a lot of hamburgers or pancakes warm but it will not cook seven pizzas at once. Make arrangements so that you can serve everyone at one time.

Devotions, spiritual growth, and worship. Determine if the youth sponsors or members of the youth group will be in charge of these sessions. The atmosphere of the room sometimes plays a part in sensitive spiritual times. Setting the stage for a serious spiritual time is especially important if you have been running relays in the area you now plan to worship in.

Balance spiritual times with social and physical sports times.

Sunrise devotions seem like a natural but they may be hard to pull off effectively at the end of a lock-in. Physical fatigue becomes a competitive factor to spiritual sensitivity in the early morning hours. The peak spiritual time should come three or four hours into the lock-in while the mind is fresh and the emotions are still responsive.

Select music in advance. If you use a guitar be sure the guitarist can play the songs before the song leader teaches them to the group.

Bible studies or training programs. If your lock-in has a theme and you plan three or four sessions around that theme, you can separate each serious session with recreation, food, free time or a film. If free time precedes a serious session, be sure everyone is clear about when and where they are to meet next.

It is difficult to do serious, concentrated thinking much after 3 a.m. Plan to meet your major objectives before that time. Be creative in your teaching method and use a variety of methods to stimulate interest. If small group discussions are planned, break down into small groups by age so that the older kids will not dominate their group's discussion. If your youth group is large enough, and you have qualified leadership, you can offer optional activities during your lock-in and allow kids to choose a session that appeals to them the most.

Place a guest speaker on the program early and allow him or her to leave during a later session.

Discipline. It is impossible to come up with a set of rules that would cover every possible circumstance. It is best to keep the rules few and simple. Be specific in advertising and in prelock-in sessions about appropriate dress at the lock-in. Electronic games, radios, comic books and TVs are not a problem at a marathon rocking session, but strict controls should be placed on them at lock-ins where group and individual participation is crucial to the lock-in's success.

Telephone use should be restricted. Youth should expect to stay for the entire lock-in when they come. Check with parents if a teen must leave early.

Finances. Mention the cost in every lock-in advertisement. Plan how and when to collect money so that no one fails to pay. It is a good idea to close registration two or three days before the lock-in so that final food plans and financial arrangements can be made. If possible, collect all monies before the lock-in. This gives the teen an added incentive to come to the lock-in even though some other optional activity came up at the last minute.

Starting with a bang. What happens at the lock-in during the first hour sets the tone for the entire lock-in. Plan the first hour to involve every person. Schedule surprises to excite them about the rest of the lock-in.

Four things need to happen at the beginning of the lock-in:

1. Reduce tension and nervousness while building community. This can be done many ways but usually involves doing strange and unusual things together such as crazy songs, unusual exercises or weird games. Acting silly reduces tension and it is fun.

2. Get in touch with the overall group feelings, attitudes and expectations about the lock-in. Simple, nonthreatening questions allow people to express something about their current emotional state. (Such as: "The color I most feel like..." or "The things I hope to get out of this lock-in are...")

3. Clarify rules, purpose and schedule. Answer questions about the rules and schedule.

4. Determine teams for relay and sports events to break down existing cliques and contribute to the overall unity of the youth group. Random drawings or fun exercises help the young person identify with and belong to his or her new team. Controlling the team formations reinforces the similarities among the members in the group and allows them to discover important things about other kids in the group.

With your purpose clearly in mind and a well-planned, well-prepared program your youth group can create life-time memories—and short-term fatigue at your most successful lock-in!

How to Build "Community" in Your Group

Activities for Increasing Group Trust

by John Shaw

Do you ever wish your group were closer? Do you ever see a lack of cooperation hindering your group? Do you ever find discussions stalling because members are afraid to share their real feelings? Perhaps your group could use a little work on trust.

Trust is often the missing ingredient in group functions. Christian growth demands sharing—and sharing requires trust. People who trust each other can develop understanding and acceptance. They learn that it's okay to take risks that lead to being close to others. Trust builds bridges between persons.

Trusting our fellow Christians can also lead to deeper trust in God.

Building trust in the youth group is important. But there are no easy formulas. Trust-building is a process. It takes time. But there are activities that will help you get started.

The following activities will help your group determine the present level of trust within each person, help develop an awareness of trust within the group, and give each person an opportunity to try some trusting experiences in a controlled situation.

Choose the activities that seem best suited for your group.

Trust walk

This activity begins with the leader suggesting that members choose someone they would like to know better, or someone for whom they feel a lot of trust. The leader should then instruct the participants to concentrate on the feelings of trust or lack of trust they experience during the exercise.

Next, one person in each pair is blindfolded. His partner will lead the "blind" person around the room, building or yard, trying to help him experience as many sensations as possible, such as touching and identifying objects. Those who lead should be cautioned to assist their partner very carefully—the "blind" person must be able to trust his helper.

Very definitely, no one is to talk during the entire experience so that people can concentrate on their feelings.

After ten minutes, the pairs should switch, and the leader becomes the "blind" person.

Following the exercise, the group should talk over the feelings experienced in both positions, with specific attention to the level of trust within themselves and between each other.

Trust fall

Six people stand in two parallel rows, about three feet apart. One other group member then stands with his back to them and falls backwards into their outstretched arms. Once the person is caught, he should be lowered carefully to the floor and given a chance to concentrate on what he felt, 1) while falling, and 2) after he was caught by the other group members.

When everyone has had a chance to be caught and do the catching (although no one should be forced to take a turn), the members should share their feelings in a group discussion.

Trust talk [pairs]

Pair up with someone you can talk with. First, share something someone else did that is important to you. After both persons have shared, tell each other how you felt during the sharing. Then decide if you want to go on to the next level. If you do, tell something that you did in the past that has importance in your life. Discuss how you felt while you were sharing. Then decide if you want to go to the next deeper level. If you do, share something that is important to you right now. Discuss your feelings. If you felt comfortable sharing, consider sharing some other important things. Your level of trust is good if you can feel comfortable sharing things that are very important to you right now.

Trust talk [group]

First, decide as a group if you want to keep all information confidential. If so, each person must agree not to tell others outside the group what was shared.

Use the three levels described in the Trust Talk (Pairs) above. Open up the first level to all who want to share with the group. After everyone who wants to has shared, discuss feelings that were experienced. Consider how it felt before, during and after the sharing. Discuss whether feelings about yourself changed or about others in the group.

Have the group decide if it wants to go to the second level. If so, give everyone an opportunity to share and then discuss. What feelings were experienced? Were feelings the same as or different from the first level? Any other changes?

Have the group decide whether or not to go to the third level. If so, repeat sharing and discussion. What different feelings were experienced during the three levels? How have feelings changed? How much trust appears to be present in the group? Is there any need to develop more trust?

Trust development inventory

1. *How do you develop trust with others?* List every way you have used to develop trust. Which way works best for you now? Which way would you like to improve? Which of your friends fits best with each of the activities you use to develop trust? Write each friend's name by the activity or experience that fits best.

2. *How do you develop trust within yourself?* List what you do to build self-trust. (Practice a lot? Listen to others? Check for comfortable feelings?) Decide which two of your approaches are your best methods and place a check by each one. Identify the one on the total list you would like to improve. Place a plus by that one.

3. *What new activities can you think of that could develop self-trust and trust with others?* List activities for each category: for others and for self. Which activity would be easiest to start? Which activity could be completed the fastest? Which activity would be the most meaningful to you? Choose one of these activities to work on beginning now.

Spiritual trust inventory

Write out your answer to these questions:
1. What do you trust God to do in your life?
2. What do you trust yourself to take care of?
3. What do you trust others to do for you?
4. What changes would you like to make in each of these areas of trust?

Trust-o-gram

You'll need two sheets of paper and a pencil for each person. Take a sheet of paper and list all the people you trust, along with what you trust about them. (Their ability to drive, their willingness to keep a secret, their lasting friendship, their understanding, etc.) Then take another sheet and place an X in the center. That's you. Place the person's name you trust the most closest to the X, and the person you trust the least farthest from the X. Locate names of the others on the page to represent the degree of trust you have in each person.

When you're done, study the sheet to see if it is accurate. Then consider if there are people that you would like to trust more. List those people. Then decide what you would need to do to develop more trust with each person. Share your ideas for developing trust with the group.

Trust level

Have the group sit in a circle. Turn off the lights and have the group experience the darkness. Ask them to think about their feelings as they sit silently for a few minutes. Then ask the group to share what they are feeling while it's still dark.

After everyone who wants to has talked, turn on the lights. Ask the group to identify how they feel now and whether or not they feel differently than when it was dark. Ask them to share with the group.

After feelings have been described, discuss possible reasons for the differences in feelings. Explore areas such as the need for eye contact, self-consciousness in front of others, fear of the dark, etc.

Meaning and effects of trust

Have the group sit in a circle. Each person should have a candle. Ask members to think of what they trust about the group or what their trust of the group means to them. Turn off the lights. One person then lights his candle and shares his statement. He then lights the person's candle to the right and that person shares. Repeat this process around the circle.

A group leader can then point out how the statements of trust represented by lighting the candles combined to make the group shine brighter as each person contributed.

Then have the last person to speak blow out the candle to his left and repeat that process back around the circle until it is black.

The leader can then point out how a lack of trust can hinder the possibilities in the group, just like darkness does. Trust enables people to work together. A lack of trust prevents or slows growth and progress.

Exercises for Building Unity in Your Group

by John Shaw

Simulation games and experiences will help your group get in touch with feelings and ideas that can lead to growth and insight during your group sessions. The following activities focus on unity. Groups that can feel a deep sense of unity within members' relationships to God and each other will be able to grow and change effectively. New insights from scripture and the leading of Christ's spirit will be met more fully by strongly united groups.

Use these experiences to pinpoint where your group is with unity, and then work to increase your ability to unite in worship, service and relationships.

Each activity can be customized to meet your plans. You can do half the activity one week and after a brief rehashing, complete it the next week.

These activities can be used for regular sessions from week to week in a series, planned into your meetings at regular intervals, or set up for a retreat of one or two days. Discussion times can be adjusted to fit activities into your schedule.

Be creative and flexible, using ideas that come up during planning or while the activities are happening. Your group can discover God's creative presence more and more fully as you engage in action together.

Effects of individuals on unity

- Leadership: one designated leader for each group of up to 25 people.
- Materials: one ball of yarn containing at least 150 yards for each group of 25 people or less.
- Theme scripture: Philippians 2:1-8.

You can see the importance of individuals to group unity by creating the often-used yarn circle. Form a circle with elbows touching. The person starting the activity holds the end of the yarn and without mentioning about whom he's speaking, states a quality that a person has that contributes to the unity of the group. He then tosses the ball of yarn to that person, holding onto the loose end himself. This process is repeated, with each person holding onto the yarn and tossing the ball to another person, until everyone has been included in the yarn pattern. You can continue until you run out of yarn, if you want.

Look at the beauty of the patterns created within the circle. Then ask two or three people to let go of the yarn and step back. Point out how the absence of some people makes the patterns sag and turn ugly. Then have the group tighten up the yarn by stepping back slowly. Then ask two or three more to drop out and repeat the process. Ask the group to observe what is happening to the closeness and the patterns as more and more people drop out.

Read the theme scripture and ask the group to pick out qualities and actions that contribute to group unity. You may want to read it more than once. Discuss the scriptural suggestions that could help your group build more unity. Record the ideas for planning sessions.

Close the session with prayers thanking God for the contributions each person makes to the unity of the group and for their presence in the group.

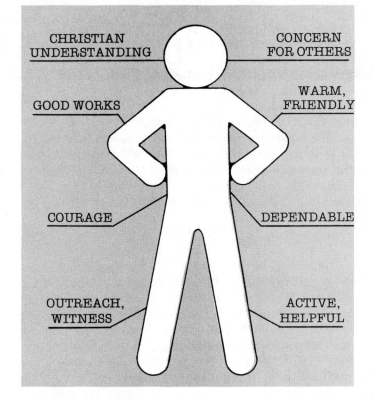

One body, many gifts

- *Leadership: one designated leader.*
- *Materials: large sheet of newsprint, posterboard or chalkboard; chalk, markers or crayons.*
- *Theme scripture: 1 Corinthians 12:4-13.*

Reproduce the body drawing (above) on a large sheet of newsprint, posterboard or a chalkboard. Have your group think about the qualities that are present in individual members of the group. After a few minutes, ask whoever is ready to start the activity by writing the name of a person in the group under one of the qualities that is noted in the drawing. The person whose name was listed then goes to the drawing and lists another person, and so on.

When everyone has been listed on the drawing, invite the group to add more names to the lists, until no more additions come up. Then, look at the chart to see where qualities need to be developed within the group. Ask for volunteers or suggestions of persons who could develop the qualities that would make the group better.

Discuss ways to develop those qualities through group programs or activities.

Close by reading the theme scripture. You can repeat this activity in three or four months to see how improvements are going.

Creating unity

- *Leadership: one designated leader.*
- *Materials: in retreat setting, explore for materials; in church building, provide your choice of materials, such as boxes, pipe cleaners, balloons, clothes hangers; also watercolors, crayons, markers, pencils, Scotch tape, rubber bands, string.*
- *Theme scripture: Ephesians 4:1-16.*

Read the theme scripture and ask the group to brainstorm ideas for creating unity in your group. If you're in an area where you could search for materials and objects, give the group 20 minutes or more to look for ways to symbolize the elements that would build unity in the group. If you're providing materials, ask everyone to choose materials to create a symbol of one element of unity.

Build a group unity sculpture by combining the individual symbols one at a time. People can add a symbol as they see a place that it would fit. As the sculpture grows, adjustments and improvements can be made until you have the finished art form. (You may need to use the string, rubber bands or Scotch tape to attach the symbols together.)

A volunteer can begin the sculpture and other symbols can be attached or placed beside it. As a symbol is added, the person should explain its meaning. After your unity sculpture is complete, discuss a title for your masterpiece and make a title sign. If you think you might want to leave the sculpture on display, create it on a table that can be moved, or in a place that will be suitable to leave it.

Discuss what thoughts people had about building unity in the group. What is necessary for unity? What would help build a feeling of unity? What might prevent unity? Does the sculpture represent your group? Is anything missing? What would God want your unity to look like?

Unity evaluation

- *Leadership: one designated leader.*
- *Materials: pencils and paper, at least three sheets per person; sealable envelopes, one for each person; chalkboard and chalk.*
- *Theme scripture: John 17:20-23.*

Give pencil and paper to each person in the group. Ask them to diagram the closeness of the group by placing X's on the paper to represent each person in the group in relation to the others. Initials placed by the X's can identify where you placed each person. (Identifying marks can be erased or marked out later.)

Exercises for Building Unity in Your Group CONT.

Tell them that their identifications of people in the group may remain confidential.

After the diagrams are complete, ask the members to place a circle or circles on the diagram to show where Christ is in the group. Positioning is important, since he could be at the center, on the edge, with some individuals and not with others, etc.

With members using their diagrams as a reference, use group suggestions to draw a diagram on the chalkboard that would represent the general feeling of the group. Disagreements on positioning of X's and circles may be settled by voting.

Read the theme scripture or have the group read it in small groups or individually. Give members a sheet of paper and ask them to list three activities that would improve the unity of the group. Ask them to list the easiest activity first and the hardest last. Then discuss what could be done to improve the unity of the group. Also, how could the group use its present unity to help others?

Give members another sheet of paper and ask them to write a prayer for the unity of the group. Give each person an envelope and ask the group to form a circle. Ask those who want to share their prayer to read it to the group. Then have everyone place his/her name on the envelope and seal it.

Take up the envelopes and store them so you can return them to the group in two or three months. At that time, you may discuss together how the unity of the group is going, according to the lists and prayers. You could again diagram the group closeness, and compare the two diagrams.

Types of unity

• *Leadership: activity organizer; discussion leader*
• *Materials: crepe paper, enough for each person to have a two-inch wide streamer long enough to reach from the center of the room to the corner of the room; Scotch tape; paper sacks of various sizes, one for each person; scissors, pencils, papers, crayons, markers [enough of these for everyone] chairs, one for each person and one extra; Bibles, one to every six people.*
• *Theme scriptures: Galatians 3:23-28; Colossians 3:12-15.*

The discussion leader may introduce the session by pointing out what follows is a way of experiencing the feelings that go along with different types of unity. Then read Galatians 3:23-28 to lead the thinking about the first activity.

The activity organizer will then ask for two or three observers who will watch and take notes for later discussion. Ask each member to take one streamer of crepe paper to use for both activities. Ask the group to

get together in a big bunch in the center of the room. Each person should hold the end of his streamer and pass the tail to those on the outside of the group so all the streamers can be wrapped around the total group, tucking the ends into the wrapping. Care should be taken to avoid breaking the streamers. When the group is all wrapped up, ask them to work together to outline the shape of a heart with folding chairs in the room, being careful not to break the group wrappings.

When the group has finished the assignments, ask them to unwrap, returning each streamer to the person holding the end. Broken streamers can be taped back together. The discussion leader then asks the group to divide into groups of six and discuss what happened. After five minutes, get the group back together and have the observers give their descriptions of what happened. Then open the discussion up for everyone. After about ten minutes, or whenever the discussion slows, start the next activity.

The discussion leader then reads Colossians 3:12-15 to start the thought processes. The activity organizer asks the group to tie one end of each streamer to a chair placed in the center of the room. (You can place a Bible on the chair for a little added symbolism.) Then ask the members to again form a heart from folding chairs, while holding one end of their streamers. The observers will again take notes for later discussion. (Pick new observers, if you like.)

When the heart is formed, ask the group to divide into groups of six and discuss for five minutes. Get everyone back together and have the observers report again. Open the discussion for everyone, and cut it off after ten minutes or when it slows down. Be sure to point out the increased freedom in the second activity because the ties were not binding people together.

The discussion leader then asks that at least one person from each group of six writes down these questions for discussion: 1. How do different types of unity affect action by a group? 2. What kind of unity fits your group best? 3. How can your group build unity? 4. What can the group do in the next three months to build unity?

Ask one person from each group of six to pick up a Bible and have the groups start their discussion by reading the two scripture passages again. Give them 15 minutes and ask that a reporter be prepared to share the group's ideas with the total group.

Share the small group ideas for about 15 minutes. Then ask the total group to pray silently about the unity of the group. After a few minutes, ask the members to maintain silence and pick a paper sack and whatever else they need from the materials to symbolize their own prayers. Suggest that they try to capture the main feeling of their prayer for the unity of the group and make the sack represent that feeling, using color, shape, words, placement, and so on.

Close the session by forming a circle around the symbols placed on a table or on the floor and offering brief prayers for the unity of the group.

Ways to Help Members Accept Themselves and One Another

by John Shaw

The quality of personal experience in your group can make or break all of your activities together. If group members can accept each other personally, projects that flop or have overwhelming success will be handled effectively. Members in the group will see that the life of the group is what happens between the members more than the planned activities of the group. Self-acceptance and accepting other people form the foundation of a good youth group. Insight into this reality will help you plan for experiences that meet the basic needs of your members.

People in your group are trying to get their heads straight about themselves. They are struggling with what or who is important to them personally. They want to know as clearly as possible if other people care personally about them. Too often, youth groups ignore these concerns or assume that doing things together takes care of the needs of persons in the group. Activity may or may not be personally enriching, depending on how direct and open the relationships are between the persons who do the activity together.

Second only in importance to loving God is the concern to ''love others as you love yourself.'' Can all of your group accept and encourage the growth and success of each of your members or are there put-downs, sarcasm, even jealousy and resentment among your members? Do some people try to control others by bossing or manipulation? Is there a scapegoat or two who always get the heat if something goes wrong? Do the less capable people in your group get help or ridicule? Loving others as you love yourself means freeing yourself to positively encourage and assist the other person in his growth and personal needs.

If you feel your group could improve its personal relations by taking seriously the basic need for acceptance, you could use a series of four experiences that focus on self-acceptance and accepting others. One evening for each experience will be needed, since it takes an hour or more to get things going, depending on the size of your group. Each evening should include three steps: (1) An introduction of the purpose of the experience with regard to the need for acceptance. The activity should then be explained and members given the chance to ask questions or respond with their concerns about the activity. Participation should be voluntary and usually people will take part when they understand fully what will happen and its purpose. (2) Then experience the activity. (3) Follow up with a discussion that gives an opportunity to share the feelings that members had while the experience was happening and the feelings of the members now that the activity has happened.

Ways to Help Members Accept Themselves and One Another CONT.

Activity number one:

Personal Ten Commandments

People have their own personal do's and don'ts. Your group members can begin feeling acceptance by sharing their personal Ten Commandments. Have the group sit in a circle if possible. You will need to give two sheets of paper and a pencil to each member. Ask them to write their ten personal commandments on the first sheet and to not sign their names. Give a few examples, such as: "I shall not cry in front of other people," "I shall not get angry," "I shall always be honest." Encourage the group to think seriously about their commandments and take as much time as they need to write them out.

After everyone is finished, take up the sheets and read each one to the group and see if they can guess who wrote that set of commandments. Do this by reading a list of commandments and then ask the members to write down on their second sheet of paper who they think owns that set of commandments, matching the name with the number. After all the commandments have been read, begin with number one and see what names were chosen for that list. (A blackboard will help with the tabulation.) When a person is matched up with a set of commandments, place the sheet in front of that person and go on to the next sheet.

After the lists have all been identified, discuss what happened. In particular, ask the group to share their feelings about the experience and what insights they had into their own lifestyle. Then, ask them to try to determine if their own commandments fit them here and now, or if some of them are old messages that don't work too well anymore. This last part could be delayed until the next meeting.

If your group is too big or parts of the experience take too much time, you can plan this exercise for two meetings by taking up all the sheets after discussing the feelings about the experience. Then, at the next meeting have each person read his or her own list and let others ask questions or make responses. After everyone has had an opportunity, discuss whether the commandments still fit.

Activity number two:

Positive and Negative Messages

It's fun, at times, to overhear people talking about you. This activity structures that kind of experience. The group sits in a circle and each person is given the opportunity to hear the group talk about him. When a person is to be talked about, he can choose to sit outside the circle with his back to the group or he can choose to sit in the middle of the circle. Encourage people to make their choice according to where they would be most comfortable. If they choose to sit inside the circle, they should keep their eyes closed and simply listen to the conversation. The group will be responsible for agreeing on three positive messages and two negative ones. Beginning with a positive message, the group will alternate between positive and negative messages. If there is disagreement about a message within the group, the message must be explained or changed until all can accept the message.

When the five messages have been completed, the person talked about can discuss the experience and his feelings while it was happening. This sharing should be completely voluntary. If a person would rather wait or not share at all, the group should respect his choice and move on to the next person. After everyone has had his turn, the total group can discuss the total experience. Since there were both positive and negative messages, the group will need to determine the effect of each. It can be reassuring to know the negative feelings others have about you do not keep them from accepting you. The group should work to make clear its acceptance of each person, even though there are some things people don't like. It is also a relief to know that everyone has negative messages as well as positive ones. The positive messages should also be emphasized, since a lot of people discount their own good points and have trouble accepting the good feelings others have about them.

Activity number three:

Who I Would Like to Be

This activity takes place in three parts: (1) presentation, (2) feedback, and (3) contracting. The presentation involves each person in clarifying in his own mind how he would like to operate as an "ideal" person. He tries to answer the question, "What would I be like if I were exactly the person I would like to be?" Then, he tries to express this "ideal self" to the group —how he would relate to other people, how he would handle problems and disappointments, how he would operate in the group, etc.

The group should ask questions until they get a fairly clear picture of this member's ideal self. First, the progress the group sees in the person should be shared in terms of encouraging certain processes and behaviors that could lead to achieving the kind of life this person wants. For example, the one person might say, "I feel that your willingness to face problems directly helps you in becoming the kind of person you would like to be." (The group should be cautioned to not make judgments on the person's goal.) Then, group members can share their feedback about what they see as obstacles to growth in becoming the ideal person each wants to be. For example, "You seem to be too hard on yourself and don't accept your own achievements," or "You're too worried about what other people think." Encourage the person to look for the opposite approach to each obstruction to his growth. As in the examples above, he could look at rewarding himself for his successes and work to decide for himself what is important without worrying about others' opinions.

Contracting can then firm up this process of sharing. The group and the individual can clarify an agreement that will state, first, what the person will attempt to do and, second, what the group will attempt to do. The contract can be oral or written, and it should set whatever period of time is agreeable. (If the contract has not been satisfactorily completed during a specified period of time, it can be renewed or restated. Time periods should be short, such as two weeks or one month.) The contract can be for rewards: "If I do this by a certain time, the group agrees to reward me by doing that." The contract could be for mutual effort: "I agree to try this, and the group agrees to try that." Or, the contract can be supportive: "While I work on doing this, the group will help me by doing that." At any time, the contracts can be revised if they are not reasonably effective. Care should be taken so that people don't get involved in constant contract revision just to avoid working on any contract. If this happens, point out what you think is happening and talk about it.

The group should evaluate the contracts after a set period of time, usually one or two months. You could have a special "Reward Party" for those who complete their contracts or make good progress. Hopefully, all of the members will complete their agreements and the whole group will be able to give itself a big reward with some fun time.

Activity number four:
Positive Feelings

Expressing positive feelings on a personal level is hard for many people. But this kind of expression is essential if your group wants to feel acceptance between each other. Too often feelings are given second-hand, they are talked about without actually experiencing the feeling. This activity focuses on feelings without talking. Because feelings are hard to handle for some people, special care should be taken to introduce this experience.

Try to point out the importance of personal feelings. Your feelings are the most unique gift you can give. No one else can give someone else your feelings. And withholding your feelings is often seen as a negative message by others. Persons who can appropriately share their feelings—especially their positive ones—can build acceptance and trust quicker and deeper than those who can't. Encourage your group members to try to be creative and express their own feelings in their own way. A small gesture from one person may be more effective in expressing feelings than a dramatic production by someone else. And again, if someone feels he can't handle this activity or any part of it, respect his right to decide not to participate but encourage him to talk about his choice after the activity is over. And encourage the members to share their acceptance of him even though he didn't participate.

The activity is fairly simple to set up. Have the group stand and form a circle. Ask for people to go to the center of the circle one at a time when they are ready. When a person enters the circle, the members of the group may individually express a positive feeling to the person *without talking*. This does not have to be done one at a time. For example, one person may want to stand beside the person in the center to express his feeling while the others are expressing theirs. Or, if one person shows his feeling by hugging, another may choose to join in hugging at the same time. Dancing, handshaking, smiles, anything nonverbal can be used to express a positive feeling.

When everyone has had an opportunity to receive the positive feelings of the group, discuss the feelings during the experience. Try to assess what this activity means to your group as individuals and as a total group.

Overview the activities

After completing these four activities, it would be helpful to discuss what each of them did or didn't do for the group. Perhaps you can arrive at some feeling about how all four experiences have affected your group. What level of acceptance was achieved? How much self-acceptance did it take to participate? How do you feel about your plans as a group in light of your personal feelings?

Loving others as we love ourselves means no put-downs are necessary within a group. Differences are accepted simply as differences—a part of the variety and fullness of life. No one needs to control others where there is acceptance along with the opportunity to care and share what is going on inside us. If we understand and accept others in the group, we can trust each other to be what we are. And with that kind of acceptance, people will grow "in favor with God and man." That kind of love frees us to live with each other.

Getting it together can mean working at the processes that make any experience meaningful. Why not help your group by giving it an opportunity to begin getting it together?

CHAPTER

Meeting the Special Needs of New Group Members

by John Shaw

S cott was a friendly, intelligent guy who came into our group not long ago.

Before the first meeting was over, he made a couple of quick comments that came across as opinionated, but possibly helpful. Then, at the next meeting, Scott came on strong and took over one conversation completely. During the next few weeks, our youth group developed some resentment toward Scott because of his aggressive efforts to take charge of discussions and strong-arm his way into the activities of the group.

What happened? Scott was obviously a person who could become a real strength in the group. But instead of making a place for himself in the group, he faced a power struggle that resulted in feelings of rejection, confusion and anger. He could become a dropout before he ever really got started.

Scott's feelings those first few weeks help explain the way he acted. He confessed later than he felt "left out," even though the group was very willing to include him in the discussions and activities from the start. He found himself becoming argumentative and always having to be right. Scott didn't know where he fit in the group, and his efforts to make a place only made things worse. He felt bad about the way things were going, but he didn't know what else to do.

Could the kids in the group have helped Scott find his place in the group before things went sour?

While thinking about Scott, I remembered when Susan entered the group. She was very quiet during the group's discussions and activities, but she always appeared to be interested and listening to what was going on. Susan never volunteered her ideas or energies, but she seemed to be enjoying the meetings.

Even though Susan was usually smiling, I remember feeling uneasy about her involvement in the group. How long would she last as a spectator?

Susan shared with me several months later that she almost quit coming several times because she felt no one cared whether she came. The group did not face a crisis with Susan, but she didn't get much help with her struggle to feel that she "belonged" in the group.

Could the group have taken the initiative in some way and helped Susan feel accepted?

Our youth group had several things to deal with while Susan and Scott were trying to become a part of the relationships that made up the life of the group. Group members already enjoyed deep friendships with one another, and those relationships had developed over many years in a lot of cases. It was easy to overlook Susan with good feelings already happening. Scott was seen as a threat—he might break up a good thing. The group resisted these newcomers without realizing what was going on. Then, too, a lot of the kids were uncertain that the new people would like them, and it was not easy to take the risk of offering someone else an opportunity to "put you down."

For various reasons, newcomers may not be able to make a place for themselves in the group. They often feel alone and left out of the warm feelings they see in the friendships around them. And if the new members don't become a part of the friendships within the group, they will typically quit before they get going. So, let's look at some possible ways to open the door for new members to become a real and lasting part of the group.

The first thing that can help is an awareness of the problem that people like Scott and Susan face when they begin attending group meetings. Sometimes it's hard for group members to realize that a new person doesn't "feel like" a part of the group. Regular members often see themselves as open to new kids and willing to form new friendships. But in the busy life of an active group, it is easy to be unaware of a new person's feelings. And, it takes effort to look for clues that will reflect what someone is feeling. Only a sensitive, concerned group member will take time to look beneath the new kid's actions to try to understand what he is trying to accomplish on the personal feeling level.

What does it mean when a person is too reserved and reluctant to engage in group functions? What does it mean when a person is too aggressive and tries too hard to make a place for himself?

Both reactions grow out of the need we all have to be accepted by other people. One reaction is aggressive, and the other is withdrawn, but both are attempts to handle the question, "Will they like me?" Only the group members can furnish the answer to that question, and too long a delay in giving a clear answer may mean the loss of new members. Let's look at specific ways group members can help new kids feel accepted more quickly.

To begin with, nothing takes the place of personal effort. A few words offered with a warm and caring attitude can be the foothold that a new person needs. And a few words from several people multiplies the feeling of acceptance. So, if five people take the risk and make the effort to open a new relationship, a new person will feel included five times quicker or five times stronger than if only one person tried.

Inclusion in the meaningful jobs of the group will also increase a new member's feeling of acceptance. This sharing of meaningful responsibility will help a new kid begin to believe, "I'm important enough to do something for the group." It's good to know that others trust you with a job and that they are relying on you to get it done.

The whole group can prepare itself to receive new members by role-playing the experience of a new person entering the group. It might work best to have one of the members who has been in the group the longest play the role of the new kid coming for the first time. This set-up will help the older members feel what it is like to have to learn a lot of names while trying to find a place in the activities and relationships that are already in full swing. It would be helpful to role-play two situations: First, with the other members not trying to do anything to help the new member; then, with the other members working on ways to help the new member feel accepted. After both situations have been acted out, the group can share insights and feelings experienced in the exercise. Hopefully, the group will become more comfortable with new members and more able to help them feel accepted during the crucial first few meetings. It would be helpful to use a role play at least once a year.

Prayer may be the one thing that pulls all the other efforts together. Open prayer in the group will clarify the seriousness of the need to include everyone in the group who wants to be included. Sincerely asking God's help for yourself, the regular group members and the new members will assure something more than going through the motions without caring. For God is love.

43

Ideas for Effective Group Communication

by John Shaw

Have you ever seen people in your group suddenly stop talking and stay quiet the rest of the evening? Have you ever seen someone take over a conversation and do all the talking? Have you ever felt hurt or confused while you were discussing something in the group? If you have had these kinds of experiences, you are a pretty sensitive and aware person—and you've seen a problem with communication.

Usually when people withdraw, become aggressive or feel hurt, someone is not being understood or, at least, feels misunderstood. How can we help each other to avoid misunderstandings in a group? And, when misunderstandings do occur, how can we work through them to mutual understanding?

The group itself is one of the best resources for helping people to learn to communicate. A group can provide relationships of trust. Group relationships can offer enough stability and commitment between members to allow them to practice and develop communication skills.

But maybe your group isn't sure better communication would help them have better group discussions. If there is uncertainty about whether further skills would help, try this activity. Before the meeting, take a piece of paper and cut out a cross, or some other figure, about eight inches long. Then cut the cross into five pieces as illustrated. Using these pieces as patterns, cut colored pieces from construction paper to form Set A. Then cut another set (designated B) with colored pieces that do *not* correspond to the colors in Set A. Place the cross of Set A in an envelope marked A. Place the cross of Set B in an envelope marked B. Now you are ready for the meeting.

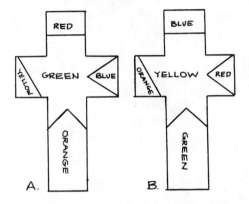

At your meeting, select two people who know nothing about this exercise. Everyone else will serve as observers and should be asked to watch the exercise carefully in order to be able to discuss what happened. The two people sitting back to back should be designated as a sender and a receiver. The receiver should be told not to say anything during the exercise. He is not to communicate with his partner in any way. The sender is instructed to describe *how* to place the pieces of a puzzle together, but that he can't tell the receiver *what* the figure is. In addition, neither partner is to look at what the other is doing. Then, place an A envelope in front of one partner and a B envelope in front of the other. Then, the leader should go to the sender and empty the contents of the envelope in front of him. The leader should form the pieces into a cross and let the sender begin instructing his receiver how to place his pieces.

After the sender has completed his instructions, he can look at what the receiver has formed with his pieces. Then, the total group can get together and discuss the experience with the observers reporting first. This experience usually shows the problems caused by 1) lack of feedback (the receiver can't respond), 2) a different frame of reference (colors are different for the pieces in the sender's and receiver's crosses), and 3) making assumptions that the receiver understands what has been said (no way to check out what the receiver has heard).

Once the group sees the value of feedback, understanding the other person's frame of reference, and not making assumptions about what people have heard, you have a good start in developing good communication. A second step will be to practice a "feedback" model of communication. You can set up this activity with pairs of people who take turns sending messages. The model operates like this: the sender gives a message, such as, "It sure is a nice day today." The receiver then feeds the message back in his own words: "You really like the kind of day we're having." The sender then acknowledges that the message was received accurately: "Yeah, I really like days like this." Or he clarifies the message by restating it in different words if he feels the receiver didn't catch the actual intent of the message. Once a message is given, received and acknowledged as accurate, the partners switch functions and begin again. Let the group practice for several exchanges.

Next, share the concepts of content, command and context. These "three C's" involve the skills of listening. Content means paying careful attention to the words; command means trying to catch the feelings of the speaker; and context means taking into consideration the circumstances in which the message was given. The feedback example used above concentrates on the content, or the words. To go beyond the words to the feelings of the speaker would involve awareness of the command aspects of the message. For instance, if the speaker appeared to be irritated (in his tone of voice or facial expression or posture) when he said "It sure is a nice day today," the listener could respond with an awareness of both parts of the message: "You're aware that the weather's good, but you seem to be irritated about something." If the speaker is ready to talk about his feelings, he will probably explain more about what's happening inside him. The context also may influence the meaning of a message, as in the different meanings the "nice day" message would have if the speaker were 1) in the hospital with a broken leg, 2) putting his skis in the car, and 3) looking at a stack of homework.

Have your group practice communicating with the feedback model while paying attention to the three C's. Then see if they would be willing to spend a month or two concentrating on their communication. If the group agrees, ask everyone to try to help each other clarify feelings and increase accuracy in listening by using feedback and checking out their impressions of what is happening within conversations.

With this deepening ability to hear and understand, your group may experience what Jesus was talking about when he first quoted from Isaiah, ". . .For this people's heart has grown dull, and their ears are heavy of hearing, and their eyes they have closed, lest they should perceive with their eyes and hear with their ears, and understand with their heart." And then Jesus said, "But blessed are your eyes, for they see, and your ears, for they hear" (Matthew 13:15-16).

Let's sharpen our seeing and hearing so our group will feel understood and accepted. Then we'll be Christ-like groups.

DUD DISCUSSIONS:

How to Prevent Them

by John Bushman

Julie was a neat kid, but she wouldn't talk in our group discussion. But Julie wasn't the only one.

Many of the kids simply didn't open up. I realized our group needed some activities that would help kids remove their inhibitions in discussion groups.

What happened next was very interesting. As I introduced these activities to the group, Julie began sharing her concerns. She said she hadn't participated because she really didn't know the group very well and didn't know just how the others would react to her comments. So, she simply refrained from talking.

It seems that we don't like to share our feelings and ideas in discussions until certain conditions are met: we must know each other and we must have established a limited amount of trust. Once these human relationships have been obtained, additional skills can be introduced to the group. These include the need to participate, listening skills, awareness of roles and masks that people often use, and techniques that all participants need in order to discuss a particular issue in-depth.

What follows are specific activities that participants in youth groups and their adult leaders can use in order to achieve effective group interaction.

Building relationships

I can imagine that many of you are saying: "Hey, we already know each other; we don't need to go through these activities to find out who we are—we're already there!" Well, maybe so. But sometimes we really don't know any more than our friends' names and where they live. To me, to know means more than just knowing names.

To know each other well helps build the relationships needed for the sharing of open and honest responses. The following are but a few of the many activities that can be used to help you get to know each other.

ACTIVITY: The group is in a circle. Fit your names and an item that begins with the same initial sound as your first name in an introduction. Example: "I'm Terry; I'm going backpacking; and I'm going to bring a tent." Steve, the next person in the circle, introduces himself in a similar way: "My name is Steve and I'm going on a backpacking trip with Terry. I'm going to take a sleeping bag." The process continues around the circle until all have participated.

ACTIVITY: Share three things you enjoy doing ending in "ing."

ACTIVITY: Write "I am. . ." on a sheet of paper, followed by five items that would accurately complete the statement as it applies to you. Sample: I am. . .anxious about school; eager to play football; pleased with my family relationship; concerned about Fred's operation; silly.

The following activity is rather fun and exciting since it asks you to recall thoughts and feelings from your childhood.

ACTIVITY: Think of your childhood and complete the following partial statements:
When I was a child, I was crazy about. . .
The TV shows that I liked were. . .
When I think of my childhood, I think of. . .
The most exciting time of my life as a child was. . .

ACTIVITY: Again completing partial statements, tell a bit more about yourself:
I like people who. . .
In my spare time I love to. . .
It makes me mad when. . .
I feel best when I'm with a group of people who. . .
I feel worst when I'm with a group of people who. . .
Strangers make me feel. . .
If I were an instrument in an orchestra, I would be the. . .
I feel squeamish about. . .
I will absolutely not eat. . .
I see myself right now feeling much like. . .
Other people regard me as. . .

DUD DISCUSSIONS CONT.

It's important for the group to evaluate how each other responds to this last item, "Other people regard me as," since this item forces you to think how others see you—a process that is not always easy. This activity helps to determine the amount of trust that has been established.

ACTIVITY: Members of the group have a paper bag. The bag represents yourself. Using magazines, crayons, glue and scissors, share on the outside of the bag how you feel others see you. On the inside of the bag indicate how you see yourself. Share your bag.

ACTIVITY: The group responds to the following question: "What can each of us do to make each other feel comfortable and free to respond in discussion?"

Functioning as a group member

After you have achieved a trustful relationship with each other, it is important to consider three other areas so that the group can function effectively: the need to participate, listening, and the roles we play and masks we wear.

Membership in a group carries quite a responsibility. To be a nonfunctioning group member is not fair to the other people in the group as well as not being very productive. Therefore, each participant needs to evaluate his/her participation so that contributions are made. Also there are times when people talk too much! So the group may suffer from too much talk rather than not enough. The following activity helps group members become aware of the need to participate in groups.

ACTIVITY: The group selects a topic for discussion and discusses it using the following guidelines: During the discussion each person must contribute at least once and at random. No person can participate twice until all have participated once.

Have you ever been in a group in which everyone is intent on talking, but no one listens? I remember such a group. We had quite a discussion about the motivations of the various people in the Parable of the Good Samaritan. Two of our members were so intent on getting their point across to each other that they failed to listen. It wasn't long before they were close to agreeing with each other, but they didn't know it because they weren't listening. I have found that there are many times when the interactive process breaks down because members are preparing rebuttal statements rather than listening to the other's contributions.

ACTIVITY: Each person in the group discusses a problem using the following pattern: 1) Summarize the preceding person's statement, 2) state points with which he agrees, and 3) give his opinion.

We wear many masks and play many roles in our varied activities from day to day. That process doesn't stop when we become members of a group. For whatever reason, the masks and roles continue. Example: Henry talks most of the time and monopolizes the discussion. Jane is quite aggressive and doesn't mind stepping on a few toes to get her point across. Don, on the other hand, tends to agree with whomever is doing the talking; he simply doesn't have an original thought. Beth, the mediator of the group, tries to help bring the discussion together by being very diplomatic. Then, of course, there is Fred. He talks to hear himself talk. He pokes fun; he makes irrelevant comments; he's simply a cut-up. I'm sure you can see the common roles and masks that are found in any group: Dominator/Monopolizer, Hostile Aggressor, the Yes-Man, Diplomat, and the Clown.

The following activity is quite enjoyable and can be most helpful as you evaluate roles and masks.

ACTIVITY: Participants create cards with the name of a specific role on them: Diplomat, Yes-Man, Silent Member, Clown, Hostile Aggressor, Dominator/Monopolizer, Humanitarian, Logical Reasoner. Each member gets a role to play. He discusses a topic from the point of view of and in the manner of the role suggested on the card. The group should discuss the activity following the role playing. The discussion should include the advantages and disadvantages when groups are made up of people with a variety of these traits or just one.

Getting below the surface

Well, the group is functioning most effectively by now. The relationships are built, the interaction is moving smoothly, and the group is having effective discussions. But, is it? One final question comes to mind: Is there any depth to the discussion? If after all the skill-building activities are completed and the group still doesn't get to the core of the problem in discussion, then the following activity may be helpful.

ACTIVITY: During the discussion of a particular topic, incorporate the following statements/questions at random. Due to space limitation, only one example is given; additional statements/questions should be created.

Elaboration: "I'm not sure how that applies. Could you build on that idea more?"

Clarification: "What exactly do you mean?"

Comparison: "I see the following similarities in the ideas presented so far. . ."

Contrast: "In contrast to your statement, I think. . ."

Justification: "I think the idea/solution would work because. . ."

Evaluation: "What do you think of that idea?"

Balancing Peer Pressure and Individual Identity

by John Shaw

"Why can't you let me run my own life?" "You act like I can't even make decisions for myself." "I can hardly wait until I can get out on my own so I'll have a chance to live the way I want to."

These statements and thousands of others like them reflect the drive for individuality and independence. Probably everyone in your group feels the need to be his own person. And usually, parents are the ones who get in the way of the opportunities for freedom that are so deeply desired during the teen years. But what about other sources of pressure that prevent independence and individuality?

Have you looked carefully at the pressures that a group of people your own age place on you? Often, these pressures prevent independent choices even more than parents do. How many people do you know who have done things to go along with the crowd? How many times have you felt uneasy about something you were doing with friends? How likely is it among your circle of friends that each person will make an individual choice to not go along with the crowd?

A lot of rebellious actions take place as a result of the pressure to be accepted by a circle of friends. I've known people who engaged in shoplifting, drinking parties, pot parties, and took other serious risks as a result of the pressure to be a part of a group. At a less severe level, staying out too late, hassling teachers and going to a movie that doesn't interest you can be examples of a lack of independent choices.

Group pressure takes many forms. For example, it can prevent positive individual efforts when others tease about "brownie points." And, as a result, group conformity seems to block out either high or low achievement and discourage individual, independent action. Both the "dummies" and the "eggheads" are regarded as "weirdos" in order to press everyone into "the crowd."

But what is at the root of this vulnerability to conformity? Why do people demand the right to be individuals one minute and then go along with the crowd the next? What basic need is being fulfilled by "belonging to" a group of friends?

Usually, the need for acceptance is at the root of the group's power over individuals. And that power can be tough to resist.

If individuality really is important, how can a person be both independent and a part of the group? The key to that combination grows out of a feeling of acceptance by the group along with the ability to state your position clearly without putting anyone down or allowing yourself to be pushed into unwanted activities.

Your group can set up some experiences that will help develop the feeling of acceptance. Then you can practice stating your position in ways that will develop confidence in self-assertiveness.

Acceptance experiences attempt to open up the group to direct processes of giving and receiving acceptance. Once the planned experiences start the feeling of acceptance, hopefully the group will be able to continue relationships in a way that will keep the feeling flowing.

Balancing Peer Pressure and Individual Identity
CONT.

Respond

A good activity to begin with points out the importance of responses in creating a feeling of acceptance. Have your group divide up into pairs. Ask each person to tell his partner three things (abilities, skills, etc.) he likes about himself. After each thing is shared, the partner is to respond simply by saying, "Thank you," and nothing else. After everyone is through with this process, tell the total group what kind of feelings each of you experienced when you received a simple "thank you" as a response. Usually, people feel cheated or uneasy or that something was lacking. At this point, you can discuss the importance of responses. People need positive feedback that at least lets them know they've been heard. And, hopefully, the feedback will begin to include some genuine responses that support and encourage the sharing.

If the group is uncertain about which types of responses are helpful, you can let someone share something he likes about the group and then let members of the group brainstorm to find responses that support the person who shared. Several people could try this until the group has a clear understanding of what works best for people in your group. An example of this interchange might be, Member: "I really like the group when we talk openly about tough problems we all face." Group responses: "You really appreciate the chance to share ideas about problems," or "I like those opportunities, too," or "I really appreciate knowing you feel that way, since you're usually so quiet when we talk about problems." These responses tend to aid further conversation and a growing feeling of mutual understanding and acceptance within the group.

Activity 2:
Dealing with Disagreement

A second activity attempts to help people in the group clarify a feeling of acceptance during a time of disagreement. Perhaps you've seen hard feelings develop during a time of disagreement. Perhaps you've seen hard feelings develop during a discussion or planning session when members disagree with each other. During these times, feelings get wrapped up with differences of opinions, and it would be helpful to be able to distinguish between the two. This clarification can take two forms: 1) separating a difference of opinion from feelings about a person, and 2) clarifying the difference between feelings about behavior and feelings about the person. These two distinctions will need to be role played in order to get into a personal understanding of the differences involved.

For the first situation, ask two people to role play a discussion in which they disagree on what kind of party to have for New Year's while each one carefully makes certain that the other person feels accepted during the disagreement. Statements like, "Even though we disagree, it feels good that we can share our differences personally," or "I respect your opinions, and I need to know if you've heard mine." Actually, your own statements will have to grow out of your group so they won't sound phoney. A role play is a good way to discover spontaneous statements that give a person acceptance in the middle of a disagreement. This kind of role play may take several different attempts, so discuss each effort and then try again from a different approach. Be careful to identify the statements that reflect acceptance.

The second situation can also be role played, but be sure to make the distinction clear before you begin. In other words, you can dislike what a person does without disliking the person. For example , a role play could be set up in which one person is getting more and more angry during a discussion or during a work project. Another person will try to reflect back to him in awareness of his anger without judging or condemning it. Simple statements that reflect the feeling will help like, "You seem to be getting pretty uptight," or "I can understand that you're getting upset with so many pressures." Accepting a person's feelings by identifying them communicates respect for the person and acceptance of his right to have feelings.

Activity 3:

Motivation

A third activity shows the need for motivation and effort in developing a feeling of acceptance. This situation helps people experience what it feels like to work to be accepted into the group. Members will have to use their ingenuity, skills, strengths, or all three to gain a place in the group.

Ask for a few volunteers who want to experience the need for acceptance. Have these volunteers stay in another room and bring them one at a time to the place where the group is. The group should form a circle— standing with their arms locked together around each other's waists or shoulders. The person outside the group is then told to try to gain entrance into the circle of the group while the group tries to prevent his entering. Some people will try to force their way in, others may simply give up or not try at all. The important thing will be to discuss the feelings members experienced during the activity. How do those feelings relate to the actual feelings of acceptance within the group? What methods might work to get a feeling of acceptance within the group? How does the group keep others from feeling acceptance when they first start attending? What skills could be used to gain acceptance into any group of people? Try to record some of your answers to these questions and others that come up. See if these insights help in your planning for the new year.

Now that you've begun to engage in feelings of acceptance, it will be helpful to look at ways of using those good, secure feelings in effective ways that will allow for individuality within the group. When a person feels accepted, he may dare to be himself within the group. The concern now is how to assert himself effectively.

Assertiveness basically involves stating your position, need or feeling in a way that does not put anyone else down and that doesn't allow others to ignore you or pressure you into unwanted experiences. The goal of assertiveness is to be able to make clear your feelings or thoughts in a way that doesn't threaten others into defensiveness.

Role play

It will help if you discuss these concepts and then role play some circumstances that help members get the feel of assertiveness. Everyone should get a chance to role play, so you may have to divide your group into subgroups and after the role play, share what happened in the subgroups. Give all of the subgroups the same situations so you can compare the different ways the situation was handled. Some role play situations could include: 1) Your sponsor wants to run the group, and you feel the members should make their own plans. 2) You and your friends at school are planning a party and they are suggesting activities you don't want to participate in. 3) You have agreed with your parents that you would not ride in a car driven by a friend who had been drinking. On a double date, the driver had several drinks and appeared "high" when it was time to leave. 4) Pick a situation that is unique to your group and role play it.

As you can see, the purpose of these group experiences is not solely related to the life of the group. Your members can benefit in any setting from a feeling of being accepted and the skills of assertiveness. The more effectively your group members handle their relationships, everywhere, the more their quality of life will be enriched by their group experiences. Hopefully, the purpose of your group includes the total life experience of your members and not just their "church" involvements.

Consider the parable of the talents which pointed out Jesus' concern that his followers invest their skills in ways that multiply their value and effectiveness. Christ expects that we will multiply our abilities and use them in every possible way to make life better for ourselves and those we meet while we try to fulfill God's expectations for human experience. Our love for our neighbors as well as for ourselves depends on its expression through the skills of assertiveness and the feelings of acceptance. In these experiences you may find yourself not only being an individual within the group, but also growing "in favor with God and man."

The struggle for personal freedom and identity within the pressures of expectations from friends can be one of the most important efforts of your life.

17

Helping Group Members Clarify Values

by Roland Larson

Just imagine for a few moments that you are 13 years old and your friends mean more to you than almost anything. Five of you are at a friend's house, and the parents are gone. One of the girls suddenly appears with an opened bottle of whiskey and quickly pours five small glasses. You really don't want any, but suddenly one friend holds out a glass to you and says, "You're not a baby, are you?"

What can you do? What are some ways you can respond? There are many possibilities. For example, you might shake your head and refuse it; you might say you don't want it; you might take it and pour it down the sink; you might drink it; you might leave the house immediately; etc., etc. The point is that you have many possible choices at that moment, and you must decide what to do. You are facing a dilemma that requires your response.

Or, consider this situation: you are a young scientist working alone in a laboratory on an experiment which has to do with prolonging life in older people. Almost miraculously you stumble upon a compound which prolongs life indefinitely in human beings. You keep it a secret while you gather evidence that it works. There is no question as to the importance of your discovery. It works—people can be kept alive forever! You can scarcely contain your excitement. What are you going to do?

One small group brainstormed this dilemma and came up with these possible solutions: don't tell anyone; sell the idea to the highest bidder; patent the formula; tell the whole world; publish the formula in a medical journal; start a company and sell it; give it to a task force for study and recommendations; run a pilot program to show how effective it is; throw it away; give the formula to the United Nations.

Again, here we have a values-laden dilemma. Suppose you make a snap decision as to what you would do. If you did not think carefully about this, your hasty choice might not take into consideration the many possible choices as to your best course of action. Therefore, in solving a problem of this kind it is important to think about your many possible options. Further, you want to consider the consequences, or what might likely happen if you decide to solve the dilemma in one way or another. How does your choice affect others, your family, yourself, society, mankind? Is your choice a responsible one, one that you can live with? Further, is your choice consistent with your religious faith?

That's what clarifying our values is all about—making responsible choices about life's important issues. To make a responsible choice I must concern myself with getting as much information as possible when there is a decision to be made. I consider the results or outcomes of each possible option. Then I make a choice in the light of my background, traditions, beliefs, opinions, and the best information I can get. My choice is a responsible one, a decision with which I am comfortable.

Daily choices
Every day we make judgments or choices. Every day we express opinions or do things that are guided by our values. For example, this morning I opened the kitchen cupboard to select a breakfast cereal. Five or six brands looked down at me. Quickly I chose Brand X. Why? My selection was guided, in part at least, by my personal value system. Health is important to me. I had recently read a study which gave nutritional comparisons and sugar contents for various breakfast foods. Brand X was given a strong, positive rating. I chose it.

There are many definitions for the word "value." The one most useful for me is this: "Values are basic beliefs about what is good or ought to be—beliefs that serve as criteria or guidelines for decision-making and actions." In my breakfast food example, Brand X linked most closely with my basic belief about the desirability for me to maintain my good physical health. The older I get the more important my physical health becomes to me. I consider certain alternatives, options, and the consequences of my choices in the light of my health values. My value guides the action I take. I feel good about selecting Brand X.

A method for clarifying
What is "values clarification"? Simply, it is a way of dealing with the everyday choices that people make. Values clarification is an educational approach designed to help individuals of any age examine, discover and develop their own opinions, attitudes, beliefs and behavior and share their thoughts and feelings about important issues in everyday life. It is commonly used in small groups such as in church, school, or in family life.

Value-clarifying exercises can add interest, zest, and depth in youth religion classes, Bible study groups, retreats, confirmation, parent groups, special interest groups, and church boards. For example, a leader may precede a discussion on faith by using the "interview" exercise. Students might interview a pastor, youth worker, group member, or recent confirmand to learn about that person's life, experiences, beliefs, and values.

By using these exercises group members learn and practice a decision-making process leading to more responsible life choices when considering questions such as:

Whom shall I choose as my friends? as my marriage partner?

How shall I use my leisure time?

To what religious beliefs do I choose to commit myself?

What are my political beliefs?

What career and life work shall I pursue?

How important is money going to be in my life?

What do I believe about war and peace?

How do I define male and female roles?

What lifestyle shall I choose?

How important is independent decision-making in various areas of my life?

What is responsible social behavior?

How do I view health? Will the use of drugs and alcohol be a part of my life?

What does the Christian faith have to say about these things?

We could go on and on, for there are many important issues which face both youth and adults in this complex and changing world. It's not an easy time to be alive, but it certainly is a challenging and fascinating time in which to live, to learn, and to serve God and the people around us.

Helping Group Members Clarify Values

Springboards

A method being used by more and more youth groups is one that helps participants clarify their own attitudes, beliefs and values by sharing and learning with others—using value-laden exercises as springboards for sparking interest and discussion. The resources of the Christian faith (including the Gospel, pastor, youth worker, fellow Christians, and the Holy Spirit) become part of the clarifying process, helping individuals find answers to difficult questions and issues. Through game-like exercises persons are challenged to examine what they think and believe. This is a process to help persons clarify what they believe, what they value, and what their behavior will be—in light of their Christian faith.

The dilemma story mentioned before is one example of a "springboard" exercise to help people think about the many choices confronting them when faced with a decision. Among the types of exercises more commonly used are Values Voting, Ranking, Either/Or, Interviewing, Listening, Dilemma and Goal Setting.

Let's try a few exercises that are taken from my book **Values and Faith** (Winston Press). You might want to use one or more of these as a discussion starter in your own group—or to think about yourself, in private.

Ranking

Ranking exercises present three or more possible choices for participants to rearrange and prioritize—from best to worst, or from most important to least important. Try ranking each of these in order of your priority, writing in a number 1 for the most important, 2 for the next most important, etc.:

1. Which is most important in your life?
.......happiness
.......security
.......success

2. Which is grace most like?
.......God's acceptance of the past, allowing us to move into the future without guilt
.......God loving us with no strings attached
.......a reward from God

3. How is the Christian faith most often passed on to others?
.......through words
.......through personal witness
.......through the Holy Spirit
.......through loving actions

4. Which statement is most important in relating to God?
.... doubts are okay; God understands them.
.... faith becomes even stronger when it is tested through doubt.
.... we should never doubt.

Either/Or

This is a forced choice between two options. Each person selects the option with which he or she most closely identifies.

Often a choice boils down to one of two alternatives. Sometimes neither choice is appealing; sometimes both are. Nevertheless, each person is asked to choose one of the two options. These are examples of Either/Or exercises to get people involved in discussing, sharing, and learning together about their faith:

Which is faith more like? (Choose one)
    Action / Surrender

Which is praying more like?
    Thanking / Asking

Love for God is more like which of these?
    Outer acts of love for people / Inner devotion to God

Which best describes our relationship to God?
    God needs us / We need God

Which is your faith more like?
    A butterfly/A cocoon

Which is following Christ most like?
    Riding / Walking

Which is death more like?
    A dark closet / A sun-filled doorway

Which do you think Jesus is more like?
    Lion / Lamb

When used with groups, values-laden exercises should be fun. But they are not merely games to be played, and should be used responsibly—keeping in mind that this method provides a chance for participants to grow in their ability to listen with acceptance, understand and communicate. Thoughts and feelings are shared so that each individual person has a chance to learn and practice the difficult art of making mature, wise and responsible decisions.

Working Out Problems with Role Plays

by John Shaw

Nancy is having trouble with her parents. She wants to take off for a workcamp over Thanksgiving break. But her parents want her to stay home to spend time with the family.

The conflict has upset Nancy. She's talked with her youth group about it. And now the group is helping her through the problem by enacting a real-life scene from Nancy's family situation.

The group uses role plays to develop more skill in personal relationships and for clearer understanding of Bible passages. Role playing is the process of assigning group members the roles of people involved in real or hypothetical situations. The "actors" spend a few minutes "in the shoes" of their characters—to explore feelings and find solutions for problems.

The simple process of role play can have dramatic results. In Nancy's case, she was able to practice talking with her parents in more effective ways while learning to control her feelings. Group members were able to give support and offer her positive suggestions. She developed insight into her situation, set goals for her approach to her parents, got rid of some of the problem feelings she had and felt more confident about solving her problem.

"Please, Mom, this is really important to me!"

"I know it is, Nancy, but this may be your last Thanksgiving dinner at home. We really want you to spend it with us."

"Besides, Nancy, you went to a work-camp just this last summer. I can't see why you need to go on another one so soon. Your mother and I like to have you around some of the time."

"Dad, this camp is set up only for the kids who went to last summer's camp. I was chosen for my enthusiasm in helping others. It's something I've always wanted."

"But, Nancy, your Aunt Martha is coming just to see you and she'll only be here at Thanksgiving. She'll be awfully disappointed if you aren't here."

"Mom, you know Aunt Martha just gives me a big hug and a kiss. Then she talks to you all the rest of the time. I could turn into a pumpkin after the first ten minutes and she wouldn't even notice."

"But she feels better just knowing you're there. I know she'll be upset if she can't see you."

"Think of your family. Aren't your mother and I as important as a bunch of strangers with broken down houses? I can't see why you have to work for people who should take care of themselves."

"Dad, we've been through that. You know these projects are carefully chosen. We only help the ones who can't do it on their own. And I am thinking of my family.

I just feel that being gone for one holiday won't hurt our closeness. Besides, I'll spend a lot of time telling you all about it after I get back."

"I know. You rattled on for days after the camp last summer."

"But you'll be so busy with school and church activities. It won't be like last summer when you had more free time. It's also Dad's busy time of the year. He may not be free to talk when you aren't busy."

"Oh Mom, we can work that out. If we want to talk, we'll take the time. I think we'll talk all we can when I get back. I'll have pictures and everything."

LEADER: "Okay. Let's cut the action here and talk over what's happened. Nancy, what was going on inside while you were playing the part of your mother?"

NANCY: "Well, once I got into it, I began to understand how my parents feel so strongly about holidays. They must hurt a little every time I'm gone on a trip or something."

LEADER: "What about you, Julie, how did you feel in Nancy's place?"

JULIE: "I felt ganged up on. It's hard trying to answer one point after another with two parents firing at you. I felt like crying or something to bring things to an end. And they kept bringing up family so much that I began to feel like a traitor."

Role play gives people a chance to experience new, unusual or problem situations in a protected, caring group. They can try new approaches and correct mistakes.

To get started, Nancy described the situation as it usually happens, with herself getting upset and giving in to her parents' wishes. Actors for the other roles were chosen and Nancy described how her parents usually act and what they might typically say. She set her goal: to stick to the issue and control her feelings. The players then acted out their roles spontaneously.

Nancy acted her own part the first time around, but had trouble controlling her feelings under pressure from her mother to stay home. After discussion and suggestions from the group, the leader asked Nancy to take the role of her mother. This role reversal gave Nancy a new look at the situation, and you can see the results in the discussion that follows the role play.

Read the action between Nancy and her "parents" and pick out Nancy's best statement. Also identify the statements that sound more defensive than helpful.

After you've read the role play, you'll see the processes that lead to creative changes. These processes can be applied to many different learning experiences.

Problem solving is a natural. New behaviors and statements can be tried with the support of the group. Alternatives can be discovered so people don't feel locked in by old methods. Tom's and Ann's suggestions offered new avenues for Nancy to reach out to her parents. Practice also builds confidence and shows a clear plan of action for dealing with problems. Nancy was already feeling better about her efforts as she approached the third role play.

Release of feelings and replacement of problem feelings with more positive ones also can result from role play. Nancy could see how she began to feel guilty and then was less capable of discussing the issue. Talking about how feelings got started (such as when Gordon pointed out Nancy's reactions to her dad) can help people be alert for certain pitfalls. Nancy also could see how Julie felt when both parents were talking to her. It's a relief to know others feel the same way you do.

Understanding another person's point of view also helps prevent negative ideas about motives. Nancy could see her parents' side of the issue better when she realized they weren't just being judgmental.

You can also get involved in scripture by acting out a situation or parable. Take Luke 5:1-11, where Jesus

NANCY: "I feel that way a lot. It isn't fair to be made to feel guilty when I'm trying to help other people."

LEADER: "So Julie was into your role pretty well. Did you think she responded like you usually do?"

NANCY: "It was really freaky hearing my arguments from the other side."

LEADER: "Well, Roy, how did it feel to be the dad?"

ROY: "I guess it's hard to let go as a parent. I wanted to just say, 'No' after a while. But I knew Nancy said her dad was willing to talk and keep an open mind. It would have been easier just to be the authority and tell her what to do."

JULIE: "But I felt really important and respected when both parents were listening to me. I can't believe parents can be that way. Mine just make a decision and that's it."

NANCY: "My parents are good about talking. But I still feel overmatched when they both come at me with their arguments."

LEADER: "Was there anything that Julie said that gave you some new ideas?"

NANCY: "Yes, I hadn't thought about pointing out how much I talk to them after a trip. That ought to help make up for my being gone. Also, I don't think Dad would complain about my working on the homes. He understands the importance of this kind of service. It's just that I'll be gone on a holiday and he's so strong on family holidays."

ROY: "I just threw that in 'cause my dad thinks poor people just won't help themselves."

LEADER: "Any comments about how the action went?"

GORDON: "I thought Julie handled Nancy's part really well when she didn't get all teary after Nancy's dad started the bit about thinking about the family. Nancy seems to get hooked into feeling guilty when her dad gets into that."

NANCY: "You know, you're right. Dad can get to me with that stuff better than anyone."

GORDON: "You seemed pretty quick to defend him about understanding the service projects, too. You must be pretty close to him."

NANCY: "Yeah, I love my dad. It's hard to resist his wanting me to stay home more."

LEADER: "Okay, Nancy, try to think through what you say to your dad before you say it. It'll help you stick to the issue. Are you ready to run through the role play a third time now? You could take your own part again this time."

NANCY: "That's good. I feel more confident now than I did the first time. Playing Mom's role helped me see that they're not putting me down, but just expressing their own feelings. I think I can stick to the issue better now."

LEADER: "Great! Now, are there any suggestions any of you have for Nancy?"

TOM: "Maybe you could offer to plan extra time with your family during Christmas to sort of make up for being gone Thanksgiving."

NANCY: "Yeah, I think that might help."

ANN: "You might offer to write a note to Aunt Martha explaining why you'll be gone."

NANCY: "Oh that's a great idea. Aunt Martha doesn't really spend all her time talking to Mom. I'll miss our chance to talk."

LEADER: "Any more suggestions? Okay, who would like to play Nancy's mom this time around?"

SHARI: "I know her mom pretty well, so I'd like to try."

LEADER: "Excellent. Nancy, give Shari some idea of how your mom might react to new suggestions and firmness on your part. Roy, think through your role again with the new information about her dad. We'll start in a few minutes. The rest of you continue to observe so you can make suggestions and share what you see happening. Remember, Nancy's goal is to stick to the issue and not get upset."

called his first followers. You could assign roles and act out this situation. Encourage everyone to make his own comments from the point of view of his role. Getting into the role will produce instant feelings about the incident and a deeper understanding of the power of Jesus' call. The group also will understand better how the disciples decided to leave their jobs and follow Jesus. Your group's feelings about deciding to follow Christ will be stimulated by the decision.

Leading role play

To lead role play, just follow these steps:

1. The main character describes the situation and then states a goal or goals. He then identifies the roles to be played. Actors for each of the roles are picked or volunteers are used. The main character gives each actor a brief description of typical behaviors, statements or attitudes for his role. For instance, "Dad always comes across pretty gruff and pushes for all the facts. But he usually gives in if the request makes sense and is possible." Have the rest of the group observe what happens, be able to give suggestions and identify the helpful efforts of the main character and actors.

2. Play out the situation until the roles are being presented effectively. It should take only a few minutes. The leader then stops the action and asks for responses from the main character and actors. Then, the observers are invited to describe what appeared to be helpful, give feedback on how the process went and offer suggestions for improvement. It is important to offer encouragement for those actions that were productive. Sharing feelings about the situation is appropriate here.

3. Replay the situation, switching roles if that would be helpful. If the main character needs only practice, he will not need to switch. Again share feelings, encouragement, suggestions and identify effective actions and statements.

4. Check out how the main character and the group feel about the goals and efforts made. Replay can be used again, if necessary.

5. Set a time for feedback by the main character to tell the group how the situation went in real life.

Role play can be an effective, exciting way for your group to grow. Body, mind and spirit are all used to deal with a situation. Everyone can be involved. Support and creative help can be developed.

Be sure to ask God's help as you enter this process. And thank him for giving the growth when you're done.

What would you think if you could take your group into the world of the cults for an evening and return without having to shave your head, sell flowers on a street corner or wear a white shirt and narrow black tie? All you need is one evening, a few hours of planning and your youth group.

Even though we don't hear as much about cults as we once did, they're not exactly sitting back and thinking up new ways to be weird. Most cults are stronger than ever. In fact, pollster George Gallup writes in his book **The Search for America's Faith**, "Christian churches are losing their youth by the thousands to other religions and cults. The Christian churches of America, liberal, conservative, evangelical and fundamental, must now perceive a common enemy in the cults or expect serious decline in their current membership and their future prospects."

That's pretty strong language, especially when it comes from a guy whose research data has a great track record of predicting trends in our nation's youth.

There are several reasons we haven't heard much about the cults lately. One of the best explanations has to do with the cults themselves. They're smarter than ever before—they look more like us. While it's not terribly difficult to spot a Hare Krishna's bald head and flowing robes, young people aren't prepared for the nicely-dressed, scripture-quoting, soft-spoken style of most present-day cults.

CULT NIGHT:

An Evening to Help Young People Recognize Marks of Cults

by Gary Richardson

Rev. Dan Berger and his youth leaders at Grace United Methodist Church in South Bend, Indiana, have designed a one-night session to help young people recognize the marks that separate cults from Christianity.

"This session turned out to be the most successful meeting of the year," comments Dan. "The discussion that followed our 'indoctrination' session was fantastic. Our kids picked out all 10 marks of the cults from this experience."

First things first

Dan emphasizes that surprise is a key element in making this meeting successful. "We told our group we were going to do something on the cults. But we didn't

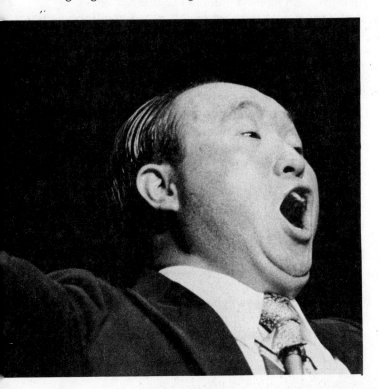

let them know they'd actually experience some of the methods the cults use. And they walked right into it."

A first giant step toward making Cult Night a powerful experience is for you to become familiar with the marks of the cults. Check some of the books on cults listed in the "resources" section at the end of this chapter.

Dan and his leaders decided to have two cult groups that had the same basic beliefs, but used different sayings, dress and had different rules of conduct. "We had two groups because we wanted our youth to have the choice of which group to belong to," Dan said. "They probably could have gotten as much if we had used only one group. But we felt they should make a 'free' choice."

If you decide to use more than one cult group, have your Maras decide how they want to adapt the basic beliefs to fit the various groups. You'll also need a separate room for each group.

Cult Night—the enticers

As young people come into the room, the first things they see are snacks. (Use different snacks for each group if you choose more than one cult.)

You'll also need to plan how to set the mood of the session and which "beliefs" you'll use to indoctrinate your kids.

Once you determine your set of beliefs, your cult leaders (Dan called the leaders "Maras"), will need to prepare themselves thoroughly on what they want to say and do with their "followers." "Mock seriousness and commitment to the cult are necessary in getting the young people to go along with you," Dan said.

Each cult has its own host or hostess, a well-dressed, good-looking girl or guy who oozes friendliness and love.

As the kids enter the room for the snacks, the host or hostess asks each person to sign a register. The regis-

CULT NIGHT: CONT.

ter is harmless looking, but it contains fine print. (Few, if any, will read this print.) The fine print contains such rules as, "I agree to give 50 percent of what I own to my Mara," "My only desire is to please the Mara," and "I denounce my family and friends and understand that this group is my only future." Use the different marks of the cults to come up with your own fine print.

Warm fuzzies—the bait

After the snacks, the host or hostess introduces the adult leader by saying something like, "Please meet our divine master, Mara (leader's last name)."

The Mara leads the group in new games and creative interpersonal experiences. The last activity before the indoctrination session should be fairly serious and heavily relational.

MARKS OF THE CULTS

1. Extra-biblical revelation
2. A false basis of salvation
3. Uncertain hope
4. Presumptuous messianic leadership
5. Doctrinal ambiguity
6. The claim of "special discoveries"
7. Enslaving organizational structure
8. Financial exploitation
9. Denunciation of others
10. Syncretism: the taking of ideas from diverse places

(Taken from **Know the Marks of Cults**, by Dave Breese, Victor Books.)

Mara! Mara!—indoctrination

This part of the cult experience is the most serious and requires the greatest amount of preparation by the adult "Mara."

He introduces himself by saying something like, "As your leader I have spoken with God, and I alone am the one who has received this divine insight. When I speak I want quiet. Be serious, for I am God's chosen instrument for this age. Our group is not like any other, for we have God's word that we speak the truth. All other groups are perversions of God's revelation. Trust in me, for I am your savior. I am the one who can lead you to salvation."

The Mara places small gold stars on each of the kid's foreheads as he explains the group's "beliefs." (If you use two groups, you might consider using washable ink to draw the stars on each person's wrists.)

The Mara's beliefs are:
1. We believe in self-improvement.
2. We believe that we should love one another.
3. We believe that we give to receive.
4. Our leader is all-knowing and we must follow him no matter what.

5. We only sin when we go against the wishes of Mara.

You could have diagrams of the cult's beliefs drawn on posterboard and hang them around the room.

Other ideas for indoctrinating your young people are:
• Continually refer to them as "disciples" or "followers."
• Give the members sayings, such as, "Mara knows all."
• Develop rituals: gestures, special handshakes, incense, candles, low lights, Indian music, special songs, and so on.
• Use peculiar dress. Check your church's storage area for old robes and Christmas and Easter costumes. You could also use arm bands, hats or anything that gives people a group identity.
• Make them do work they don't want to do. Point out that their allegiance is to the Mara. What he says goes.
• Take some money from them. Point out that when they signed the register they agreed to give half of everything to the Mara.
• At the end of the indoctrination period, come up with something the group must do to signify allegiance to the Mara. Dan had his group drink Kool Aid from Dixie cups. You could have everyone sign a formal-looking ledger or memorize a brief incantation and recite it in unison for the Mara.

Deprogramming

Stop the exercise and have people express how they felt as they were drawn more and more into the cult and into the Mara's control.

Discuss ways in which the cult was like or unlike their church. List ways in which the cult was both similar to and against biblical principles.

Also have the group list and discuss the different marks that separate the cult from Christianity.

This discussion would make a great springboard for getting into a more in-depth study on the marks of the cults.

Dan and the young people at Grace United Methodist Church learned an important lesson about the cults that evening. They also learned about themselves and how easy it is to become involved in something evil.

Try this one with your youth group. It works.

Resources

1. **Know the Marks of Cults**, by Dave Breese, Victor Books.
2. **Cults, World Religions, and You**, by Kenneth Boa, Victor Books.
3. **Youth Brainwashing, and the Extremist Cults**, by Ronald Enroth, Zondervan.
4. **The Kingdom of the Cults**, by Walter Martin, Bethany Fellowship.

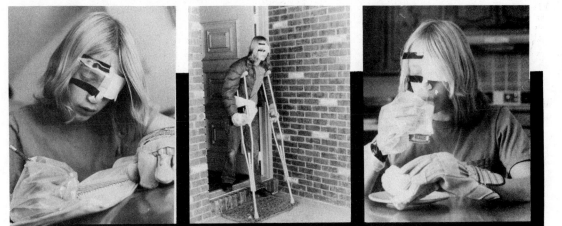

I WAS A TEENAGE GRANNY:

A Simulation for the Younger to Understand the Older
by Thom Schultz

What's it like to lose your hearing? Or your eyesight? Or your sense of taste? What's it like using hands that are handicapped by painful arthritis?

Millions of old people know the answers to these questions.

But those of us who are younger often have a hard time understanding the plight of the aged. And, sometimes we just don't care.

Young people in Saginaw, Michigan, decided to learn, firsthand, what kind of life an old person leads. They became old for a day to see how they felt and how others acted toward them.

The kids used earplugs to impair hearing, noseplugs to stifle smell, gloves and plastic bags to make hands awkward and slow, as they might be with arthritis. And they used splints and bandages to make leg and arm movements difficult.

Some kids put patches on one eye. Others put foggy plastic over one or both eyes to give the impression of eyesight blurred by cataracts.

"I found myself getting very irritable because I couldn't get around as well as I normally do," said Mike Russell.

The experiment was modeled after one designed by Dr. Tamerra Moeller of the University of Michigan. "We tend to forget all of the adjustments a person must make as a result of the physical process of aging," Dr. Moeller said. "Declining vision or hearing, chronic illness, memory loss—these processes are painful and unnerving."

Young Mike said, "The eyepatch was my biggest problem. I kept misjudging distance. The first surprise was that I couldn't catch a table tennis ball. Then I tried to pick up a pencil and missed. I even misjudged steps."

Terry Colby said, "When I went home my mother said, 'You're not coming to the table with those gloves on.'

"I told her I had to—it was part of an experiment. The gloves really cut down on movement, and even though I was slow and careful, I still spilled my glass of milk."

Holly Neuman had a plastic bag over her right hand and a bandage on the left eye. "I couldn't turn the pages of my books," she said. "I also found the eye that wasn't covered got tired."

Ray Lucas spent the day with tape across his nose, and that helped him discover how closely the sense of taste is linked to the sense of smell. "At noon, I had a deviled egg sandwich that tasted blah," he said. "Even the water tasted funny. My candy bar wasn't good either."

Many youth groups are involved in a ministry to old folks in nursing homes. If your group is interested in showing a little love to shut-ins, you might want to try becoming old for a day.

Or, you may want to plan a weekend retreat where you must remain "old" for the entire weekend. Such an experience would not only enable you to develop empathy for old people, but will help you appreciate and celebrate your young years.

CHAPTER

21

HERE LIES OUR GROUP:

An Experience to "Bury" the Old Group and Celebrate the New

by Henry Sawatzky

In the back of my mind was the experience of Rev. Richard Wilcox. He was in his office when a man came in for some counseling. Mostly the man just sat there and muttered that he felt dead.

So, Rev. Wilcox reached over and took out his service book and read the burial section and, in effect, buried this man who said he felt dead. The man said nothing. He sat there until the "commital service" for him was over. Then he left. He made no further appointment and Rev. Wilcox didn't know what would happen.

Several weeks later this same man appeared, sat in the same chair and said "Last time I was here you buried me. Now we can talk about resurrection."

The senior high youth group of Hampstead Congregational Church was in the midst of another kind of death. But it didn't want to die. Before September, a group barely existed, but with the help of a core of committed senior highs it began to thrive. We worked hard, played and studied together. We went on bike-a-thons, retreats and talked about the meaning of

our lives and what relevance the Christian faith had for us. We became a very close group. The climax of the year was a trip to New York City, and I assumed that the group would end for the summer at that point. But it didn't and we kept going through July.

Between April and July there were rumblings about not wanting to have the incoming group of freshmen join us in September. "They would ruin it," was voiced by the group.

I thought of Rev. Wilcox's story.

It seemed to me that the old group had to die in order that the new group could be born. So I planned a meeting of just the old group in early September. At that meeting we did what, in effect, often happens at a funeral. We remembered. We listed all the good times we had had in the past year. We also remembered the hard times that were a part of our history. A funeral is a time for remembering, so we did just that.

Then I told them what we all knew, namely that this had been a great year but that this group had to die so

62

that a new group could start. I took out the committal service that I had used so often and read it over to the group committing the "Hampstead Congregational Church's Senior High Pilgrim Fellowship to the earth, dust to dust, and ashes to ashes in the sure and the certain hope of the resurrection."

You could have heard a pin drop. After a few moments I said to the group, "Okay, now we can begin to talk about resurrection, about a new and possibly better group than we've ever had before."

And so we did. We began to share our dreams of what we could do in the new year—projects, trips, studies, etc. But more than that happened. We began to include in our thinking the new people who would be joining our group. We focused on people specifically who had expressed an interest in joining our Pilgrim Fellowship. We named them, and the people in this group said they would take responsibility to make sure they were invited to the next meeting. We planned ways to make sure that the new group would be a welcoming and warm group. We talked about how "the old guard" could help the new people without forming

into factions of "the old" and "the new" groups. The members talked about how they should behave.

The group really turned around. In biblical terms, they repented of their past ways. They began to get excited about their resurrected group. Grumbling turned to more glowing possibilities.

And so they went to work.

Next week at the new Pilgrim Fellowship meeting the group had doubled in size. I could hardly believe it. We did what we said we would do and "the old guard" basically carried out what they said they would. We did some get acquainted games and thought of things we could do together.

But more than that happened. The older senior highs were very conscious of what was happening. They went out of their way to be sensitive to the needs of the new people. They also acted as a kind of force to keep everything from becoming chaotic—a socializing force.

This approach of Christian burial and resurrection helped move this group from a point of grumbling to the point of seeing new potential.

How to Plan and Do Creative Retreats

CHAPTER

22

Ten Ideas for Group Retreats

by Virgil and Lynn Nelson

Retreats can bring unity, purpose, direction, fun and Christian growth to your group.

Sometimes, though, retreats become routine. So, we've compiled an assortment of ideas for retreats, suggestions for new formats, and ideas for specific retreat focus.

It is fun to share ideas and suggestions. We trust that some of the following will be new to you and that you will give them a try.

Your part is to have some idea where you are headed [the purpose or goals] for a given retreat. The following ideas are like balloons without strings, they can be "tied" to many different things and used in/for many different purposes.

the world with new eyes.

Spend a whole weekend creating your media resource bank for use in slide-sound programs, creative Bible study, and reporting to your church on your group.

Let different individuals (or small groups) take different areas of focus. For example, one group might take "hands" as its focus and shoot a whole roll of slides just showing different hands, contrasting age, size, what the hands are doing, etc. Other groups might consider feet, faces or children. Emotions can be included as well as feelings—love, tension, anger, happiness.

Tools and techniques can vary with the equipment you have available. The simplest way to start is with slides: you can get slide film even for Instamatic cameras, or you can borrow a 35mm camera. Slides can be made without a camera, and some individuals or groups can do this while others are using the photo equipment (see chapter 37).

If you have access to a super 8mm camera, one group or person can be shooting footage around the above themes or recording the whole process of the media retreat for later use in worship celebration of the life of the group, and God's gifts to it.

One of the best resources for those just starting out in multimedia is Ed McNulty's **Gadgets, Gimmicks and Grace** (Abbey Press). This volume includes hundreds of practical how-to-do-it suggestions and theological/scriptual basis for our use of media in the church (see also chapter 36).

3. Lock-in Retreat

Right after school, everyone comes to the church and is "locked-in" for the night until school time the next day. Or, try a week-long lock-in. (This may also be planned for a weekend.)

This gives a group a unique opportunity to live, study, and play together. People agree not to leave the church once they have arrived, and there are no incoming-outgoing calls once the week has begun.

The focus of the week can vary as widely as the needs of your group. The results can be fantastic in spiritual growth; people getting genuinely acquainted with each other, learning to work together, etc.

You can choose whether you want to let the group do its own cooking as part of the learning experience, or to find someone to handle that for you.

You might even consider a lock-in retreat at a special place, for example at a rest home, or mental hospital, or juvenile hall, where the group would be involved each evening in a special ministry with the folk who live there.

Lock-ins can also include special program features:

1. *No talking* for one whole evening through breakfast the next day. Here's a genuine opportunity to experience the frustrations of being handicapped, and the opportunities for nonverbal communication, the lack of pressure to "talk" or have "something to say."

1. A Weekend with the Shrink

Arrange with a Christian psychologist, psychiatrist, or counselor to be with your group for the weekend and administer a variety of personality tests for individuals in the group, such as the Taylor Johnson Personality Inventory. There are a number of such tools which can help an individual better understand him/herself and the unique gifts God has given him/her.

The rest of the focus for the weekend could be Bible study and worship celebrating the uniqueness/similarities God has created in us. If appropriate, small groups could also generate development of trust and love in discussing/sharing what we have learned about ourselves through the tools we have used.

2. Media Retreat

Whether your group is only four or five members or you have 150 members, media can be an exciting way to celebrate your group life and to see scripture and

Ten Ideas for Group Retreats CONT.

2. Or a *no see* (or *no hear*) time dividing the group into partners, possible one for one evening and switch for the next.

In considering any one of the following retreat ideas, you must keep in mind the particular needs and characteristics of your group and your community. Each idea can be adapted to your particular situation with some thought. Each format can be used for many different purposes or goals.

4. Planning Retreat

Do you get frustrated planning your programs for your group at the last minute? Is it a hassle getting people to look ahead and take responsibility for some aspect of your group's life and spiritual growth?

A planning retreat might just be what you need to help you determine your purpose, to clearly identify your focus for the next few months or a year.

Identify the persons you feel should be involved. Do you have elected officers or coordinators? If so, they would be a core. Others might be invited as well. Sometimes the whole group can be involved in planning ahead for the year.

Some possible questions for group focus during the retreat:
- The purposes of our group are. . .
- This next year I feel our group needs to. . .
- God seems to be telling us to. . .
- One of the prime opportunities we have is. . .

These open-ended questions can lead to input and goal statements that can then be specifically translated into program ideas and suggestions. The retreat can even include calendaring of events and the division of labor for implementing them.

5. Star Power Weekend

Encourage your group to create a simulation game that you would live/play for a whole day or weekend.

Dennis Benson's book **Gaming** (Abingdon Press) is a fantastic resource that will help you experience the fact that you can create your own exciting simulation games. It also contains eight complete simulation games.

One simulation that we have had good experiences with is **Star Power**, developed by Garry Shirts, Simile II, Box 910, Del Mar, CA 92014. This game simulates a three-class society based on wealth. The wealthy gain advantages as the game progresses, which ensures their continued position. The format is a do-it-yourself kit.

Others:

Baldicer: simulates the problem of feeding the world's people (John Knox Press).

Credit and Debt: sets up the experience of being in debt and the frustrations that can come trying to meet the bills (Brethren Press).

The Poverty Game: (Brethren Press).

6. Action Weekend

Does your church have special mission projects with which your group might organize to serve? Do you live near (within 200 miles) a large city that has community centers, or special programs for youth, adults, elderly citizens?

Do you have any special concentrations of people near you—a rest home, a juvenile placement facility, a half-way house, a treatment facility for alcoholics, a hospital, a child-care center, a seniors' center, a mental institution?

You have a unique opportunity for Christian action and involvement. Have your group make a list of such institutions and organizations. Do several Bible studies on some of the following scriptures: 1 John 2:5 and 4:16-21; John 13:34-35; Matthew 25:37-41 and 5:43-48; 2 Corinthians 5:17-18; Luke 4:16-17; and Ephesians 5:16.

Have someone contact several of the organizations to find out what kind of involvement they might appreciate. Encourage the group to select one.

You could contact them and arrange to work together for a day, a weekend or a week. Have the joy of learning to be Christ's reconcilers and healers!

Explore the possiblity of going to another country for mission service. Select a group of two or four or more. Go, return, and share.

7. Travel Retreat

Have a yearning to see the world? to go to new and distant places? There are lots of ways to travel.

Determine the cost you can afford for the weekend and then figure out how far you can go on that amount of money. The possibilities are endless, and the fun and creativity in stretching the dollars is fantastic.

Bike it. The bicycle has been determined to be the most efficient and ecologically sound means of transportation ever devised. Ross Chenot of University Baptist Church, Bakersfield, 2512 Church Ave., CA 93306, leads several bike trips each year, some short, and others over 500 miles.

Road show. Your group, large or small, can create a 20- or 30-minute program that you can share with other groups along the way. Write to other churches and arrange to sleep in their fellowship halls, and to perform for them. Great fun, and a neat way to make new friends.

You don't have to be professional actors. One group started with the Peanuts theme "Happiness is. . ." and created 20-second scenes illustrating the different ideas, plus many that they created on their own. These were interspersed with appropriate short scripture readings, poetry and other creations from the group.

Backpacking and foot washing can make an exciting and meaningful activity of fellowship.

8. Discovering Your Community

A home retreat can give you new eyes to see your neighbors.

Send out several people with cameras to photograph parts of your community that few people ever see.

Call and arrange for 15-minute interviews with several community leaders—chief of police, a policeman, a barber or hairdresser, a business-person, a welfare worker, a lawyer, a psychologist/counselor, a labor-union leader, a farmer, the mayor, a school board member, a newspaper reporter, etc.

Ask them three questions and record their answers on a cassette tape recorder and take notes:

1. What do you see to be the genuine strengths/assets of our community?

2. What do you see to be the needs or problems, issues that face our community?

3. What can the Christian community do to be part of the solutions to our community's problems, from your perspective?

Map your community. Ask members of the group, using crayons, to draw your community as they see it—significant groups, structures, "dividing lines," etc.

Do a newspaper collage. Create collage from back issues of the paper showing strength and problem areas.

The above information can be the basis for continuing discussion and reflection of our opportunities as Christians to influence the communities in which we live as ministers/servants of Jesus Christ.

The pain/problem areas can be listed during the report time. These could be ranked and one selected for possible group action.

The above information might be the focus for a special reporting session to the whole congregation regarding what you have learned and what opportunities you have to love the people God has created.

9. 24-hour Fasting Retreat

Several groups have organized fasts as part of their serious look at world hunger. During the time together, the group can study, view films, and share experiences related to the magnitude of world hunger, and the alternative responses we have as individuals and as Christians.

Rev. A. T. Meyer, Our Saviour Lutheran Church, 2101 N. Fruit, Fresno, CA, 93705, coordinated such a program, and involved other churches in doing it simultaneously around a Walk Against Hunger held near the time of the fast. Response was beautiful.

10. Multi-cultural Extravaganza

Do people from another racial or ethnic background share your community? Possibly many different heritages? Even if it is only one, you can have a ball finding out more about each other and experiencing what it would be like to be part of that culture.

Plan the weekend to include the foods, the folkstories, the history, the dances, the games, and the religious heritage of the cultures in your community. (Maybe the other cultures are non-Christian. This will give you an opportunity to share your faith with them).

If there are ethnic churches nearby, be in touch and work together in joint planning.

You might have only 10 participants total, or you might have over 100, as did an event in the Philadelphia area that involved five different ethnic groups.

You are the only ones who can determine what you need and what a particular retreat experience can do for you and your group.

You have the opportunity to use your God-given creativity to adapt the ideas for your group.

23

WHO AM I?:

A Self-identity Retreat Idea

by Virgil Nelson

The question "Who am I?" becomes a crucial issue for each of us at various times in our lives. The way we answer that question determines much of our openness and response to God, our feelings and actions toward others, our decisions about a career and a life partner—and even our sense of meaning in life.

While the focus in this retreat is self-discovery, the process of answering the question "Who am I?" from a biblical perspective demands that we hear from "God's people"—Christian friends—about our unique talents and abilities.

This retreat design assumes the need for group interaction and sharing as a necessary basis for helping individuals answer the question of "Who am I?" for themselves.

Before we can end up with personal answers to the "Who am I?" question, we also need to take a general look at some of God's answers. Without his perspective, we risk ending up with a distorted picture of who we are and what gives our lives meaning.

Theme scripture: 2 Corinthians 5:17-18

Before the retreat

In planning for your group's retreat, consider a number of items: budget, the place, food preparation, adult leadership, youth leadership and the balance between the structured and unstructured interaction.

You'll also need to complete the following:

1. Before the retreat, encourage individuals in the group to try something they've never tried before. New experiences might include playing different games, variations of familiar games, trying out a new talent in a talent show, reading something in front of the group, praying aloud, creating a retreat menu and purchasing the food, registering campers, handling money, and so on. All of these are valuable opportunities for self-discovery.

2. Ask at least three people to do specific planning for the Sunday morning "Needs Reporting" session. For additional details see the program ideas for that time period later on in this article.

3. Prepare the "Journal Reflection Sheets." See the Saturday morning session for ideas in designing these worksheets.

4. Encourage each person who comes to the retreat to bring a favorite thing as a vehicle for letting the group know something about him or her. The item can be anything: a song from a tape or record album, a photo, a poem, a book, a sample of a hobby, a rotten tennis shoe—anything.

5. If most people in your group don't know each other well, you may want to spend time building a solid basis for trust by helping the kids get to know each other better.

Getting there

Traveling to the retreat area can be an important part of the self-discovery process. To help your group get to know each other better, try the following "Traveling Scrambled" game.

1. First, pick names out of a hat to scramble the riders in the different cars and vans. If you're traveling by bus, divide into groups of eight.

2. Create a "Scramble Puzzle Sheet"—a crossword puzzle you've copied from a newspaper will work nicely. Beside the puzzle, print the headings "ACROSS" and "DOWN." Leave quite a bit of blank space beneath each heading.

When riding, the group is to try to
• get every person's first name to fit somewhere;
• get at least one descriptive adverb or adjective for each person in the group;
• get at least one favorite activity listed for each person.

At the end of the trip, each team should have its puzzle completed and clues to the puzzle written out. For instance, the "Across" clues could read, "Jane's hobby;" "Name of a girl who is very friendly;" "Bob's favorite sport" and so on.

WHO AM I? CONT.

Have each team score its own puzzle. Each team that fits all the names of its members into the puzzle gets 50 points. Award 100 points to the teams that get adverbs or adjectives for each member and 200 points for including at least one favorite activity for each person. Allow 10 bonus points for each additional adjective, adverb or favorite activity the team includes.

Award a crazy prize to the winning team during the Friday evening program.

Possible retreat schedule

FRIDAY:

3:30 p.m.—Register at the church; final payments; cabin room assignments here or later at the camp.

4:30 p.m.—Departure for the retreat (actual time depends on the driving distance to the center).

6 p.m.—Dinner on the road: individual cars on their own, or agree on a specific location and all meet there.

8 p.m.—Arrival at center: get unloaded and move in.

9 p.m.—Opening session: "God's Handprint, My Hand."

10:30 p.m.—Free time: snacks, games.

Midnight—In the sack, lights out. (This and other ground rules need to be agreed upon in advance of the weekend. Rules depend on the age/maturity of the group, rules of camp, program goals, morning schedule, etc.)

1 a.m.—Absolute quiet.

SATURDAY:

7 a.m.—Up and at'em.

7:30 a.m.—Personal devotions.

8 a.m.—Breakfast.

9:30-11:30 a.m.—Morning session (with break): "Who Am I? God's Word Speaks to Me."

Noon—Lunch.

Afternoon—Free time, with some structured optional choices: group games (see references); tournaments; swimming; outings; etc.

5:30 p.m.—Dinner.

7-9 p.m.—Evening session: "Who Am I? Self Discovery."

9:30 p.m.—Free time: (see Friday evening).

SUNDAY:

9:30 a.m.- noon—Morning sessions including break and worship: "God's People Speak to Me."

12:30 p.m.—Lunch and evaluation: most/least valuable activity for me; most/least valuable activity for our group in its spiritual development; changes I would suggest; other comments.

WEDNESDAY:

Leaders meeting to look over evaluations and reflect upon the strengths and weaknesses of the weekend.

Friday evening session (1½-2 hours)

1. 9 p.m.—Making handprints (45 minutes). For this activity you'll need water-base printer's ink, a small rubber roller, a piece of hard plastic or linoleum approximately one foot square, sheets of colored construction paper and one handkerchief. All of these supplies are available from a paint or artist supply shop.

Have each person choose a sheet of construction paper and sign his name at the bottom. Then place a small amount of ink on the hard plastic or linoleum and smooth the ink to even thickness with the roller. Also roll the ink onto the palm until it covers the fingers and the palm evenly.

Crumple the handkerchief and place it under the colored paper. (The handkerchief helps lines in the palm to print clearly.)

Press the inked hand firmly on the paper with the palm directly over the crumpled handkerchief.

Put the handprints in visible places around the room.

2. Begin group singing while the handprinting is being finished.

3. Fun 'n games: Pick a partner, sit back-to-back and lock arms. On signal, everyone sits down. On signal, everyone stands. Repeat this exercise in groups of four. Then try groups of eight. How about having the entire group stand back-to-back, lock arms and sit down, then stand up?

4. Who's here: Try this exercise in circles of 8-12 people, or everyone if the group numbers 25 or smaller. The first person gives his or her first name, describes one activity he enjoys and acts out that activity: "I'm Sue and I like to swim." (She makes swimming motions.)

The next person introduces himself and reintroduces Sue: "My name is Bill and I ride motorcycles," (he acts as though he's riding a motorcycle) "and this is Sue who swims" (he makes swimming motions).

Go around the circle and have kids introduce themselves and all the people who've been introduced earlier, including the actions. Don't embarrass someone who forgets a name. Have fun, but be sensitive to those who are shy.

5. Scrambled awards time: Report the winner of the "Traveling Scrambled" game and award the crazy prize. You might want to read some of the more creative puzzle entries before placing all the puzzles on the walls with the handprints.

6. My arrival, God's handiwork: In groups of two or four, tell about *the earliest birthday I can remember* and *a special gift* or *my most memorable birthday.* In groups of eight, tell *when the word GOD became more than just a word in my life.* Point out that not everyone has experienced a personal relationship with God, and that it's okay to mention questions they have about God or issues about God they're struggling with.

7. Mini-presentation: Have two volunteers read 2 Corinthians 5:17-18 and Jeremiah 1:4-9 aloud. Then say something like: *As we try to answer the question,*

"Who am I?" we need to know what God wants for us. What does he think about us?

We also need to look at ourselves—our interests, abilities, weaknesses.

As we go about answering this question we also need to talk with other people. Hearing about our strengths and weaknesses from others often tells us things about ourselves that we overlook.

Tonight we completed handprints. During the rest of the weekend feel free to write on someone's handprint qualities you appreciate in that person. Everything you write should be positive—no jokes or putdowns.

Remember who's in your group of eight. We'll get back in these groups tomorrow.

Saturday morning session (2 hours)

1. Group singing (10-15 minutes).

2. Have people get in the same groups they were in Friday evening. Then give each group a 200-piece puzzle without the picture of the puzzle. Challenge them to see how much they can assemble in five minutes. At the end of five minutes count the number of pieces each group has assembled.

Then give each group the picture of the puzzle and see how many pieces they can add to the puzzle in the next five minutes.

Possible discussion questions: *In what ways is putting the puzzle together like or unlike putting my life together? In what ways is the puzzle like or unlike answering the question, "Who am I?"* (10 minutes;

73

allow an extra 10 minutes for total group interaction.)

3. Studying God's finished picture: Divide the following six sets of scriptures among the groups. Give the following directions: Take 15-20 minutes and

a. read the passages out loud in your group;

b. discuss what you think the passage says;

c. explain what you think the passage means in each of your lives today;

d. describe what the verse says we are in God's eyes.

The person whose birthday is closest to April 1 is the group's recorder and is responsible for reporting back to the entire group at the end of the study session. Use large sheets of newsprint to record answers.

The passages to be studied are: Group 1—Genesis 1:26-31; Group 2—Isaiah 43:1-3 and Colossians 3:5-17; Group 3—Luke 4:18-19 and Ephesians 5:15-16; Group 4—John 6:21-40 and 1 Thessalonians 4:3-5; Group 5—Ephesians 4:11-32; Group 6—Galatians 5:13-26.

Be sure to read through these passages ahead of time. You may need to help when different groups get stuck in their studies.

After each group of eight has finished discussing its set of verses, get the total group together and have the "reporters" report on what their verses meant to different group members.

4. Mini-presentation (5 minutes): Comment that we are to practice all of what we just studied in whatever we do. Provide an opportunity for young people to talk with you about making a commitment to Jesus Christ.

Close this portion of the session with prayer.

Take a 15-minute break. You might want to serve simple refreshments at this time.

Saturday morning session continues

1. Favorite things: With kids in the same group of eight as before, have each person share a song, poem, rotten tennis shoe—whatever they brought. If people forgot to bring their items, have them tell about their "favorite things." (10-15 minutes).

2. Personal journal: Have each person create a personal journal for the retreat, which can be as simple or as elaborate as individual creativity and available supplies will allow. Bring construction paper, laundry markers and old magazines to cut up. Have kids put their name on the front and back covers.

Introduce the journal as an important part of the self-discovery process. Indicate that it is to help each person begin putting down thoughts, feelings and decisions for future use.

The journal's ground rules are simple: a.) What is written is strictly personal. No one is to read someone's journal unless he gets permission from the journal's owner. b.) No one will be forced to share what he's written. There will be opportunities for sharing what has been written, but each person is free to choose what to share and what not to share.

Hand out "Journal Reflection Sheets." (Produce these before the weekend, allowing ample space for each question.)

Journal Reflection Sheets

1. List 10 things you love to do.

2. List 10 things you'd like to try sometime.

3. If I had my choice, I'd rather work with things or with people. (Circle the number that best describes the way you see yourself.)

Things   1 2 3 4 5 4 3 2 1   **People**

4. I enjoy working with my hands less than I enjoy thinking about problem-solving.

Working with hands   1 2 3 4 5 4 3 2 1   **Problem solving**

5. Go back to questions 1 and 2. Rank the top five in each question.

6. List five things you don't like to do.

7. Put a check mark by those entries in questions 1 and 2 that might be related to a possible job or future career and list specific jobs. For example, if you "love kids," potential career areas could be child care, teaching, parenting, counseling, pediatrics, and so on.

8. List what you like and don't like about your parent(s) or job.

9. Write the name of one person you know who is working in a job you'd like to know more about.
Name: Job:

10. Three things you like about yourself are:..............
Three things you don't like about yourself are:.............

11. List five jobs you'd consider. Give each a percentage of hand/problem solving and things/people.

12. If you could do anything for God and knew you couldn't fail, what would you do?

Before adjourning the morning session, ask people to:

a. finish their journal covers;

b. complete questions 1-4 during the afternoon (you may want to have your kids complete these questions before ending this session);

c. remind everyone to add positive comments to the handprints on the walls;

d. bring journals to the evening session;

e. come up with gags, skits and acts for the evening talent show.

Saturday evening session (3 hours)

7 p.m.—Group singing. During the singing have each person tear a name tag from a piece of construction paper that says something about him or her (a basketball, a roller skate, a TV, whatever).

Spend the first hour or so of this session putting on the talent show. Keep in mind that this event can be an important opportunity for people who haven't performed well in the small discussion groups (1 hour).

8 p.m.—Self-discovery session. Have everyone pair off and compare handprints, noting similarities and differences.

1. Allow 15-20 minutes for the group to finish journal questions 4-11.

2. In the original groups of eight, allow each person two minutes to talk about his or her feelings and thoughts about a future career choice.

3. Spend a few minutes letting the entire group ask questions that came up in the smaller groups and add comments that might interest everyone.

4. Place a small candle in the center of each small group and allow for a few minutes of silent reflection. You may want to read some scripture or have someone share a reflective song.

Sunday morning session (2 hours)

1. Group singing (10-15 minutes).

2. Hearing God's words: Ask volunteers in advance to read Psalm 139 and Luke 4:18-19 aloud to the group.

3. Reports on needs and challenges: In advance of the retreat, get a team of youth "reporters" to make presentations on specific needs in your community or area, in addition to global needs such as world hunger, threat of nuclear holocaust, refugees. (Examples of community needs are poverty areas, senior citizens and transportation and daycare.) If time permits you may also want to show the film "Tilt," a 20-minute animated film on global concerns. This film is available from CROP, Box 968, Elkhart, IN 46514.

4. Allow about 10 minutes for everyone to finish journal question 12.

5. Have two volunteers read John 14:12 and Ephesians 4:1-16 out loud.

6. Speaking and hearing: Ask the entire group to circulate among the handprints and add additional characteristics, strengths or qualities they have observed in the person.

7. Have each person find his or her own handprint and take it to the group of eight.

One person at a time hands his handprint to the person in the group whose first name begins with the letter closest to G. That person reads everything that is written on the paper out loud. The group has an additional 30 seconds to write in other strengths and special qualities. Repeat the process until each person has heard what people wrote describing him.

8. Happy birthday: Say something like: *Whether or not you've made any decisions or commitments this weekend, you are invited to this birthday party. God offers us new birth each day and gives us the special gift of his spirit to share with each other and the world.*

Have each person think of gifts he'd give to each person in his group of eight. The gifts can be material goods, skills, or qualities. For instance, someone might give someone else the gift of patience to deal with a difficult life situation.

Go around the groups, with everyone focusing on one person at a time.

Sing "Happy Birthday" to "the new you" and have people point to someone as they sing. Sing the song a

second time and have kids point to themselves.

9. Provide an opportunity for volunteers to tell about decisions they've made during the retreat. Encourage each person to complete the sentence, "One thing I want to do next is. . ."

10. The gift of service: Close with communion within the groups of eight in celebration of God's sacrificial love, and the new life he has given. (As an alternative ending, you could end the retreat by conducting a hand- or foot-washing ceremony similar to the one recorded in John 13.)

11. Close with a song.

Resources

1. Game ideas for group recreation time: **The New Games Book**, edited by A. Fleugelman, Doubleday. **Fun 'n Games**, Rice, Rydberg & Yaconelli, Zondervan. **The Best of Try This One** and **More Try This One**, Schultz, GROUP Books.

2. Songbooks: **Songs**, Songs and Creations, Box 559, San Anselmo, CA 94960.

3. Activities: **Recycle Catalogues 1 and 2**, Benson, Abingdon. **Values Clarification: A Handbook**, edited by Simon, Howe and Kirschenbaum, Hart.

4. Retreat planning, philosophy and program ideas: **The Retreat Handbook: A-Way to Meaning**, V. Nelson and L. Nelson, Judson.

EARS: A Wee

by Thom Schultz and John Shaw

Two of the most effective tools in your own personal Christian ministry are stuck on the sides of your head.

Listening is the primary tool used by psychologists and Christian counselors when dealing with people with various problems. Many burdens can be eased tremendously simply by "talking them out." But somebody has to listen.

Listening is also our primary way of getting to know a person. Sometimes we're really surprised to find out we like someone who, on first impression, really turned us off. All it takes is a little listening.

The "Ears" retreat is an unforgettable, high-impact experience in listening. Groups should be eager to benefit from this experience before ever making plans for the retreat. The retreat demands many hours of strict-discipline—you will be unable to speak.

Schedule

FRIDAY NIGHT:

After you arrive at your retreat site, break into a rousing mixer or game. Have fun and celebrate the weekend you're about to experience.

Then, determine the diads. There are many ways to do this, so your group should decide which way is best for you. You may agree to number arbitrarily off by having someone pass out numbered slips of paper to everyone. Each slip would have a matching number, so all you need do is find the person with your number.

Another method involves a more personal approach. The group is given four or five minutes of silence to think about the partner each person would like to have for the rest of the weekend. You may decide to pick someone you'd really enjoy being with for the weekend. Or you may want to select somebody who you feel really needs to be listened to by someone. After the period of silence, walk to the person you've selected. Obviously, not all diads will fall naturally into place, so you should have a second and third choice of a partner in mind. Remember, no one is required to reveal his reason for selecting the partner he did. This is not a popularity poll.

After the diads are determined, agree who will be the 'A' partner and who will be the 'B' partner. Then hit the sack.

SATURDAY:

Before breakfast, it should be announced that all 'A' people will be restricted from speaking from now until 3 p.m. Then proceed with breakfast. Mealtimes will be among the most meaningful experiences of the week-end. The talking partner will have to be aware of the silent partner's needs for sugar, more milk, etc.

During breakfast, the 'B' people may feel tempted to ignore their silent partners and converse freely with other 'B' people. The common social phenomenon of shutting out naturally quiet individuals may become all too obvious.

After breakfast, each 'A' person is given a note pad and pencil. This will be available to them should they want to make notes about things 'B' will tell them.

Now, from about 9 to 10:30 a.m., each diad should find a spot to talk and listen. The topic for 'B' will be your group. He should air feelings about what's right with your group, what's wrong with your group, what direction it's taking, and what kinds of things it should be doing in the coming year.

Then, from about 10:30 to noon, each diad should remain together for some fun and games. Activity will depend on what's available at your retreat site. A diad may engage in a game just for themselves, such as ping pong, or several diads may join for a team effort such as volleyball or tug-of-war. Several different types of activities should be offered.

Lunch will again be a very important part of the listening experience.

Then, from about 1 to 2:30 p.m., the diads should again each find a place to talk and listen. This session will be the heaviest. The topic for 'B' this time will be himself. He should describe to 'A' who he is—not just what he is. His description of himself should go beyond, "I'm a junior at Lucille Ball High School." 'B' should share what sets him apart from every other person on earth. He should also share his faith with 'A'. And, 'B' may also use this period as a "dumping time"—airing his gripes, problems, etc. Remember, 'A' must remain silent.

Planning

Before setting up the retreat, have at least one discussion on the importance of listening. Discuss problems often arising with friends, parents and teachers where a bit of listening by one or both sides would help a great deal. Then, discuss the idea of a weekend retreat where everyone must spend a certain block of time just listening. During the retreat, the group would be divided into diads (pairs). One person would be free to talk, but the other would say absolutely nothing. At a certain point during the weekend, the listening-speaking roles for the diads would be reversed.

Your group must really want to experience this type of retreat. It won't work if everybody sees it as a joke. This is not to say it won't be fun. There will be plenty of fun and funny moments.

After the group decides to do the retreat, select a site. The retreat works well in either a rural or urban environment.

At 2:30 p.m. everyone should gather for some light refreshments. At this time, the leader announces the role reversal. From this time forward, 'B' is silent and 'A' may speak. (Be prepared for some loud vocalizations from the 'A' people—celebrating their voices.) Give a pencil and pad to all 'B' people.

From now until about 4:30, each diad should again find a spot to talk and listen. The topic for this session will again be your group, covering the same feelings 'B' was invited to share during the morning session.

From 4:30 to 6 p.m., again engage in recreation, remaining in your diads.

Then, experience dinner. With the roles reversed, you may notice some differences.

Follow dinner with some singing. Remember, only 'A' people may use their voices. The 'B' people may wish to become the rhythm section—clapping, stomping, or dancing.

Then, from 7:30 to 9 p.m., each diad should again find a spot to be alone. Now 'A' will share who he is with 'B'. And, like before the roles were reversed, this is also a time for sharing faith, gripes and problems. And, of course, 'B' may only listen, and take notes, if he wishes.

Now, at 9 p.m., everyone is free to talk again. Be prepared for more hollering.

At this point, the leader should outline the elements of effective communication and "active listening." Basically, this process involves a simple confirming of thought. When someone says something to you, as an active listener you should say what you interpret the other person to be saying. For example, if someone says, "I sure feel uncomfortable in this room," you might say "Do you mean it's too hot in here?"

Now, the diads should again go off alone. But, this time, both people may speak. Be sure to take your note pads. Now is the time for feedback, telling your partner what you heard his saying throughout the day. Be sure to use the confirming process in this session. During this time, you'll really have an opportunity to use your active listening ministry skills with your partner, as you discuss each other's personalities, hopes, dreams, frustrations, and problems. The notes in your note pad will help you remember what your partner said to you during the day.

Close the day with a group prayer.

SUNDAY

Enjoy breakfast where everyone may speak.

After breakfast, get your diad together with another diad. Discuss the value of the retreat. How did you feel? What did you learn? What was the most difficult part of the experience? Appoint one person in each foursome to report your feelings back to the total group.

Then, bring the entire group back together for celebration/worship. Give time to the recorders from each foursome to contribute feelings and hopes for your group for the coming year. Discuss the person of Christ as listener. Join in an agape meal.

Follow-up

Since this retreat is really a powerful one, you may want to reserve the next one or two group meetings for debriefing. Reserve a time during these meetings for your original diads to get back together for a private talk. You may have some additional deep feelings that should be shared with your diad partner.

I CAN'T SEE:

A Retreat to Exp

by Joe Fowler

All right now people, shut those beady little eyes of yours and imagine staying like that for 18 hours. Let me tell you, it's a real experience and I recommend anyone trying it. Well, 14 other people and I did it and in this chapter I'll tell you all about it.

The idea of a blind retreat had been in the making for quite a long time, but finally the idea began to work up to a reality. We had been trying to develop a caring community among ourselves to help us face day-to-day problems in life and one way of going about this might be to experience how others not so fortunate manage to get along in society and everyday life.

Planning meetings started to take shape. The facilities and weekend were finalized, menus made, food purchased and program developed. All of this was done by both youth and advisors.

We all met at Salem Church on a gloomy April night to set forth on one of the most unforgettable excursions of our lives. The "top egg" was our best friend (and associate pastor of Salem United Church of Christ) Roger Lawarre. This is one guy everyone should have the good fortune to be touched by in some way. All of us who were associated with him grew so much from him.

Back to my story. Before the blindfolds went on, we all agreed to a contract, which essentially is a statement of the ground rules of the retreat. Then one by one, each of us lost all touch with our most indispensable sense—sight. It was the last daylight we would see until Saturday afternoon. Some of us were pretty bold in the beginning, until we learned that one wrong move could land somebody in the hospital.

"I felt awkward, clumsy and terribly dependent." Those immortal words of Ken Daniel say what a good many of us in the group felt.

Next on the agenda was getting from Salem to Camp Adams, where the retreat was to be held. This was an experience in itself. The members were completely dependent on the driver and the voices of each other. It was a slow trip because we were traveling through mountains and it was extremely foggy. After what seemed a long time, we finally made it to the one-room cabin in the Pocono Mountains.

erience Blindness

The cabin's features were ideal for this retreat: one room with the kitchen area on the left, and tables in the middle and an open area on the right. A fireplace was in the front wall with bathrooms on the opposite wall. The ceiling was high and above the bathrooms was a balcony for sleeping, overlooking the rest of the cabin. Leading up to the balcony was a spiraling staircase.

The cabin's structure limited the extent people could pullout of sessions, although in the blind portion of the retreat it would have been next to impossible anyway. Everything that had to be done was just a short distance away, so it simplified movement.

For a good number of people it was the first time they had been there. They were living in a place they had never seen, which I guess isn't really that awful, since blind people never see their surroundings either.

Then the advisors unloaded everything, which was an accomplishment in itself because 20 persons' clothes, sleeping bags and food is a lot of unloading for only a few advisors.

After settling in, we did some awakening exercises that involved doing some crazy things. At first I was a little reluctant to do them for fear of the others watching me. But then I came to realize that everyone was in the same position, except for the advisors. Anyway, we were paired off with another person and we then had a personal discussion with that individual.

After that there was a short break in the schedule. Oh boy! That's free time! Big deal! We sat and sat and maybe once in a while someone actually spoke! It was really strange, you didn't know when to talk or really what to say. You were never sure if anyone was listening. Free time never went so slow.

Then came the pizza. Oh, brother! That you should try. It's hot; it's greasy; it's slimy and when you can't see, it's a mess! You're never sure if you're getting it in your mouth or on your lap. Since you usually don't say much when you're eating, it's like eating alone.

Did you ever have an affair with an orange? We did! We felt it, caressed it, top to bottom, moved it between our hands and rolled it on our faces. Peeling it with care along with listening, feeling, and smelling it,

proceeded tearing it apart, eating some and squeezing the rest all over your hands until they were good and sticky. In this experience we used all our senses but sight, and there really was no use for it.

Clean is a sensation you really don't fully appreciate until you are blind. We washed each other's hands with soap, water and salt, dried them and rubbed them in baby oil. After that treatment my hands actually tingled.

The last thing for the night was to experience a cup of water. Each of us was handed an empty cup and we were to realize its condition. Empty, light and round. Our cup was then slowly filled with water. Listen. . . feel the weight change, and slowly drink it being aware of it moving down your body.

Bedtime! That's easier said than done. According to one advisor, it was a real dilly.

First we had to describe each sleeping bag and duffle bag to find out what belonged to whom. It never occurred to us to put identification on personal belongings. Once we got the gear to the person and the person up the circular steps to a cot, we thought we had it made. Oh, yeah! Judi HAD to go down and brush her teeth. Debbie HAD to go down and wash her face. And numerous other nightly chores in the bathroom too numerous to mention had to be done by almost all the other youth. . .use your imagination.

Now, waking up blind is really a hairy experience when you don't know what's coming off. But we all managed to figure out what was going on quickly. Judi and Debbie said what they felt, "As we undid our sleeping bags to prepare for bed, I had a feeling of fear to know that when I woke up in the morning it would still be dark for me."

Come 8 a.m.! It was time for a good hearty breakfast. Most of us were moaning about how the bandages itched. And they itched as long as we sat and thought about how much they itched.

After breakfast we went on one of the most "eye opening" (har!) experiences of the retreat, a blind walk in the forest. We broke off into groups, one leader for every five blindees. All six of us held hands and started out on our trip. While walking along I had a compelling fear that I was going to walk into a tree.

We then began to explore nature's wonders. Jean, our group leader, found different things and let each one of us try to figure out what it was. For instance, a mint leaf. We smelled, tasted, and felt it. And because of its distinctive flavor and smell, it wasn't too hard to figure out.

Judi had a good point. "Noises seemed a lot louder. Driving up in the car, the traffic, and rain seemed louder. I heard things that I never took time to hear before." We walked for about one half-hour. In that half-hour we became unbelievably closer to nature.

One of the final blind experiences was foot washing. We each went with a partner and washed another's feet while a story about a similar situation with Jesus and his disciples was read to us.

Now is the time for all good people to get rid of the blindfolds. Debbie and I sat face-to-face and slowly removed each other's blindfold, keeping our eyes closed. Boy, did that hurt! We then counted three and opened our eyes for the first time in 18 hours, together. I imagined everything to be dull and dark. But, due to three large skylights, the room was bright. My initial sight was a flash of light that lasted for a fraction of a second. Then I saw Debbie, and for some unknown reason, I almost started to cry.

After our sight was restored, relationships and friendships seemed much more genuine and real. Here is a statement by Roger that might help you better understand what feelings came out of the retreat: "It's hard to say what made the experience such a high point for me as well as the other participants. I can only say that when we cut off the dependence of vision, the group members became quieter and less willing to do their own thing. They gradually began to support each other so that they could walk without falling. They centered their discussion on their feelings and "observations" and almost no time on trying to impress each other with their physical, social, or intellectual abilities. In essence, the group freed themselves from the bondage of 'what will others think of me?' "

Now it's time for us to do some mind finding, soul searching or whatever you want to call it. One thing we got into was the love process, which is basically a good set of guidelines to follow when dealing with people. The five basic steps are: I see you, I hear you, I accept your right to be you, I need you and I love you. I'll end my explanation of it there because an entire chapter can be written on it.

We also did a value clarification, which is deciding in your own head what ideas or values held the highest priorities in your life and which ideas hold the least importance to you.

On Sunday, after breakfast, we had a celebration. To start, some sections of the number one best seller were read. Then we did "Live-Die Sheet," which is really fantastic. How it works: Each of us took a sheet of newsprint and wrote on it our name and two columns—"Live" and "Die." We all put them anywhere on the wall and began. Taking a marker, we went to each sheet and in the "Live" column wrote a good characteristic about that person that he should let live. In the "Die" column we wrote a bad point about the individual that we thought the person should consider doing something about. At the end we all took our own sheets and read them, and if inclined to do so, rapped with other people about them. I find this an excellent way of learning about yourself and is something you can refer back to later to see if you have changed in either column. It is also a way of restoring confidence in yourself and taking a good honest look at yourself and other people.

To close the celebration we did a love circle, which is quite an experience. Everyone stands in a circle. One by one each member stands in the middle of the circle. One by one, members go into the circle and greet that person in any nonverbal way. It sounds easy, but it's really risky when it comes to doing it. Reluctance is prevalent in the beginning. It takes a lot of guts to walk out into the middle, and once you get there you get the feeling no one is going to greet you. But everything goes fine and you come out of it with a really great feeling.

For the rest of the retreat we had a cleanup, lunch, and a quick evaluation of what we thought about the retreat. We loaded the cars up and headed for home. Like all retreats, going home, back to civilization, and school, and leaving this fantastic environment, was a real kick in the teeth.

What's that? You say you'd like to have a blind retreat like that in your group? Great! Let me offer a few suggestions. First, in planning our retreat we considered having half the group blind for half the retreat with the remainder of people partners of sight. Then we would switch roles for the rest of the retreat. We ruled this out because that would create a feeling of superiority among those with sight. This would put the participants on different levels.

With everyone blind, everyone was in the same position.

The smaller the housing for holding the retreat, the better.

Use bandages with adhesive tape for blindfolds. They are not so easily removed. Otherwise the temptation to remove them might be too great. We did allow a rule that permitted a blindee to remove the blindfold if the situation became unbearable. The need, although, never came up. Keep in mind that in having a retreat, there is no right or wrong way. Use your good judgment and decide among your group what exactly is going to be done and what you are going to try to accomplish.

As you ponder into the realm of a blind experience, remember the immortal words spoken by nearly everyone at some time or another during the retreat. . . "I Can't See!"

A Fall Retreat to Help Unify Your Group

by Virgil Nelson

Fall is a great time to give special focus to helping your group members get to know each other as persons and to develop a common sense of purpose and commitment to God, each other, and the goals of the group for the year.

In retreat planning, some basic decisions need to be made in light of the "givens" in your group at the moment, and your goals for your group and the weekend.

Fall Retreat CONT.

The place

You may have a regular place you go for retreats and all you need to do is check schedules and make reservations. Or, someone in the group may have a home that could accommodate the group. You may have a friend in a distant church and your group could arrange to stay in that church building for its retreat. Or you may have state or county parks that would be ideal. Make your choice, and make your reservations.

Structure

If a primary goal is helping your group members know and love each other, consider determining room assignments before the retreat so that persons who do not know one another well will be together.

If you choose to structure group contact tightly in other parts of the program, then you may want to give participants free choice regarding rooming arrangements and let natural friendships be honored. For example: If people are together in small groups during group sessions, and are assigned to work together in food preparation, then somewhere in the weekend they need to have a "no pressure" choice.

Theme scripture: Colossians 3:12-17

In travel

The process of travel can be a conscious part of building and developing friendships and group process. Try this game entitled "Chicken Roulette."

Step #1. Each car is given a number. Slips of paper with that number are put into a hat. If you plan five passengers in car #1, then put five #1 slips of paper in the hat. Each participant draws a number which assigns him/her to a car.

Step #2. Once in the assigned car, each person writes his/her name on a piece of paper, which again goes into a hat. The hat goes around and each person draws a name.

Step #3. One at a time, each person reveals the name drawn. The people in the car then try to guess the answers to the following questions about the person whose name was drawn. Each passenger gets one guess for each question. Go one question at a time. After hearing all guesses, the named person can give the real answer. If there is further discussion/sharing, let it continue.

Questions: 1. Guess how this person likes his/her chicken prepared (barbecued, crispy, old-fashioned, boiled, broiled, etc.). 2. Guess birthdate. 3. Guess favorite TV program. 4. Guess color of eyes (without looking). 5. Guess favorite hobby.

Step #4. The second and fourth persons whose names are drawn get to answer the "Chicken Roulette question of the day." Each person guesses a question that #2 or #4 might be "chicken" to ask. Persons #2 and #4 are free to acknowledge if each question is truly one they'd be afraid to ask or not. If not, they may respond with another question that they really would be afraid to ask someone. If a genuine question is asked, you shouldn't feel any compulsion to answer it. Move on; it can come up again later as appropriate.

If the trip is over two hours, plan to change cars in the middle, using the same process twice.

Possible retreat schedule
FRIDAY

3:30 p.m.—Register at the church; final payments; cabin room assignments here or later at the camp.

4:30 p.m.—Departure for the retreat (actual time depends on the driving distance to the center).

6 p.m.—Dinner on the road: individual cars on their own, or agree on a specific location and all meet there.

8 p.m.—Arrival at center: get unloaded and move in.

9 p.m.—Opening session: "God's Chosen People: Who's Here?"

10:30 p.m.—Free time: snacks, games.

Midnight—In the sack, lights out. (This and other ground rules need to be agreed upon in advance of the weekend. Rules depend on the age/maturity of the group, rules of camp, program goals, morning schedule, etc.)

SATURDAY

7 a.m.—Up and at'em.

7:30 a.m.—Personal devotions.

8 a.m.—Breakfast.

9:30-11:30 a.m.—Morning session (with break): "God's People: Clothed With Compassion."

Noon—lunch

Afternoon—Free time, with some structured optional choices: group games (see references); tournaments; swimming; outings, etc.

5:30 p.m.—Dinner

7-9 p.m.—Evening session: "God's People: Macramed (or Woven Together) in His Love," including film, "The Nail."

9:30 p.m.—Free time: (see Friday evening).

SUNDAY:

9:30 a.m.-12 noon—Morning sessions including break and worship: "God's People: Thankforgiveful-ness"

12:30 p.m.—Lunch and evaluation: most/least valuable activity for me; most/least valuable activity for our group in its spiritual development; changes I would suggest; other comments.

WEDNESDAY:

Leaders' meeting to look over evaluations and reflect upon the strengths and weaknesses of the weekend.

Friday evening session (1½-2 hours)

1. Group singing. (10-15 minutes.)

2. Put all the participants' names into a hat. Each person draws a name, and becomes a "secret friend" to that individual during the retreat, without the other person guessing that he/she is in fact a "secret friend." During the worship service on Sunday, there will be an opportunity for revelation of who the secret friends have been during the weekend.

3. Find your identity: Number the group by counting around to end up with groups of eight persons. Each number is assigned a song tune to hum in finding the other seven persons in the group. This should be done with eyes closed, on your knees, on the floor. (Possible songs: "Old McDonald," "Clementine," "Home on the Range," etc.) When all the group is found, stand and sing the song out loud at the top of your voice. (10 minutes.) Stay in this group.

4. Names Are No Game: Ask the groups to sub-divide into groups of two persons. Share around the following questions:

A. How do you feel about your name? Anything unusual about it? How did you get it?

B. If you could change it would you? To what? (5-7 minutes.)

5. Names—What's the Fame? Have the groups of eight reassemble.

A. Share briefly about the person you met and his/her name. (5-7 minutes.)

B. Individually share with the entire group: If you could be famous for something, go down in the Guinness Book of Records, be written up in the annals of history, end up in future editions of the Bible, what would you like it to be for? Allow two minutes of reflection before starting. Begin with the person whose eyes are bluest. (15 minutes.)

6. Mini-presentation (5-7 minutes) on the theme passage. Or, simply read the passage aloud to the entire group from two different translations without comment.

7. Prayer by leader for the total group, or within small groups using sentence prayers.

8. Announcements and overview-reminder of ground rules/assumptions for the weekend. Tell people to remember which persons are in their group.

Saturday morning session (2 hours)

1. Group singing. (10-15 minutes.)

2. Form same groups as Friday evening. Read aloud to the entire group the theme scripture Colossians 3:12-17.

3. Reflection sheet on key theme words: Print 8½x11 sheet with the following words listed down the left side (space out over the entire length of page): COMPASSION/KINDNESS, HUMILITY, GENTLENESS, PATIENCE, FORGIVENESS, LOVE, and THANKS-GIVING. Vertically divide the page into three columns with these headings at the top, from left to right: WHEN I HAVE EXPERIENCED THIS, WHEN I GAVE THIS, A TIME WHEN I NEEDED THIS.

A. Have each person reflect and make notes in silence. (5 minutes.)

B. Divide into pairs and share feelings and responses. (7-10 minutes.)

4. Bible study based on Colossians 3:12-17. (30-45 minutes.) Print Bible study instruction sheet as follows (or read instructions to the group).

A. Reread the scripture to your group of eight. Focus on what the Holy Spirit is saying to you about the meaning of the passage in your life. Reflect on the meaning of this passage in the life of your group. Share. (10 minutes.)

B. Then create a way to share or demonstrate the meaning of the passage using the vehicles/tools suggested below. Groups must pick different categories until they are all taken and then there can be repeats. Creations will be shared during the Sunday morning session with the entire group.

Pick one word from the list of theme words in the passage listed above and:

a) LETTER-WRITING: Pretend you are Paul writing a letter to your group on the meaning of this word and this passage in the life of your group. Now read this letter as though it were the year 2,180. You may want to write individual letters and then compile a "group letter."

b) POETRY: Pick one word and use the French poetry form "cinquain" (sin-kane) to express the meaning of this passage. It is difficult for more than two people to work on one verse, so work as individuals and in pairs so your group can create several.

A Fall Retreat CONT.

CINQUAIN FORM:
```
—— ——          title (one word)
  —— ——        describe title (2 words)
—— —— ——       feeling (3 words)
—— —— —— ——    action (4 words)
———————————    one word summary
```

Members of the group may want to use other poetry forms also.

c) CRAFTS: Using the craft materials available, make something that symbolizes, represents, or demonstrates the truths of our scriptural theme passage. (Have available an assortment of colored paper, string, glue, wire, rubber bands, paper clips, straws, crayons, Play Dough sticks, toothpicks and the like.)

d) SLIDES AND/OR MUSIC: Select slides (bring a bunch from family trips, etc.) to express the meaning of this passage. Or select one song from a record and pick slides to go with it. Or you may choose your own music and sing it live along with the slides.

e) SONG CREATION: Use the tune of a popular song, or TV ad, and create new words to express the meaning of this scripture in your life as an individual or as a group. (Several may want to work with one tune, others with another. Or you may want to work in pairs writing different verses for the same tune.)

f) COMMERCIALS: Think up ad lines from radio, TV or magazines. Take the line and convert it to convey meanings around our theme and the truths of this scripture.

g) SOAP OPERA: Create a skit, pantomime or role play that illustrates or demonstrates the meaning of the passage in a real-life situation.

5. Closing prayer by leader with the total group, or within small groups (sentence prayers).

6. Announcements, includes a request for crazy skits for tonight, talent to sing, dance, etc., as a part of the evening session.

Saturday evening session (2 hours)

1. Game: Divide group in half, on either side of an imaginary line, or use a line of chairs or a rope. Play balloon volleyball or Nerf volleyball, using two balloons or Nerfs at once. Play to 7 points.

2. Singing as a group.

3. Fun 'n dumb skits, plus musical and other talent. You'll need one coordinator and an emcee for this event. Watch your time limit.

4. One or two songs as transition to the film.

5. Show film "The Nail." (20 minutes.) In pairs (does not have to be someone from your base group of eight) share:
• feelings about the film
• if you were a person in the film, which person would you most likely be?
• what does this film tell you about being God's people bound together in love?

6. Prayer and close.

7. Announcements, reminders, etc.

Sunday morning session (2½ hours)

At breakfast announce that each person is to bring something to the morning session from outside the building—for example, an object from the world of nature.

1. Group singing.

2. Small groups of eight meet to review or prepare their creations from the Saturday morning session. (15-20 minutes.)

3. Come back together in groups of eight all in the same room. In pairs share the object you brought and how this object reminds you of God. Then share how this object reminds you of your group as it has been in the past.

Then, share one final question: "How does this object reflect how I want our youth group to be in the future?" (20 minutes.)

4. SELF RATING SCALE: On a scale of 1-10 rate yourself in the following:

I feel loved:	I am patient:	I am loving toward:
.....by self	.....with self	.....self
.....by parents	.....with parents	.....parents
.....by peers	.....with peers	.....peers
.....by God	.....with God	.....God

I am thankful for:	I express my thanks to:
.....self	.....self
.....parents	.....parents
.....peers	.....peers
.....God	.....God

Share responses to these with one other person in your group of eight. (10 minutes.)

5. Each group shares its creation from the Saturday morning session. Affirm each in a way appropriate—applause, etc. (15-45 minutes.)

6. In groups of eight, share: Who in our school, our community and our church needs to have our love (and God's love) given to them? Make a list of specific groups and even individuals. What are we going to do about it? List possible actions. (10-20 minutes.)

7. Revealing of secret friends—go to your secret friend and share with him.

8. Close in song and prayer.

9. Provide evaluation forms at lunch.

Resources

1. Games: **The New Games Book**, edited by A. Fleugelman, Doubleday. **Fun 'n Games**, Rice, Rydberg & Yaconelli, Zondervan. **The Best of Try This One** and **More Try This One**, Schultz, GROUP Books.

2. Songbooks: **Songs**, Songs and Creations, Box 559, San Anselmo, CA 94960.

3. Film: "The Nail," available from American Baptist Films, Valley Forge, PA 19481.

4. Retreat planning, philosophy and program ideas: **The Retreat Handbook: A-Way to Meaning**, by Virgil and Lynn Nelson, Judson Press.

A Spring Retreat to Focus on Helping Others

by Bill Ameiss

Spring brings new life and is a time for new starts. This retreat design is intended to help young people discover that they can help others, think through the kinds of help their friends need and practice ways in which they can help each other.

A Spring Retreat CONT.

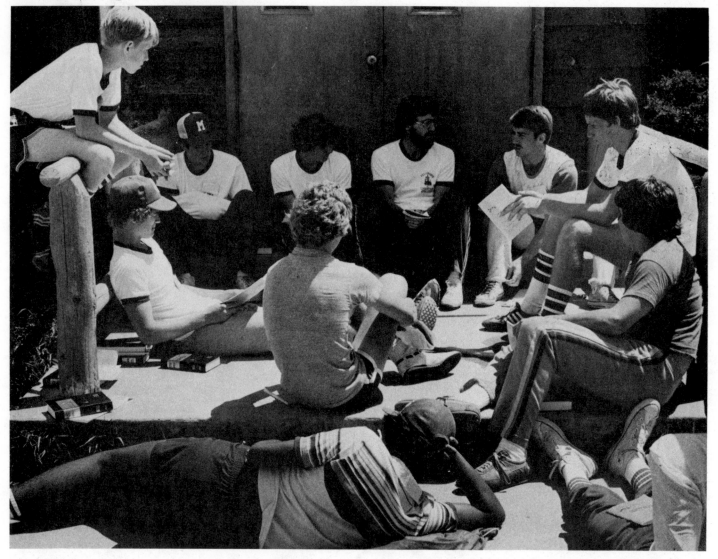

The people

Don't impose this retreat design on your young people. If you think the topic and direction are useful for your young people, share the idea with them. Let those young people help design the retreat's goals and purposes. If the young people don't become involved in setting the retreat goals, you may be wasting everyone's time. But if they meet needs and speak to concerns, get ready for an exciting time!

The place

Retreat sites vary greatly in what they offer and what they leave for you to do. This retreat design is intended for a place where meals are prepared by staff and not by the group itself. Should your retreat facility require time for cooking meals, setting tables, etc., adjustments can be made easily both before and after meals.

Get your retreat site booked as early as possible. Many good retreat sites are booked six months to a year in advance.

If a retreat center is too expensive, think of other options such as visiting a church in another town or someone's house. Many retreats have flourished with sleeping bags on gym mats for housing. Whatever you do, don't let the cost of a retreat center keep you from a valuable retreat experience.

Structure

Weekend retreats help build good group relationships. At the same time they depend on good group interaction. Give some thought prior to the retreat to at least two meetings with those committed to the retreat experience.

Use or adapt the following ideas for those optional meetings:

Goal setting—Share the retreat's goals and purposes with the entire group. Then pass out paper and pencils and have everyone answer the following questions: What are my reasons for attending this retreat? What's one thing I hope to gain from this retreat? What am I willing to do to make this a good experience for myself and for others in the group?

In groups of four to six, allow time for people to

share their responses.

What really bugs me—The first retreat session calls for role plays on the topic, "What really bugs me about other people." Divide into groups of three or four and have each group secretly practice a two- to three-minute skit to be presented at the retreat.

Creative devotions teams—Divide volunteers into two teams. Challenge your devotion groups to use themes that deal with our helping, supporting, caring relationships. Among others, the teams might consider Luke 15:11-24; Luke 10:25-37; Galatians 6:1-2; John 13:4-9. Teams can use music, records, skits or readings to close the day's activities. Allow plenty of time for practice. You may want to help in the planning stages.

A *"typical situation"*—Try a fun activity that will help your group see a need for the retreat. Come up with a typical youth group activity. Then write on pieces of paper different roles to be acted out. For instance, the activity might be "deciding which group game to play." The goal is to come to a group consensus. Different roles can be "leader, wants to play volleyball," "leader, wants to play charades," "sad over lost lover," "angry with any leader," "doesn't like anything," "will agree to anything," and so on. After the activity has become totally frustrating, stop it and ask the different actors their feelings about themselves and the other actors.

Group Covenant—A retreat *covenant* (a promise between at least two persons) can be a meaningful commitment made by group members to each other. Have each retreater complete and sign the following covenant.

1. We commit ourselves to treat each other as follows:

2. We will support and be responsible for each other by:

3. We expect our retreat leaders to:

4. We agree to handle any group behavior issues or concerns (such things as noise, sleeping times, drugs, alcohol, hassles/disagreements, and breaking the covenant) in the following way:

5. As a group on this retreat we want to accomplish: (List the group's goals.)

Signatures...

A brief meeting prior to the retreat can reaffirm the covenant and firm up the details of meeting times, departure times, equipment to bring, etc.

Possible schedule
FRIDAY EVENING
5 p.m.—Meet at church to load and pack; final payments due
8 p.m.—Arrive at retreat center and get settled
8:30 p.m.—Games
9-10 p.m.—Session 1: "Honesty—The First Step in Helping"
10-10:15 p.m.—Devotion
10:15-Midnight—Night hike or free time
Midnight—Sack time

SATURDAY
8-8:30 a.m.—Breakfast
9-11 a.m.—Session 2: "What, Me Lost?"
11-Noon—Organized fun 'n games.
Noon—Lunch
1:30-3:30 p.m.—Session 3: "Getting in Over Your Head"
3:30-5 p.m.—Fun 'n games
5:30 p.m.—Dinner
7-9:30 p.m.—Session 4: "Don't Just Stand There"
9:30-11 p.m.—Fun 'n games
11 p.m.—Live options: devotions and singing
Midnight—Sack time

SUNDAY
8-8:30 a.m.—Breakfast
9-11 a.m.—Session 5: Optional sessions
11-11:15 a.m.—Evaluation
11:15-Noon—Clean up, pack up, get ready to leave
Noon—Lunch and depart

Friday evening session (½ hour)
You won't have time to complete all the options in this outline. Using key young people in your planning team, plan activities and studies that will best suit your group.

1. 8:30 p.m.—Begin with a crowdbreaker: "Spring Beauty Contest." Provide stacks of old newspapers (you'll need plenty), several pairs of scissors, rolls of Scotch tape and an abundance of straight pins.

Divide into groups of four or five persons each and make sure each group has the necessary supplies. You'll also need a separate room or corner where each group can work secretly.

Each group selects one person to be its entrant in the "beauty" contest. After deciding what person, place, thing or animal the entrant is to be, everyone goes to work—cutting, crumpling, bunching, rolling, piecing, pinning, taping.

Allow 15 minutes. Then call everybody together for a costume show and an awarding of prizes (a Barbie doll makeup set, a bottle of cheap perfume, a McDonald's gift certificate).

2. *Name tags*—Provide a large piece of construction paper, a straight pin and a laundry marker for each person. The object is to tear the construction paper into an animal that represents you. (Use a large piece of newsprint to show, step by step, what you mean.)

On one-half the large name tag, have each person write two little-known facts about himself and then a lie. On the other half of the name tag, each person follows these directions: 1. Write a brief definition of help. 2. Jot down one reason people need help. 3. The kind of person I look for when I need help is. . . 4. When people come to me for help, it's usually because. . .

Allow enough time for everyone to complete each item.

Divide into small groups and have each person explain what his or her "animal" is. After guessing which statements are true and which one is the lie, each person shares answers to the sentences on helping. Encourage people to explain why they wrote what they did.

3. *What Really Bugs Me About Other People*—If you practiced the skits outlined earlier, put them on now.

4. *Forehead feelings*—Stick a large gum (or mailing) label to each person's forehead. Use a laundry marker to write a feeling on each one ("happy," "sad," "angry," "depressed," "love sick," "lonely," "dumped on," "happy go lucky," and so on). Have each person try to guess what feeling he has on his forehead by the way people act toward him. For instance, people would treat the person with the "happy" label as though he's happy. After the exercise, ask different people how they felt being treated the way they were.

5. *Bible study: "Honesty: The First Step in Helping"* —The following Bible study will work best when you use it as a worksheet which includes both the passage to be studied and the discussion questions.

Complete the Bible study in the small groups, with each person completing the response questions after reading the text. (Allow 30 minutes for this exercise.)

A. "Logs and Specks": Read Matthew 7:1-5. Then answer the following questions.

B. My first reaction to "Logs and Specks" is: (Choose one.)

☐ Surprise! I never thought of my own weaknesses as "specks in the eye," not to mention "logs."

☐ Concern! I'm wondering if some folks see "logs" in my eyes, and I think they're just "specks."

☐ So what's new? Everybody has problems.

☐ Other:

C. One of my problems with "Logs and Specks" is: (Choose one.)

☐ I never really seem to spot any specks in others. I guess I'm just too trusting.

☐ You wouldn't believe the kinds of specks I see in others. Everyone is full of faults. It's unreal!

☐ It's hard to notice that log in my own eye, even when I strongly suspect there is one there.

☐ I don't look beyond the specks or logs sometimes but just tend to judge the person on what I see at first glance.

☐ Other:

D. The kind of specks I really find it easy to notice in people are: (Check any that apply.)

☐ People who are friendly in class but ignore you outside of class.

☐ People who act like they're too good for you.

☐ People who act like they're perfect, but then really foul up.

☐ Other:

E. To be perfectly honest, some of the logs in my life that I struggle with from time to time are. . .

F. Knowing I have logs to deal with makes me. . .

G. One thing Jesus is saying loud and clear to me through these words from Matthew is. . .

6. *Closing devotion.*

Saturday morning session (2 hours)

1. *Wake up or lose your socks*—Tape off a circle on the floor that's large enough to seat the whole group. Everybody who sits in the circle is shoeless, but is wearing socks. On a "go" signal, the object is to collect as many socks as possible. The people who lose their socks are out of the game (and the circle). They're also out of the game if any part of their body goes outside the circle. The last person in the circle wins.

2. *Group survey*—Hand out pencils and 3x5 cards, four cards to each person. Then ask the following questions: (one answer for each card) (a) One thing that makes me angry is. . . (b) I really like it when people. . . (c) One thing the youth group can do to make me feel more accepted is. . . (d) One thing I'm struggling with right now is. . .

Collect the cards. Use one large strip of newsprint for each question and tabulate the answers while the groups are working through the following Bible study. Post the survey responses for everyone to see. You'll use some of the responses later in the retreat.

3. *Bible study: "What, Me Lost?"*—This is a good time to arrange new groups so that relationships are extended beyond just four to six people. Have the two persons from each group whose birthdays are closest to the retreat date switch groups. The rest of the group will remain intact. Have the group read Luke 15:1-7 together. Then hand out half-sheets of paper to each person and give the following items to share:

A. The part of this scripture that really spoke clearly to me was. . . (Allow participants time to jot down an answer, giving an illustration if necessary).

B. Some of the ways people I know seem to get lost today are. . . (Again, give people time to write responses, giving examples where appropriate, such as—withdrawing from friends, getting angry over unsolved family problems, looking to drugs for help with problems, etc.)

C. I feel lost when. . .

D. Some people have been able to "find me" in my life and bring me back when I have been "lost." What they have usually done is. . . (Give people time to finish writing and additional time to share their responses in this small group. Instruct each group to close with prayer when finished.)

4. *What's That?*—A first step in helping someone is being able to understand what he or she is trying to say. To get practice in listening, try this exercise: Divide into groups of three. Explain that you'll read a statement and each person will have up to three minutes to talk about it while the other two listen. The "talker" can either agree or disagree with the statement or add new thoughts.

The "listeners" are to try to understand the speaker's feelings and beliefs. They can ask questions to clarify what the speaker's saying, but may not comment or add thoughts. They also should keep eye contact with the speaker.

After everyone has expressed himself, ask the entire group to comment on how they felt and what principles of listening they learned.

Various listening topics are: (a) Guys are better than girls because... (b) Girls are better than guys because... (c) God guides our lives every second.

Use some of the responses to the group survey if you think they'll make adequate discussion topics.

Saturday afternoon session (2 hours)

1. *Amoeba Race*—Tie a long rope around each group that formed in the last session. Set up a course for the teams to run, perhaps to one end of the room, over an obstacle and back again. Race two teams at a time until you have a winner. To guard against crunched toes, all team members should remove their shoes.

2. *Over My Head*—Read Matthew 14:22-33. Assign roles and read the passage as a dramatic reading. The roles needed are: narrator, several disciples, Jesus, Peter.

3. After the dramatic reading, pass out sheets of paper and ask them to write the following items:

a. One word that describes my feelings after hearing this story.

b. The strongest truth I see coming out of this story is...

c. Like Peter, I sometimes get in "over my head." When I do, it usually has to do with... (Possible examples are family hassles; someone of the opposite sex; making decisions, plans for the future.)

d. Think of people whom you know who seem to be "in over their heads." What are some ways in which you might be able to reach out to them? (Again, provide adequate time for sharing, encouraging each group to close with prayer.)

4. *On the Spot*—This exercise is a story or situation that forces you to make a choice. It also gives everyone practice working through an important problem-solving process.

Talk through the following problem-solving steps before working through any "on the spot" situations.

Step 1: Identify and clarify all aspects of the problem.

Step 2: Try to identify what led to the problem.

Step 3: Once you've identified the problem and its causes, look at its consequences.

Step 4: What are potential solutions?

Step 5: What's the best solution, based on the information you have?

Situation 1: A new person moves into your school. She seems as though she'd make a good friend. But as you get to know this person you realize that her outgoing personality was a big front, that she's got the worst inferiority complex in the world. Today she stops you and says, "There's just no hope for me. I'm stuck with being me and I hate it." How would you respond?

Situation 2: There is a movie you've been wanting to see for some time but couldn't find anyone to go with you. Finally you decide to go alone because the movie is playing its last day. You're about to leave when the doorbell rings. There stands John, your best friend. He looks really upset. "I've got to talk to you now," he says in a whisper. "Things are bad at home. I don't know what to do." Just then the phone rings—it's another friend, Tom. "Hey, all right, you talked me into it! I'll pick you up in 15 minutes and we'll see that show!" What would you do?

Optional Topics: Take various responses from the group survey question, "One thing I'm struggling with right now is..."

A Spring Retreat CONT.

Saturday evening session (2 hours)

1. *Teeth Teasing*—Have the entire group sit in a circle. The object is to never show your teeth. To speak, you pull your lips inward around your teeth to hide them.

One person starts by asking the person next to him, "Is Mrs. Mumble home?" The person responds, "I don't know, I'll have to ask my neighbor." This keeps going around the circle. When someone's teeth show, he's out.

Smiling is permitted provided the teeth don't show.

When asking or answering, contorting the facial muscles is okay to make the person next to you laugh.

The last one left is the winner.

2. *Conflict Is*—It's time to change two more members in each group. Have the youngest and oldest member of each group relocate. Then allow 15 minutes for each group to come up with a brief role play that illustrates a conflict people often face.

After the role plays, list different conflicts that group members have faced. Also refer to the group survey question, "One thing that really makes me angry is. . ."

3. *Bible Study: "Don't Just Stand There"*—Hand out copies of the following Bible study. When everyone is finished, begin the sharing in small groups.

a. Read 1 John 3:16-18.

b. Reading this text makes me feel. . . (Choose the best answer.)

☐ challenged to help as much as I possibly can.

☐ guilty! I don't really seem to be able to help a great deal.

☐ frustrated. I can do only so much!

☐ good. It is possible to help people from time to time.

☐ other:

c. The message that comes through the strongest to me is: (Select one.)

☐ Helping people means actions, not just nice words.

☐ It is easier to "talk" help than "do it."

☐ Helping people by actions is one way of showing your love for God.

☐ Our words about love for God have little meaning without actions of love toward people.

4. *Conflict time*—Discuss various ways of handling conflict when it arises in the group. (Denying that the problem exists, avoiding the problem, giving in to the other person, overpowering the other person, working through the problem.) List the different responses on newsprint.

Next, hand out sheets of paper and pencils and have everyone list three conflicts they have now or can remember having. Then have each person list what he

thinks is his or her personal style of handling the conflict and what he'd like his personal style to be.

Take a couple conflicts from volunteers and have the small groups determine alternative ways of handling the conflict.

5. *Closing devotions*

Sunday morning session (2-3 hours)

Use one of the two optional sessions, depending on the needs and interests of your group.

Option 1: Create your own worship service. A particularly meaningful worship experience can be created by dividing the retreat group up into work groups to create an instant worship service. The following tasks are possible: (1) the worship setting—work on design, decorations, etc,; (2) music; (3) a message or sermon from the Word; (4) a celebration of communion—if this is appropriate for your group—or prayers.

Provide appropriate materials, particularly for the music and message teams. Let all of the groups know they have two hours in which to pull the worship service together and prepare it. You'll find a rewarding experience if you've never done it before.

Option 2: Helping, one more time. Meet once more in your small groups. Have volunteers in each group read the texts used in the four previous Bible studies: Matthew 7:1-5; Luke 15:1-7; Matthew 14:22-33, and 1 John 3:16-18.

After all the four sections of scripture are read, hand out a half sheet of paper and share the following comments for individual response:

(1) The section of scripture that had the most impact on me was. . . The reason it had the impact was. . .

(2) One thing I learned about helping people was. . .

(3) One thing I discovered about being helped was. . .

(4) One thing that surprised me in these Bible studies was. . .

Allow time for the group to finish writing their responses. Then move into small groups of four to six for this last sharing. Allow ample time as the ability to share will have grown over the number of studies used. Again, ask each group to close with prayer. You might consider chain prayers, each person contributing, if your group is comfortable with that.

Evaluation: Provide a brief evaluation form which includes questions similar to the following: (1) The best part of the retreat has been. . . (2) The part I liked least about the weekend was. . . (3) If we did another retreat next week. . . (4) One thing I'll never forget about this weekend was. . .

Allow folks time to finish writing. Assure them that they need not put any names on their evaluation sheets. Read them carefully in reviewing the retreat.

The Bible studies used in this retreat appear in the study booklet "With a Little Help From My Friends" by Bill Ameiss, ©1980 by Concordia Publishing House. Used by permission.

A Fishin' Retreat

by James Rhiver

"A fishing retreat? What's that?" This question was asked many times as the publicity went out on this unique event in our group's schedule of activities.

Retreats have always been popular vehicles for Bible study in our group. And many of our members love to fish, so we planned a weekend combining fishing and Bible study.

Our fishing retreat was a big success—complete with campfire experiences, night fishing and fishing contests.

A Fishin' Retreat CONT.

Choosing the Bible study for the weekend was simple. In John 21, Jesus teaches some good lessons using fishing as a setting.

Here are some guidelines for planning a fishing retreat:

1. Find a location that provides some accommodations. We found a member who owned a clubhouse with running water, electricity, stove, etc. (Tents, etc., add adventure, but also more responsibility and planning.)

2. Check the necessity of having boats for fishing. (Be sure to check boating rules in the area.)

3. Be sure those "of age" have proper fishing permits.

4. Establish a "contract" with all participants: "We will have some Bible study time and much time to fish. If you don't like to fish, don't sign up!" (This latter statement is essential since many fishing areas offer little else to do.)

5. Limit the number of participants. We limited our group to ten, plus counselors. If you are fishing in a public area, most fishermen do not enjoy large groups around.

6. Make the cost minimal. With subsidy from the youth budget, we kept it to $5 per person. Your cost will be determined by distance, facilities, meals, etc. Bait is costly in some areas and is best supplied by the youth themselves.

7. Such a retreat requires that the leaders (or one of them) love to fish. (Sometimes only a fisherman understands the needs of other fishermen!)

8. Since a fisherman's cabin is not a room in the church, it may be better to make copies of the text rather than bring Bibles.

9. In our case, we had a communion service on Saturday evening. This is very meaningful to the community formed because it unites them in the body of Christ and offers a real chance for forgiveness that may be necessary when late hours and little sleep increase the level of irritation.

10. Prayer is essential. Anything with God's blessing is successful.

Schedule
FRIDAY

6:00 p.m.—Leave church
7:30 p.m.—Set up for weekend
8:00 p.m.—Evening fishin'
10:00 p.m.—Bible study, John 21:1-3
10:45 p.m.—Vespers
11:00 p.m.—Snacks, sleep, night fishin'

SATURDAY

5:00 a.m.—Breakfast
6:00 a.m.—Fishin'
9:00 a.m.—Donuts and Bible study, John 21:4-8
9:45 a.m.—Back to Fishin'
Noon—Lunch
1:00 p.m.—Fishin'
5:00 p.m.—Supper and Bible study, John 21:9-14
6:00 p.m.—Fishin'
10:00 p.m.—Vespers with communion
11:00 p.m.—Sleep, etc.

SUNDAY

5:00 a.m.—Breakfast
6:00 a.m.—Fishin'
9:00 a.m.—Donuts and Bible study, John 21:15-19
10:00 a.m.—Fishin'
Noon—Lunch
1:00 p.m.—Clean up
2:00 p.m.—Closing Bible study John 21:20-25
3:00 p.m.—Leave for home

(Be flexible, biting fish do not read schedules.)

Bible study on John 21:1-3

Purpose: to reflect on our relationship to the resurrected Christ.

1. Take time to share one exciting fishing trip or story.

2. Check your best reason for going fishing:
☐ I love to clean fish.
☐ I just like to compete with nature.
☐ I like to get away from others sometimes.
☐ I like the feeling of accomplishment.
☐ I really don't know.

3. Read John 21:1-3 and check the best ending for this sentence: I feel the apostles wanted to go fishing because. . .

☐ they were frustrated with the past events.
☐ they were hungry and needed food.
☐ they had nothing else to do.
☐ they needed to "get away."
☐ none of the above.

4. How would you have felt at this time if you had had the same experience (the death, resurrection, etc.)? (Check one.)

☐ great
☐ confused
☐ wow!
☐ who cares?

5. Using the same list, how do you feel about it as a Christian, today?

☐ great
☐ confused
☐ wow!
☐ who cares?

6. Close with a prayer about your relationship to the resurrected Christ.

Bible study on John 21:4-8

Purpose: to recognize the resurrected Christ as Lord of our lives.

1. Have you ever had anyone tell you "how to fish"? Share your reaction to them.

2. Read John 21:4-8 and circle the answer you feel best answers this question: Why do you think the disciples did what Jesus told them to do?

a. They felt "commanded" to do it.

b. They wanted to prove this "intruder" wrong.

c. They figured early morning fishing was really better anyway.

3. If you had been one of the disciples, what would have been your reaction to this scene? (Circle one.)

a. angry because you had been fooled.

b. eager, like Peter, to get to Jesus.

c. like the other disciples, take care of the most immediate concern, the fish.

4. Where do you feel you would fit on the continuum when it comes to the Lord's guidance?

5. Sing together the hymn, "My God, My Father, Make Me Strong." Use guitar accompaniment or bring pre-taped music.

Bible study on John 21:9-14

Purpose: to find a relationship between the presence of Christ in communion and in our daily living.

1. Share a time when you ate with someone and enjoyed the meal because of the company.

2. What makes a meal a feast? (Circle one.)

a. the food

b. the people you're with

c. the atmosphere (outdoors, fancy restaurant, etc.)

3. Read John 21:9-14. Check the statements that apply to both a communion celebration and a regular meal.

☐ fellowship with others
☐ presence of food
☐ forgiveness of sins
☐ presence of Christ
☐ bread, wine, the Word, forgiveness
☐ joy

4. Take time between now and the communion celebration this evening to meditate privately about your sins, your need for forgiveness, the assurance of the presence of Christ, and forgiveness through Christ.

Bible study on John 21:15-19

Purpose: to become aware of the "cost of discipleship."

1. Check the word that best describes your feelings when someone tells you more than once to do something:

☐ put down
☐ angry
☐ bored
☐ important
☐ other

2. Read John 21:15-19.

3. Looking back to number 1, how do you think Peter felt?

4. Share how you would feel if your promise for being faithful would be crucifixion. (Check one.)

☐ scared
☐ happy
☐ disappointment
☐ doubtful

5. How do you react to your "cost of discipleship"?

☐ scared
☐ happy
☐ disappointed
☐ doubtful

6. Close with a prayer for strength in discipleship.

Bible study on John 21:20-25

Purpose: to look at the purpose for being a part of the church—the body of Christ.

1. Complete the following sentences:

a. If I could know something about my future, I would want to know. . .

b. When others are able to achieve more than I seem to, I feel. . .

2. Read John 21:20-25.

3. Looking at vs. 20-22, check the reasons you feel Jesus answered Peter as he did.

☐ He didn't want to offend Peter.
☐ He was keeping John in the dark about his future.
☐ He felt it was none of Peter's business.
☐ He wanted Peter to be concerned about his own purpose in life.
☐ He didn't know what would happen to John.

How to Have the Group Live for More Than Itself

Worship and Service Ideas

CHAPTER

A Batch of Group Prayer Ideas

by Thom Schultz and John Shaw

Hand squeeze

Stand or sit in a circle, holding hands. A leader instructs members to pray silently for the persons on each side of them. When they've completed each prayer, they should gently squeeze the hand of the person being prayed for. The silent, gentle squeeze of the hand gives a warm feeling of Christian love and community.

Mural prayer

Tape a large piece of newsprint to the wall. In silence, one member walks to the newsprint and writes with a crayon or marker an opening sentence to a group prayer. Then, each member is given the opportunity to add another sentence, as the rest of the group watches in silence. When all have finished, the first member writes "Amen" and leads the group in praying the "mural prayer" aloud, in unison.

Picture prayer

Pictures can be a good starting point for prayer. Select some inspirational or issue-oriented pictures. In your group's prayer time, show the pictures and open yourself to the prayer concerns that are represented in the pictures. Variation: everyone brings a picture that represents a personal prayer concern. It may be a picture of yourself, a friend, family, school scene, etc. The pictures are then passed around your prayer circle for silent prayer consideration.

Anonymous requests

Many times people are hesitant to share their needs aloud with others in a group. This prayer is really for them. Everyone is given a slip of paper and pencil, and given the opportunity to anonymously write down a prayer request. These requests are then collected in an offering plate, shuffled up, then randomly re-distributed to the members. Each person is then given the opportunity to silently pray for the request appearing on his slip.

Candle transfer

Everyone should stand in a circle. Turn off all lights. You'll need only a candle. One member begins by light-ing the candle and offering a short, silent prayer for someone else in the circle. No one will know who the prayer is for until the member has completed his prayer, when he walks over to the person he just prayed for, and hands him the candle. Then the process is repeated. This continues until all have prayed, and have been prayed for. The candle light symbolizes God's presence and love.

Prayer partners

Divide your group into two equal subgroups. One subgroup should stand in a circle, facing out. The other subgroup should form a circle around the first subgroup, facing in. Then the outer subgroup walks slowly around the inner subgroup until the leader says to stop. The person face-to-face with you is your prayer partner. Everyone sits down in place and prays silently for the needs of his prayer partner. Then, if you wish, you may keep the same prayer partners through the next week.

Prayer is a special time for youth groups. Group prayer functions as a concentrated communion between the group and God. The more effectively you incorporate prayer in your group, the greater the youth will experience the bond between themselves and their Creator. Here are 13 group prayer ideas to strengthen that bond.

One word

One-word prayers are often more meaningful than long, wordy prayers. Begin by deciding upon the type of prayer to be offered by the group: thanksgiving, requests, etc. Then, with everyone in a circle, each member is given the opportunity to offer a one-word message to God. One member then closes the prayer for the group.

Random scriptures

Type or write selected, short Bible passages on little slips of paper, enough for everyone in the group. Then each member randomly draws a slip from a hat. Each person then prays for what God is telling him through that particular scripture.

Music prayer

Music can often stimulate meaningful prayer. Select a recording that contains lyrics that present some important issues or needs. In your group's prayer time, play the record and open yourself to prayer concerns that are suggested by the song.

Needs in the news

The daily newspaper always contains dozens of people and circumstances in need of prayer. Divide into groups of three or four people. Pass out newspapers and newsmagazines to each group. The groups select articles reflecting needs and later present these to the total group for prayer. The group can, if you wish, write letters to the recipients of the prayers announcing your prayerful support.

Prayer notes

Knowing that someone is praying for you is important. Open your prayer time by allowing everyone to share individual needs. Then, allow time for everyone to write short notes to those in need of prayer. The notes should be simple: "Dear Nancy, I'll be praying for you and your sister this week. Bob." The note also serves as a personal commitment by the person promising to do the praying.

Prayer committee

Some groups have a "prayer committee" that watches for those needing prayers. Needs may concern group members, congregation members, government leaders, the church, etc. The committee lists these items and presents them to the group for prayer. If this method is used regularly, members should rotate to be on the prayer committee.

Prayer target

Stand or sit in a circle. Give members an opportunity to request prayer. The person requesting prayer sits in the middle of the group. This person may announce his requests to the group, or he may simply indicate his need for prayer with silence. He closes his eyes, and the other members are given the opportunity to walk over one at a time and stand behind this person to pray for him. The members, if they wish, may place their hands on the shoulders of the person while they pray.

FLOWERS, I

A Sunrise Service

by Thom Schultz

Easter morning is a special time. Flowers and balloons are kind of special things, too.

And the youth of High Street Congregational Church in Auburn, Maine, have found a way to combine these special things for a special Easter sunrise service.

The service opens at daybreak with each member reading his/her own brief "Call to Praise." Then the Easter Story is read from Matthew.

The opening hymn is a vibrant one—to get everybody's blood flowing a little better in the crisp Maine morning. "Morning Has Broken" and "Here Comes the Sun" have both been used.

Then the group enters into a section of the worship they call "Giving Joy to Our Immediate World." Each person in attendance is given a half pint milk carton filled with dirt. Then, everyone is given time to walk to a table to pick out a flower seed.

At this point, one member of the group gives a short reading on the theme of rebirth. Now, the worshipers are invited to plant their seeds in their containers, using provided craft sticks and water. Their new plant is theirs to keep.

The symbolism of the box of dirt and seed is then explained. "This is symbolic of new life from death. A plant/flower has died so that seeds could be produced to bring new life again. The seeds bring forth flowers which will add beauty to the immediate world; they will also serve as a reminder of the Easter event celebration."

During the planting of the seeds, a light mood is maintained so that the participants aren't worrying about being proper and rigid as they poke their seeds into the dirt. Everyone is urged to help one another.

Some people plant an extra carton to take to a shut-in or relative.

The worship participants are urged to harvest the seeds from their new plant in the fall and save them for the following Easter. And the multiplication effect of the many seeds from the one seed also gives symbolic representation of the power of the early church to spread the work of the Lord.

Next, the service moves to a section called "Receiving Joy in Our Innerpersonal World." This is the communion experience. Brief prayers are said, including the Lord's Prayer. Then communion is celebrated, offering the participants their choice of the common cup or individual cups. For the bread, the youth bake several loaves for the service.

The final section of the worship is called "Sending Joy to God's World." Now a young person offers a reading, pointing out that the seeds and their potential have enhanced the immediate surroundings. And the worshipers have nourished themselves through the eucharist. The reader goes on to point out that the Christian faith is a faith based upon community, and the community encompasses the world. The Easter message is to be shared and shouted through all of creation.

Then, each worshiper is given a 3x5 card with a small hole punched in it, a pencil, and a helium-filled balloon. Everyone is encouraged to write a message on the card that they would like to share with the world. This may be a thought, a feeling, an emotion, a scripture, anything. The cards are then tied to a string on the helium-filled balloons.

Everyone holds onto his balloon as the closing hymn is sung. "Pass It On" is a favorite song here. During the singing , the people are invited to release at random their message-carrying balloons. They're told, "When the Spirit moves, then release the balloon." This develops into a very moving moment. Imagine Easter messages of joy for the world being carried aloft by multicolored balloons into the brilliance of the Easter dawn sky!

A simple benediction closes the service. Then, everyone is invited to a breakfast of rolls, coffee, tea and hot chocolate.

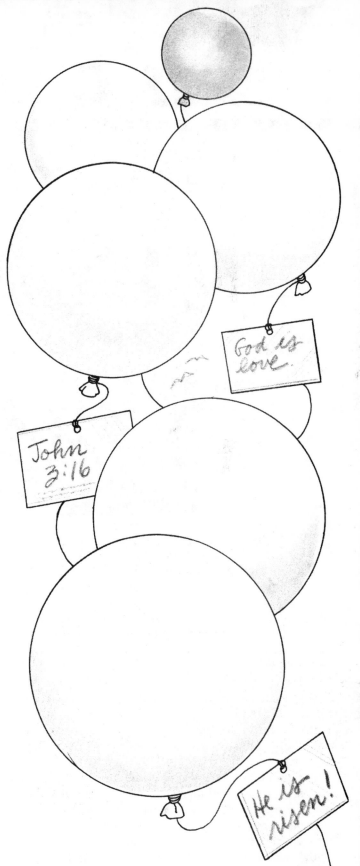

"We want to share with you, in the most vivid way we know how," announced a staff counselor, "some of the significant moments in the life of Christ." That was the only introduction we had to what came to be known as the Christwalk.

THE CHRISTWALK:

A Unique Worship Idea

by Rod Broding

The Christmas story from Luke's gospel was read and the campers sang another favorite camp hymn. But then, echoing through the chapel, came the words of John the Baptist in song from the musical "Godspell"—"Prepare ye the way of the Lord." At the leader's encouragement we clapped hands with him as he sang until another staff member rushed into the chapel, beckoning us to, "Come see! Come see some strange people who say they are from Nazareth!"

We piled over one another leaving the chapel to see these "strange people" who would take us on a walk with Christ that would extend from one end of Lutherdale Bible Camp to the other, and from Christ's birth to his resurrection.

We watched a man and woman from a distance as they stopped at a cabin. And, as they were turned away, we knew there was no room at the inn. They traveled a bit farther, and, as we caught up to them, they were kneeling at the straw bed of the Christ child. They were in a garage that looked as if it indeed might

have been a stable in its earlier years. We could hear the flutist's strains of "What Child Is This."

As we contemplated the meaning of our Lord's birth, we were interrupted by the announcement from another staff member behind us. "Come to the lakefront and listen to this man preach about the Messiah who is to come!"

We hurried across the main part of the camp to find John the Baptist, baptizing people, urging them to repent and prophesying of one to come who is "mightier than I."

Nearby, other staff members, all simply dressed in garb of the day, were in boats "fishing" or engaged in quiet conversation.

Suddenly from out of nowhere He appeared, dressed simply in a white smock and shorts. John, by his sense of awe and expression of scriptures, confirms our guess. This is the Christ!

A new mood enveloped the crowd of campers as we witnessed the baptism of our Lord. We followed him up the hill where he reenacted his journey into the desert and his temptation by the devil, again with the help of additional staff.

What began as a noisy crowd, curious to know what was going on and, in some cases, mildly apathetic, now seemed overtaken in a mood of somberness. As we walked with Christ, we were brought face to face with the woman caught in adultery, the rich young ruler, the calling of Christ's disciples, the healing of a Roman officer's servant, Christ's encounter with the Pharisees, conversations with his disciples and acts of healing. In between all these episodes Christ related to us parables and teachings as we walked with him to an open meadow.

We were quietly beckoned to sit down. We witnessed Jesus sharing his body and blood with his disciples in the Last Supper. As he left them to pray, and as they fell asleep, we were serenaded in song by other staff members.

From where we sat we watched another scene unfold. Judas was given his 30 pieces of silver to betray the Son of Man.

The drama heightened as we watched the embrace between Judas and Christ. Roman guards immediately seized Jesus and roughly carted him off to Pontius Pilate.

We followed Jesus down the gentle slope to become part of the mob that shouted for the freedom of Barabbas and the crucifixion of the Savior of the world. We watched in shock and wonder of this man as the Roman guards pushed us out of the way to lead him to a small hill 50 yards away.

Jesus, now stripped of his white smock and carrying a cross, felt the sting of the whip against his legs and back as he walked and stumbled up the hill.

The hill near the toboggan slide where we registered a few days earlier was now transformed into an ugly Calvary. We grimaced as Christ was laid down. His hands and feet were nailed to the cross. The convulsive jerks and cries of pain went through me in a way I never sensed on any other Good Friday.

Hanging from the cross, this bruised and beaten man called upon his Father for our forgiveness and his own deliverance. And it was finished. We watched in silence as the Roman soldier pierced his side.

We walked away mutely, not really knowing where we were being led.

It was all too tempting to look back. And many did as they walked. Finally, I cast a furtive glance backward to see if he was still there, hanging on that cross. He was. His nearly naked body, silhouetted against the evening sky, was eerie and disturbing. The words of the Roman army officer came to me—"Certainly this was a good man."

We went to a small clearing in the woods where a campfire was burning. Darkness was everywhere. We sang songs, listened to readings and scripture and huddled together. Those lyrics, "Were you there when they crucified my Lord," took on new depth as I had to answer, "Yes."

Then as we continued to mourn the loss of our Savior, he appeared! Stepping out from between some low hanging branches, two flashlights trained on him. The risen Christ had come to share more words with us. Then, we joined in singing "For Those Tears I Died."

This drama, of which we had been a part, brought us to an ever-deepening appreciation of God's love for us.

RECIPES FOR A H

What Your Group C

by Virgil and Lynn Nelson

"It's depressing! I try not to think about it."

"God created all people. I care about the whole human family. I want to help."

"I don't know what to do."

"Send them some food."

"Sending food doesn't do any good. There were tons of grain that rotted on the docks of India. The people are going to die anyway."

"We did hunger in last year's program. Why bring it up again!"

"If those people would only stop having children."

"Send them some more tractors and organize bigger farms."

"We've got hungry people here. We should take care of our own first."

"You know what the Bible says: The poor are always with you! It's God's problem."

Hunger is an ugly issue. Whether we like it or not, we are called by God to face it and act on his command to feed the hungry.

1 John 3:17-18 says, "But if any one has the world's goods and sees his brother in need, yet closes his heart against him, how does God's love abide in him? Little children, let us not love in word of speech but in deed and in truth."

When people are hungry as a result of a natural or man-made disaster, we feed them. This is *love* in action. It is short term help. God calls us not only to respond to crisis but to do *justice*. God's justice will be accomplished when the obstacles that keep people from feeding themselves are removed.

Among the obstacles to be removed are the misunderstandings we carry around inside us. Only when we begin to understand *why* people starve in the midst of plenty can we begin to be effective in doing something about it.

Following are some input-discussion starters. Ask someone in your church to read each myth mini-lecture into a tape recorder. Play it for your group as a "guest speaker" on world hunger. Use the process questions suggested at the end of each input. (This could be used for several sessions.)

Documentation for the following discussion of myths is found in Lappe & Collins' **Food First** and Freuden-

berger's **Christian Responsibility in a Hungry World** (see resource list).

MYTH #1: People are hungry because of scarcity— scarcity of food and agricultural land.

Can scarcity be given serious consideration as the cause of hunger when in the midst of the famine of the early 70s there was plenty of food to go around? Without even counting all the beans, fruits, nuts, root crops, vegetables and non-grain-fed meat there was enough grain alone to provide everyone in the world with 3,000 calories a day. There is not a scarcity of food.

Is there scarcity of land?

Our world's arable land *is shrinking* because of inappropriate technology for tropical conditions and greedy ignorance of ecology. However, even with the loss of *one-half* of the earth's cultivatable land since the days of Solomon, there is still *enough land* to feed the people.

Bangladesh has half the people per cultivated acre as Taiwan. Yet Taiwan has no starvation. China has twice as many people per cultivated acre as India, yet in China people are not hungry.

The problem lies not in the *amount* of arable land but in *who controls what is grown* on that land. For example, in Central America and the Caribbean where nearly 70 percent of the children are undernourished, at least *half* of the agricultural land grows crops *for export* and not food for the local people. During the famine and drought of the early 70s in the Swahilian countries of Africa, *exports* of cotton and peanuts actually *increased*!

But surely the population bombs outstrip resources to feed! Not so. Historically it has been found that high birth rate is a *result* of poverty. In poor families, having many children is seen as the only guarantee of care and food for the parents' old age. It is when countries become agriculturally self-sufficient with old age security that birth rates decline.

GROUP PROCESSING: What part of this is new information to you? What have you "heard" about scarcity of food? If food is not scarce, do you have any hunches as to other reasons people are still hungry? Any ideas for solutions grow from dispelling this myth of scarcity?

MYTH #2: The cause of hunger is a lack of technology. People are hungry because modern techniques have not been used. Large technologically sophisticated farms are the answer.

A study of 83 countries revealed that three percent of the landowners *already* control approximately 80 percent of the farmland. The large sophisticated farms are already there.

However, most of our present technology *displaces* workers and thereby intensifies the problem of the majority of people having less and less money to buy food. Much of the technology is actually *destructive* to long-range use of the land in the tropics.

It has also been shown that the *small* farmer is usually *more productive* per acre than the corporate farmer because his family's livelihood depends on getting the most possible per acre.

In Guatemala, Argentina, Brazil, Chile, Colombia and Ecuador, a 1960 study found the small farmer producing 3 to 13 times more per acre than larger farms. In Thailand, plots of two to four acres of rice yielded more per acre than farms of 140 acres or more! Japan, China and Taiwan have seen large increases in production when land was redistributed to small farm families.

Why aren't the large farms producing more? One factor is that large farms do not plant all of their acreage. A second more important reason is that larger farmers find *huge profits in food for export or in non-food items.* For example, in Sinaloa, Mexico, a farmer can make 20 times more money growing tomatoes for export to the USA than growing grain for Mexico. In Colombia, agricultural land growing carna-

tions brings 80 times more profit per acre than the same land growing corn to feed local persons.

Two of the main reasons such inequality in land holding exists are: 1) the long history of colonization by governments; 2) the recent growth of businesses based in "developed" countries buying into the economy of poorer nations.

We *do* need agricultural *technology*, but of a new kind: One that: a) puts more people to work rather than out of work; b) rebuilds land, air and water, rather than abuses them; c) uses renewable energy sources rather than the limited oil, coal and gas. Demonstration programs and rural leader training are effective means of change.

GROUP PROCESSING: Ask two persons to be a large corporation owner and wife who grow carnations. Ask four persons to be a family whose farm was taken over by the carnation growers. You see hunger increasing in your family and town and come to ask why corn is not being grown. Carry on the dialogue for 5-7 minutes, or until "finished" and share your feelings. How do the arguments given fit with scripture?

MYTH #3: Some countries have a natural advantage in growing certain crops. Those should be exported and the earnings used to import food and industrial goods.

The same land that grows cocoa, coffee, rubber, tea, sugar, carnations or tobacco could be growing food for people who live in that country—grains, high protein legumes, vegetables and fruits. The value of exported crops has not kept up with the inflation of imported manufactured goods. This is shown by the often quoted illustrations showing how much more coffee or sugar it takes to buy one tractor today than 25 years ago. Between 1961 and 1972 at least 18 underdeveloped countries earned *less* from their agricultural exports than they did in 1961 with similar levels of production.

Another problem is that money earned for export sales is used to purchase food items geared for the better-off city people rather than country people. In Senegal for example, peanuts and vegetables are exported to Europe and much of the money earned is spent to import wheat for foreign-owned bakeries that turn out European style bread for those in the cities. The rural people go hungry, deprived of land they need to grow millet for themselves and local markets.

GROUP PROCESSING: Discuss what would happen if countries first committed themselves to grow food enough to feed all their people, and then planted industrial cash crops like cotton, rubber and sugar.

RECIPES FOR A HUNGRY WORLD CONT.

How would you feel if sugar were taken out of your diet completely? What are some other sweeteners? [Sugar industry statistics show that we are a nation of sugarholics, each consuming an average of 125 pounds per year!]

MYTH #4: Hunger is a contest between the rich world and the poor world.

Is it *us* verses *them*? Labels like "hungry world" and "poor countries" make us think that everyone in a given country is uniformly hungry.

The reality is that all countries in *both* the developed and underdeveloped parts of the world have hungry people at the lower rungs of society, and well-fed people at the top.

The labels also make it easy to assume that everyone living in a "hungry country" has a common interest and commitment to eliminate hunger. Not so, as we see government business, industry and farming in the hands of a few. Foreign aid to these governments often benefits only the already wealthy.

The "rich world" verses the "poor world" also makes us fearful of our well-being. The "have-nots" will rise up and take over the "haves"! In fact, however, there are many ways in which the average citizen in the metropolitan countries and the poor majority in underdeveloped countries are the *same.*

We all experience more unemployment and higher prices for food. When agricultural corporations move food production out of industrial countries in search of cheap land and labor in other countries, farmers in metropolitan countries lose their jobs and people in developing countries lose fields for growing their own food. Five American grain companies control 90 percent of the grain flow in the world, but our U.S. farmer is losing $1 a bushel.

Multinational agribusiness firms are creating a single world agricultural system with increasing control over the most basic human need—food. The prices, availability and quality of food is already being affected.

GROUP PROCESSING: The head of an American-based multinational company was recently quoted as saying, "The responsibility of the company is only to the stock-holders to make a profit and not to the American people." In what ways can you see that the American people are getting the short end of the stick? Who is hungry in your communtiy? Who is unemployed?

MYTH #5: Our top national priority should be defense spending; since national security depends on military might.

A defense system is necessary. But *excessive* reliance on military power ties up money and personnel that could otherwise be used for health research and education.

Excessive? Every 14 hours the U.S. Department of Defense outspends the entire annual budget of the U.N. world food program. America and Russia both have power now to kill every person in the world at least 100 times.

"Every rocket that is fired, every warship that is launched in the final sense is a theft from those who are hungry," said Dwight D. Eisenhower.

Balance of military power is the preoccupation of developing countries too. The arms imports in 1975 of non-OPEC developing countries cost more than $4 billion.

One hunger project group has estimated that the jobs lost (316,550) by transferring $13.6 billion of military spending into programs to meet human needs could create 1,441,000 new jobs. We could be dealing seriously and creatively with ending hunger in a world of plenty.

GROUP PROCESSING: How much military defense of our country is enough? On what new jobs does our country need to spend money? Food in recent years has been used as a political weapon. In 1974, 70 percent of our food aid went to Vietnam and Cambodia when there was famine in India and Bangladesh. Is food something that only those "on our side" or those who have enough money should get?

MYTH # 6: Hunger should be overcome by redistributing food.

If our government believes this we are not even doing a good job. We rank 14th in our giving to the U.N. food program. We are giving less food abroad to all countries than we gave after Word War I to one country (Belgium).

Redistribution of food is not the long-range answer. Distribution problems merely reflect the problem of who controls the resources which produce the food. Who controls the land determines who can grow food, what is grown and where it goes. The basic question is: How can people *everywhere* begin to democratize the control of food resources?

Those who now control the food do have a unique moral responsibility because they control not just a *product* but a *lifeline*—an absolute need for life.

Let not the facts of our overconsumption contrasted with deprivation elsewhere produce guilt that "we" caused "their" hunger. Let these facts motivate us to redistribute where we put our energies and resources so that we move our own country toward putting food first.

GROUP PROCESSING: Who controls food in our country? How much does your family spend on groceries each month? Is that fair? How can you begin to democratize the control of food resources right here? Until then, do we need a world food reserve administered internationally? What do you know to do to reduce your waste?

SIMULATION GAME

"The World at Dinner"

Goal: To experience the sharp contrast between the American standard of living and that of the rest of the world.

Preparation:

A. Equipment and leadership needed
- time: approximately two hours
- a large room with small tables (no more than 10 to a table); or a picnic area where people can sit in groups on the grass
- a meal
- newsprint, poster paper, Magic Markers, masking tapes, colored construction paper cut into small pieces, scratch paper
- people to prepare the meal; one coordinating person to supervise distribution and give verbal leadership during the program; a coordinator of publicity and tickets.

A. Things to do ahead:

Promotion: You may choose to sell tickets or have donations making clear where money will go. Advertise that this event is a meal simulating what it would be like if the whole world sat down to eat in the same room. It is very important that people be aware that they might go home hungry.

Prepare posters (to be placed around the room) with the following information:

1. Selected facts from this article, such as "the cost of one Coke (35 cents) will feed 10 children for one day."

2. World population division and food distribution percentages. If the world were 100 people sitting down to eat. . .

USA and Canada	6 people	Over 50%
Europe/Middle East	16 people	About 20%
Africa	8 people	
South America	10 people	20-25%
Asia	60 people	

(Percentages include energy and resource use as well as food.)

Preparation for serving food:

1. If potluck, divide up the dishes according to the above statistics on different tables designated for continents.

2. If serving the food, have waiters bring out the food first to the America/Canada table; give them well over half!

If cafeteria style serving, give each American ticket a heaping tray with all that can fit; others get servings in accord with the statistics. (If served this way, people could sit anywhere—this created more pressure on the Americans however; it's usually better "political" dynamics to let continents sit together.)

Preparation for people as they enter:

1. Label the tables according to continents (if you're expecting 20 people, then two could be Americans; remember to give them an extra table on which they can "store" their food).

2. Prepare colored slips of paper according to the proportion of people in each continent, having one color for each food group. As people enter they are told to choose a color and find a table—continent that matches it.

HUNGER QUIZ

1. KWASHIORKOR is.........................
   a. a severe form of cholera
   b. the capitol of Upper Volta
   c. severe protein deficiency
   d. a nomadic tribe in Niger

2. .... percent of the world's 4 billion people are estimated to be malnourished which contributes to mental and physical retardation.
   a. 40   b. 60   c. 80   d. 25

3. ...... percent of the world's people are believed to be starving now.
   a. 10   b. 50   c. 20   d. 30

4. Of the 60 million deaths recorded each year, about .... percent are due to hunger or problems arising from hunger.
   a. 10   b. 30   c. 50   d. 70

5. Two-thirds of the world's people live on less than $....... per year.
   a. 500   b. 200   c. 750   d. 1,000

6. Historically, which has been more effective in reducing the rate of population growth?
   a. agricultural self-sufficiency with old age security
   b. family planning and birth control

7. Americans currently eat ...... percent of their basic protein requirement.
   a. 50 b. 100   c. 150   d. 123

8. The least expensive item in a can of tomatoes is:
   a. tomatoes   c. the label
   b. the can   d. advertising

9. An average American uses .... times the agricultural resources of an average African or Indian.
   a. 2   b. 3   c. 4   d. 5

10. Farmers receive .... percent of our food dollars.
   a. 5   b. 40   c. 60   d. 94

11. Jesus addresses which of these subjects more frequently in his teachings?
   a. heaven and hell
   b. sexual immorality
   c. violence
   d. poverty and wealth

12. Of the total U.S. budget, 55-59 cents of every dollar requested for military spending, ... cents is devoted to economic aid to less developed countries.
   a. under 2   b. about 5   c. 17   d. 23

13. Among the 17 First World nations giving development assistance to the Third World, the U.S. ranks ...., based on the percentage of gross national product.
   a. 1st   b. 8th   c. 14th   d. 16th

14. In 1958, a Central African earned enough money from selling 200 pounds of cotton to buy four blankets. Today he could by .... blanket(s) for selling the same amount of cotton.
   a. 1   b. 4   c. 6   d. 2

Answers: 1.c 2.b 3.c 4.d 5.b
6.a 7.d 8.a 9.d 10.b 11.d
12.a 13.c 14.a

RECIPES FOR A HUNGRY WORLD CONT.

The Meal Event:

1. Introduce the meal: This is a simulation of what it might be like if the whole world were present for this meal. State that there are no specific rules regarding what will happen or would happen; they can be as creative as they want in dealing with the situation. Pray to our loving God.

2. Distribute the food and let whatever happens happen. Do not interfere unless absolutely necessary (fist-fights or throwing food are only remote possibilities). Allow plenty of time (at least 45 minutes). Some will grumble and do nothing; others will want to do something but not know what; others will try to do things and will be thwarted; some may try and succeed.

Discussion/Reflection: (about 45 minutes)

Call the total group to order. Indicate that we are now going to take time for sharing about what has happened.

Each of the following questions is to be discussed *first* in small groups around their tables (with about 10 minutes for each cluster of questions). Then ask for one person from each group to give a brief statement to the total group to be recorded on newsprint.

A. How did you *feel* during this meal? (trapped, angry, frustrated, helpless, indifferent, passive, excited, amused)

B. What actually happened? Were there any attempts initiated at sharing? Who? Where? How? How were they received? What happened within your continent? How aware was your table of what was happening elsewhere? Did you attempt to do anything? What kind of response did you get?

C. Reflect on the facts on posters around the room.

D. How was this meal *like* and *unlike* the real world? Consider aspects such as international relations, politics, economics, missions.

E. Leader should use his judgment at this time as to whether it is important to guide further sharing of food until people are more satisfied. (Benevolent dictator.)

NOTE: De-briefing is the most important part of a simulation exercise. Allow plenty of time and opportunity for people to express and sort out their feelings.

Conclude the experience with selected scripture meditation and prayer.

FOOD BINGO

1. Someone who has lived on or visited a farm or ranch.

2. Someone who has a fruit tree in his/her yard.

3. Someone who can explain the meaning of "complementary protein."

4. Someone who has seen the waste in a restaurant.

5. Someone who knows how many pounds of coal it takes to light one 60-watt light continuously for one year. (460 lbs.)

6. Someone who has seen the wasted food in a market.

7. Someone who knows the percentage of food grown in this country that never makes it to market. (25 percent)

8. Someone who likes to cook.

9. Someone who has eaten more than one candy bar in a week.

10. Someone who knows what percentage of the world's people live on less than $200 a year. (66 percent)

11. Someone who has helped grow a garden.

12. Someone who has picked or gleaned crops.

13. A person who has talked to someone who lived during the depression.

14. Someone who knows a person who lives on Social Security as his/her primary or only source of income.

15. Someone who has tried fasting.

16. U.S. citizens are 6 percent of the world's population but use ......% of the world's energy, food, and nonrenewable natural resources. (40 percent)

Fill in a person's first name in the appropriate box:

1	2	3	4
5	6	7	8
9	10	11	12
13	14	15	16

RETREAT

Friday Evening
Arrival, food-name bingo, film (see resource list)

Saturday Morning
Bible study, plan creations to share Sunday morning, mini-lecture(s)

Saturday Lunch
Simulation game, debrief, free time

Saturday Evening
Our response, small group sharing and prayer, optional film-strips or movies

Sunday Morning
Planning in small groups—back home projects: a) family, b) our church, c) our town; worship (include creations from Saturday Bible study)

Option
Instead of simulation lunch, have Saturday a whole day of fasting (announced ahead of time so it's voluntary). Notice energy levels during the day. Encourage meditation on scripture and out-of-doors. Have plenty of books, magazines and movies available.

WORSHIP IDEAS

BIBLE STUDY:
Deuteronomy 15:4, 7-11—You shall open your hand wide unto your brother, to your poor, and to your needy, in your land.

Isaiah 58:6-8—Is not this the fast that I have chosen?

Micah 6:8—What does the Lord require of you?

Matthew 25:35-40—For I was hungry and you fed me.

Luke 12:47-48—For to whom much is given, much is required.

Romans 12:20-21—If your enemy is hungry, feed him.

James 2:15-17—Faith without works is dead.

1 John 3:17-18—If anyone has the world's goods and sees his brother in need. . .

IN SMALL GROUPS:
Process: First, READ the scripture; FOCUS on its personal message for you; SHARE with others in your group. Then CREATE a way to express the message with the large group by one of the following:

1. use craft materials available
2. use a familiar tune and create new words
3. convert ad lines you've heard to make a new commercial
4. demonstrate through a pantomime, role play or skit.

(Other options include: creating poetry, letters, litanies, slide-sound shows, and games.)

MEDITATION:
If we pray for someone else, God may decide to use us as his instruments of assistance.

If we pray that all people may know of God's love, we must offer ourselves as candidates for the job of telling them.

If we pray for the hungry, we are called upon to live more simply, to share more with others, to think new thoughts, to put all we have at his disposal.

LITANIES:
Lord make us hungry
—for your Word. . .
—for bread. . .
—for your spirit. . .
—for justice. . .
—for peace. . .
—for compassion. . .
—for action
Lord fill us
—with your hope. . .
—with your boundless love. . .
—with resurrection power
Lord, make us break bread for others
—that all people may know you as the Lord of life
—that all people may have their share of the earth's resources
—that your kingdom of justice and love be more fully realized on earth

SONGS:
"Sunday Dinner," Jim Manley, from **Take Off Your Shoes**, Newwine, Box 544, Lomita, CA 90717.

"Jesus, come to this Sunday meeting
Come and teach us how to share
Pass the cup and the bread till the world is fed
Teach us how to really care.
It's been so long, Jesus, since we tasted the life in a piece of bread.
With our mouths so full, our souls are dulled to all those left unfed."

Other songs from that album: "Take Off Your Shoes," "Lord of All Hopefulness," "The Gifts That You Gave Me."

"Everything's Just Fine," The Mission, from **Let's Get Together**, Tribute TRI 50002

"O they're starving in India, Pakistan too
That's too bad, there's nothing we can do.
When a man's reached 29 he's lived the average time
Though he dies, there's nothing we can do.
And right here, now everything's just fine.

"Take a look at Appalachia, it's sad but it's true
That's too bad, there's nothing we can do.
In a shack without much heat, children run in their bare feet
Though they die, there's nothing we can do.
And right here, now everything's just fine."

"Love Can Set Us Free" (to the tune of "We Shall Overcome")
1. Love can set us free
2. The hungry shall have food
3. Fear will pass away
4. Justice will pass away
5. God will dwell with all
6. Love can set us free

"He's Got the Whole World in His Hands" (some new verses)
He's got the rich and poor . . .
He's got the fish and the loaves. . .
He's got my good intentions. . .
He's got strength for our giving. . .
(Write your own)

"Let There Be Peace on Earth," from **Magic Penny**, by Malvina Reynolds

Mine Are the Hungry, Morse and Brumbaugh, The Brethren Press, 1451 Dundee Ave., Elgin, IL 60120

"They'll Know We Are Christians By Our Love"

RECIPES FOR A HUNGRY WORLD CONT.
GROUP PROJECTS

Detectives needed

Discover who are undernourished in your community.

Senior citizens: Ask your pastor for names of retired persons living on fixed incomes; interview them about how they are surviving inflation. Call the Social Security Administration and ask the number of seniors in the county and the average amount of the monthly checks.

Children: Call the school system; find out how many children qualify to receive subsidized breakfast and lunch programs. Call your local Boys Club, Girls Club, and other groups working with children and find out their estimate of hungry children.

Others: Public health, service organizations and drug and alcohol treatment programs can estimate numbers of others whom they serve who are in need of better food.

Report findings to your church (newsletter, sermon, program for group) and to the local clergy organization and other possible concerned groups. Write a letter to the editor of your local newspaper.

Push a little

The group raises $10 a year to subscribe to IMPACT, which will keep them posted on national legislation related to food and hunger issues. (Send to 110 Maryland Ave., N.E., Washington, DC 20002.) Appoint an IMPACTer—a person who agrees to read the issues as they arrive and get letter writing equipment ready for massive letter writing campaigns when needed. Be sure the youth group informs others in the church.

Supermarket food salvage

Talk with local market managers to see if they would allow a non-profit group to pick up the food thrown away daily (dated products, dented cans, milk, dairy products, produce). Stress that the food would not be sold but would be given to individuals and organizations in need. For more information on "how to," write: Second Harvest, 1001 N. Central Ave., Suite 303, Phoenix, AZ 85004.

Cooks for a small planet

Hold an alternative foods meal for your church. Things to do ahead:

1. Decide which recipes to use. See **Diet for a Small Planet.** Recruit the number of people needed to prepare the basic menu items for the expected attendance.

2. Sell tickets or take donations with the balance above the actual cost to go to a world hunger organization.

3. Publicity: advertise the meal and evening as a tasty meal in preparation for our better functioning on a small plant.

4. Prepare a mini-lecture or secure a volunteer to do it.

5. Decide what other program elements you want to include, such as a filmstrip, scripture reading, songs, covenant; and arrange for necessary equipment and leadership.

Procedure and timing:

1. Opening: people arrive, pray and eat, served or cafeteria style.

2. Developing the experience.

a. Call the group to order. Ask if there are any questions about what has been eaten. Share answers regarding the contents in any of the dishes.

b. Around the tables in small groups ask for discussion of the question: Why is this a hunger meal? Give about five minutes and then ask for feedback to the total group. Listen for the items that are brought out and supplement them with the following mini-lecture:

Meat, especially beef, is a "grain drain." That is, for each pound of beef protein, a steer eats eight pounds of grain protein. This grain protein would go much farther if we eat it as we have tonight rather than in the form of beef.

*There is no problem with range-fed beef, since they are eating grass that we cannot eat anyway. They are not reducing protein. (See **Diet for a Small Planet** for a chart on animal protein conversion factors. Poultry has a better ratio, about three to one.)*

These recipes are special in another way besides the fact of non-meat protein content. The proteins contained in them are "complementary." For example: the protein content of one and one-half cups of beans eaten alone equals a six-ounce steak. Four cups of rice alone equals a seven-ounce steak in protein useable to the body. However, if the beans and rice are eaten together, the useable protein increases 43 percent and the body gets the equivalent of a 19-ounce steak!

It also needs to be said that even if all of the U.S. stopped eating beef, that would not in and of itself feed any of the hungry people in the world. Grain saved would have to be shared, or the money saved would have to be used for dealing with the root causes of hunger. Reducing or eliminating meat consumption in itself is a symbolic action which may be coupled with other actions.

Progressive non-dinner

Go from house to house for courses (not food for gut but for thought) from non-appetizer through non-dessert. Use resources from this article to create the courses. Invite your friends to this odd feast!

Walk-a-thon, or bowl-a-thon for hunger

Organize a "walk for hunger" in which walkers secure pledges for each mile they walk (ride); or each pin they get (bowling). Write to CROP for information and "walk committee" organization packet. See resource list for address.

Teen gleaners

The ancients did it! Read Leviticus 19:9-10: "And when you reap the harvest of your land, you shall not reap the field to its very border, neither shall you gather the gleanings after your harvest. . . you shall leave them for the poor and stranger: I am the Lord your God." Arrange to glean the fields after the last picking. Share produce with individuals and organizations in need. For more information contact Senior Gleaners, c/o Homer Fahrner, 2606 "J" St., Apt. D, Sacramento, CA 95816.

RESOURCES

Books

Food First, by F.M. Lappe and J. Collins, Houghton Mifflin Co. Comprehensive overview of the myths and factors affecting hunger worldwide.

Rich Christians in an Age of Hunger: A Biblical Study, by R. Sider, InterVarsity. Excellent biblical study on hunger, lifestyles, and action.

Christian Responsibility in a Hungry World, by C.D. Freudenberger, Abingdon. Excellent summary of major causes of hunger and specific suggestions for the Christian community.

Diet for a Small Planet, by F.M. Lappe, Ballantine. Background statistics on the food we eat, complementary protein, the "grain drain" and over 100 recipes that take advantage of protein complementarity.

Alternate Celebrations Catalogue, Alternatives, Box 1707, Forest Park, GA 30051. Hundreds of ideas and projects.

Filmstrips

A World Hungry, five-filmstrip series with record or cassette. Each filmstrip is approximately 10 minutes. Deals with causes and myths, lifestyle changes. Complete with discussion/action guides. (Check with a denominational film library or write: ABC/PSW, 816 S. Figueroa, Los Angeles, CA 90017.)

Living Simply: Responses to World Hunger, five-filmstrip series. Shows how to live more simply so that others may simply live. Available from ABC/PSW (see address above).

A Chance for a Change, 18 minute filmstrip from CROP. Shows the work of CROP and the way Church World Service responds to need.

Films

Beyond the Next Harvest, 27 minutes, from CROP. Documents the food crisis worldwide. Emphasizes attitudes of global interdependence, and proposes realistic alternatives.

Tilt, 23 minutes from CROP and other libraries. Animated film that presents a serious view of the attitudes people hold toward the problems of Third World peoples. Excellent discussion starter.

MORE, 3 minutes. Although whimsical in tone, this film is prophetic in its vision. Film takes a hard look at the "more is better" syndrome.

The Good, Good, Life, 11 minutes. Available from Teleketics, 1229 S. Santee St., Los Angeles, CA 90015. Crammed with visual and musical satire including take-offs on TV commercials.

Organizations

CROP. Main office, Box 968, Elkhart, IN 46514. Write to them for area office addresses. Source of study materials, program packets, worship packets, ideas, films, etc.

BREAD FOR THE WORLD. A grass roots organization of folk who want to influence legislation in our country related to food issues—4600 N. Kilpatrick Ave., Chicago, IL 60630. Excellent packet of worship aids: 50 cents from same address, "Education Fund."

IMPACT ALERT. 110 Maryland Ave. N.E., Washington, DC 20002. Interfaith organization to inform concerned persons of issues before the Congress.

WORLD VISION INTERNATIONAL, Box 0, Pasadena, CA 91109. "Planned Famine," a 30-hour fund raiser for the world's hungry is a good activity for youth groups. World Vision also has several other programs.

33

"I grew closer to God this week by sharing. Everybody was sharing each other. We worked together, prayed together, cried together and laughed together."

This girl's comment is typical of many after a youth group has experienced a workcamp.

How to Plan for Workcamps

by Thom Schultz

Workcamping is one of those rare experiences that never fades from memory. And it's within reach of any youth group. Workcamps take many forms. You may work on an Indian reservation, in the inner city, at the construction site of a new church building, in a rural area such as Appalachia, at homes for the elderly, at orphanages, or in the wake of a natural disaster.

The reasons are many for involving your group in a workcamp. You're helping your neighbor in the best biblical sense. And the workcamp provides a great opportunity for personal spiritual growth in your group. The experience is usually very educational—exploring new places and cultures. There's the fun of traveling as a group. And, a workcamp can draw your members together, as witnessed by the girl's comment above.

Is your group ready for a workcamp? You'll find the answer by taking a close look at your group. Is your group able to look beyond itself? Has it learned a sense of Christian mission?

Your group should be prepared to make your Christian witness *actively*. The true workcamp concept communicates your Christian faith primarily through action, rather than through the spoken word.

Also, is your group willing to spiritually, emotionally, mentally and physically prepare for the trip? Careful preparation is needed. More about that later.

Does your project have the support of your congregation?

What resources do you have within your group? Check out your available skills, time, money, manpower and tools. Any size group can do a workcamp. And both guys and girls can participate in most tasks. You'll find that many of your female members are as skillful (if not more so) with a hammer or paintbrush as their male counterparts.

Finding a workcamp suited to your group is often one of the more difficult aspects of workcamping. Begin by

checking with your denominational headquarters or mission boards. Some denominations actually publish national lists of potential work projects for youth groups. Also check with the National Council of Churches and similar organizations.

Social service agencies in the area where you'd like to go are also good contacts, as are volunteer agencies in the area. You may also check with local churches in the area.

Inquire also at special national agencies, such as the Bureau of Indian Affairs for a source of ideas on needy Indian reservations.

Selection of a work site needs careful investigation. Is work really needed in the area? How much? What kinds? Can your group handle this type of work?

Be sure your potential work area can provide a local administrator to help coordinate your project. Many groups have been very disappointed to see their workcamp fizzle because of a lack of cooperation from local leadership.

Check out lodging possibilities. Is there a dormitory or retreat center nearby? Tenting is used by many groups, but make sure showers (or at least a lake or river) are nearby.

Investigate the needs for tools and materials. Are there local sources for these?

Determine how much time, travel and money are needed for the project.

Also investigate what the local people can give you in return for your services. In many instances, needy people have considerable pride. It's good for them to feel that they're giving you something in return for all your work. Be open to their offers to share. Indian groups will often be eager to share their music and dance. Old folks love to tell stories and legends to young people. The ladies in a particular area may be delighted to cook your group a special meal.

Preparation for your workcamp should start one year or six months in advance of your work dates.

First, check out and select your work site. Ideally, this would include a visit to the site by someone from your group.

Set the dates. Actual time spent at the site can vary from a couple of days to a couple of weeks or more. Many groups spend five or six days at the site, and another five or six days traveling.

Next, be sure to get congregational clearance for your trip.

Then, conduct in-depth research on your site and its people. Visit your local library and gather all available books and magazines on your selected site. Split up the responsibility among your members, and make orientation presentations to the total group.

Involve the whole group in setting goals and priorities for the workcamp. Determine what you want to accomplish and write it down.

Then comes the task of budgeting. Remember to include transportation, food and lodging. Also add your site expenses such as tools, materials and an advance visit if possible.

Insurance costs should also be calculated. Your church may have a medical policy covering accidents. If not, check with an insurance agent. Also ask the agent about liability insurance, to protect your leaders and the church from any lawsuits that might arise from accidents during the camp.

Remember to budget for possible emergencies. Take along an emergency fund to cover vehicle breakdowns and other unexpected expenses. Perhaps you could borrow this money from the church. Or, earn the extra dollars through fund raising, and if there's no emergency, use this money as a seed for next year's camp.

Finally, be sure to consider entertainment expense in your budget. Entertainment, or fun, is an important part of the total workcamp experience. We all do a better job when we build in a system of rewarding ourselves in some way. Research any entertainment pos-

How to Plan for Workcamps CONT.

sibilities in the area of your camp. Also check out possibilities located on the way to and from the camp. Amusement parks, beaches, natural wonders, exhibits and theatrical plays are a few possibilities.

You may also prepackage your own entertainment. Bring along films or games. Plan some sports competition, a talent night, "gong show" or "kangaroo court."

Check with churches near your work site. Perhaps you could plan an outing with the local youth—or exchange musical programs. Perhaps the local people are willing to present a cultural program—hillbilly music, mariachi band or Indian dance.

For the income side of your budget, there are a number of possibilities. Money may come from group fund raisers, of course. And, individual members can provide at least some of the income. Matter of fact, it's usually best for each workcamper to personally pay a set non-refundable amount—as a commitment to the project.

Some funds may come from resources at the site. Volunteer organizations often have money available to buy materials for local needs. Sometimes the federal government has funds available for certain locally administered programs, such as weatherization of homes in poverty areas. Also check with churches in the local area.

Your congregation, of course, is a potential source of income. Some groups take an offering during a special workcamp dedication service. And some churches provide for youth mission work in their annual budgets. Some groups sell "shares of stock" to the congregation members. These are professionally printed certificates denoting your specific work project. Church members buy these as a way of "investing" in your mission project.

Some groups are able to obtain funds from denominational mission boards.

Adult sponsor selection is another important part of preparation. Look for adults who are spiritually,

mentally and physically able to handle the trip. They should work well with your members and be willing to go through all preparation (including fund raising projects) with the group. Many groups recommend the ratio of one adult for every five youth.

Participant preparation begins with the spiritual aspect. Each member and the group as a whole should engage in prayer for the upcoming experience, and should explore the biblical concepts of mission.

Next is mental preparation. This includes orientation to the work area, skills training and interpersonal development.

Then comes physical preparation. You'll do a much better job at the site and enjoy doing it more if you're in shape. Exercise. Swim. Ride a bike. Run. Do anything that will build your stamina and strength. Also remember to get a thorough physical examination before departing.

Also, be sure to have all parents sign a permission form that transfers parental authority to your trip leaders in case the parents cannot be reached in a medical emergency. Here's the wording for a typical form: *"I/We give permission for my/our child, ..., to participate in the July 2-16, 1983 workcamp and trip of the Belleview Community Church, and to be transported in the church bus. In the event that I cannot be reached in an emergency, I give permission for a physician selected by Rev. Donald Smith to hospitalize, secure proper treatment for, and to order injection, anesthesia or surgery for my child as named above. Signed..."*

Final preparation details include securing a first aid kit, gathering tools and materials, sending a news release to your local media, and preparing a complete itinerary of your trip.

During the workcamp, many groups plan about six hours of work per day. If you get an early start each day, this will allow for some free time each afternoon.

Plan for worship in your daily schedule. Several members may volunteer to form a worship committee. Worship that grows out of the experiences, needs, hurts and joys of a workcamp can really be a life-changing experience.

When you return from the workcamp, plan to share your experience with friends, family and congregation. You may do this through a special service or dinner. A most effective way to communicate your trip is through a slide and sound presentation. During the camp, tape record the voices of residents at the site. Ask them about themselves and their reactions to your group. Also interview your own members, getting their reactions to the experience. Then edit these interviews into one tape, perhaps adding some narration. Match the tape to appropriate slides taken during the trip, and you have a very moving presentation.

Also be sure to thoroughly evaluate your workcamp in your group. Note the successes and failures. And begin dreaming of your next adventure in serving God's people.

OPERATION SANTA CLAUS:

An Outreach to Needy Kids

by Thom Schultz

Think back a few years. Remember when you were a little kid? Remember Christmas time? The twinkling Christmas tree. All the brightly wrapped gifts under the tree. Always asking Mom, "How many more days till Christmas?" Toys. The sea of wrapping paper on the floor when the big day arrives.

Great memories. But there are a lot of little kids in your own community who will have no memories like these. Poverty will deprive many families of the gift-

giving that brings so much joy at Christmas time.

Catholic young people in Philadelphia have developed a highly effective program to bring a great deal of joy to disadvantaged children in their city. It's called Operation Santa Claus. Every Christmas Eve since 1967 these youth have donned Santa and elf costumes, piled into cars loaded with toys, and delivered a little bit of Christmas into the homes of these kids.

Teresa Diamond, coordinator of Operation Santa Claus, emphasized that careful planning is needed by

OPERATION SANTA CLAUS CONT.

any group wishing to organize a program similar to Philadelphia's.

"Operation Santa Claus is designed such that a team consisting of five teenagers (usually three boys and two girls or two boys and three girls) deliver toys (collected, wrapped and sorted beforehand) along a prearranged route to approximately 10 homes," Teresa said. "Each unit travels in a car driven by an adult who serves as moderator of the team. The teenagers are dressed in costumes—one as Santa Claus, the others as his helpers (clowns and/or pixies)."

Each team assembles on Christmas Eve and departs from a base of operations where the costumes, toys and route information are picked up. After completing the entire route, the teams reassemble. It's recommended that refreshments and a worship service climax the evening, Teresa said.

Toys

Your first task is organizing a toy drive. Get started early on this. Send out news releases to your local newspapers and radio stations. Explain your program and announce the need for toys. The toys do not have to be new, but should be in usable condition, undamaged and complete. You may want to set a value minimum, so that all toys collected are worth at least $1 or so.

You'll need to determine about how many toys you'll need. This will be determined by the number of kids in your group and the number of homes you'll be able to visit on Christmas Eve.

The toy donations will come from individuals, corporations and stores.

The Philadelphia kids have learned that used stuffed animals should not be accepted because public health regulations often advise against such items because of the possibility of disease transmission.

And, of course, guns, knives, darts or other dangerous objects should not be accepted.

Each toy should be wrapped and clearly labeled as to whether the toy is for a boy or girl. The age range for the gift should also be marked. Keep careful track of how many toys you have for each sex and age grouping. This list will be very useful when you begin to separate the toys to household destination.

Each home to be visited should be registered on an index card. The card should include the family's name, address and phone number. The names and ages of each child should be listed on the card.

The Philadelphia group has found that filling out the registration cards in duplicate is a real help. One copy of the card is given to the team leader. The other is attached to the bundle of toys for that particular home.

Each home's toys should be put into a large plastic bag, the index card tied to the top. This will make your distribution system work very smoothly.

Teresa said, "A bag of approximately 15 extra toys should be provided for each route and tagged extra, since unexpected visitors or relatives may be waiting for Santa at a given home. Or perhaps the group will want to give extra help to an especially poor family. Or sometimes the team sees a needy child just on the street."

Costumes

You'll need five costumes for each team. The clown costumes can be made from Simplicity pattern 7162. This pattern requires about five yards of 35"-wide material and about one yard of elastic. You should be able to create one of these costumes for under $10.

Material and patterns may be purchased in bulk and then given to members to be sewn.

If you believe you'll be involved in Operation Santa Claus for only one Christmas, you may want to look into renting all your costumes from a theatrical supply house.

A Santa Claus costume is very difficult to make. So, you might plan to either rent or buy your Santa suits.

Families

The families you plan to visit on Christmas Eve should be determined between November and the middle of December.

Initial efforts at recruitment should be directed at seeking names of families who are in need and would desire Santa Claus to come on Christmas Eve. Contact with those people should be made through churches, community centers, social service agencies and other groups or individuals working with the poor.

You should only resort to solicitation of families through newspapers if the other methods do not result in attracting the desired number of families.

Remember to fill out a registration card in duplicate, on each family. All children up to age 12 should be listed.

Routes for each team should be marked on a map. The map and registration cards should be given to the team leader.

When Christmas Eve arrives, make sure all your members arrive at the church early enough to get into their costumes, load the cars with the bags of gifts, and get to your designated distribution area.

Your visitations should take from about 6 p.m. to 10 p.m. After that, have everyone return to the church for refreshments, fellowship and discussion on the performance of the program and improvements that might be made next year. A short worship experience is a good finale for the evening.

Teresa and the young people in Philadelphia have found that Operation Santa Claus not only provides a great service to the underprivileged, but it also tends to create in your members a more sensitive attitude toward the disadvantaged.

1 Organize an old folks' shopping day. Gather elderly congregation members and/or rest home residents. Assign each of your members to an oldster or two. Take them Christmas shopping.

2 Set up a hospitality station in a hospital waiting room on Christmas Eve. Offer coffee, punch, cookies and friendship to the worried watchers.

3 **Write and address Christmas cards for folks with arthritis.**

4 Deliver free Christmas trees to poor families. Contact your local Christmas tree dealers. They'll often donate all their leftover trees on Christmas Eve.

5 Provide a hiding place where parents can stash their children's gifts until Christmas.

6 Offer a Free Labor Day. Call a local nursing home, boarding house, orphanage or hospital and offer the time and labor of your group for a day—to do whatever is needed.

7 Loan a cassette player to a nursing home resident for a few weeks. Provide tapes of hymns or Christmas carols.

8 **Sponsor a mitten drive. Donate the mittens to an orphanage or mission.**

9 Set up a free babysitting day for parents who need to complete their Christmas shopping.

Provide a free "taxi service" for the disabled or elderly folks in your congregation. On a certain Saturday [or whenever] encourage the folks to call a number to order a "taxi." Take them to the grocery store, doctor, pharmacist, friend's house, or wherever. 10

42 Ways a Group May Give Itself to Others at Christmas

by the editors of GROUP

11 Operate your own day care center during the holiday week. You could even offer a vacation Bible school.

12 Find a lonely person. Obtain his friends' and relatives' names and addresses. Notify these people with your plan to assemble a Christmas album for the lonely person. Gather letters, notes, photos and cassettes from the friends and relatives. Put them all together and present the finished album to the lonely person on Christmas Eve.

115

42 Ways a Group May Give Itself to Others at Christmas CONT.

13 Create a Dial-a-Cheer. Record brief Christmas stories, poems, music or prayers and put them on a telephone answering device. Advertise: "Call 555-1234 for a bit of Christmas cheer."

14 Decorate a Christmas tree for a disabled person.

15 Collaborate with a local cinema to show free afternoon movies while parents are shopping. Or, set up your own little theater in a shopping center and show Christian films.

16
Chop firewood and deliver it to those who couldn't afford it otherwise.

17
Have all your group members set aside 10 percent of what they spend on Christmas gifts. Give the collected money to a hunger fund, orphanage or other charity.

18
Visit disadvantaged families and take Polaroid photos of them. Give them the pictures to send to their relatives.

19
Winterize a disadvantaged family's home. Do caulking, weatherstripping, insulating and patching to help keep the cold out.

20
Get together for a "Planned Famine." Go hungry for 30 hours and raise money to feed starving people. For more information, write "Planned Famine," World Vision International, Box 0, Pasadena, CA 91109.

116

21
Organize a toy drive. Go door to door collecting unwanted toys. Clean them up, repair them and give them to a children's home.

22 Pool all the favorite holiday recipes of your congregation. Mimeograph a special holiday cookbook and distribute to the congregation.

23
Create a giant Christmas card for your pastor. Get congregation members' signatures and present the card to your pastor on Christmas.

24
Contact Big Brother, Big Sister, or similar agency and arrange to befriend a little kid for a month, or longer.

25
Organize a Christmas party for all the old folks in your church. Provide a meal or refreshments, games, entertainment, etc.

26
Create handmade Christmas cards. Give them to those who could not afford Christmas cards. Also provide postage.

27
Open a Christmas Listening Service. Loneliness reaches epidemic heights during the holidays. Advertise a phone number where persons may call just to talk. Be sure to know when to refer a caller to another service—crisis line, pastor, etc.

28
Agree to sponsor a poor child overseas. Each member agrees to bring a set amount of money each week to help support a disadvantaged kid. Just $18 a month supplies many basic needs. Contact Compassion International, P.O. Box 7000, Colorado Springs, CO 80933.

29

Produce a "What Christmas Means to Me" radio show. Air it on a local radio station.

30

Have your group hire out as a free singing telegram service.

31

Create a special Christmas church bulletin insert. Perhaps you could assemble a series of "My Best Christmas Memory" stories from those over 70.

32

Offer to help put out the church bulletin for a month. Do the typing, folding and distributing.

33

Tape record Christmas greetings from congregation members. Send cassettes to church members who are stationed away from home in the military.

34

Deliver gift packages to your local jail, prison or mental hospital. Call authorities and inquire about appropriate gifts.

35

Give a "snow certificate" to a handicapped or elderly person. This will entitle him or her to a free walk-shoveling after the next snowfall.

Give a "spring clean-up certificate" to a handicapped or elderly person. This will entitle him or her to a free house cleaning by your group.

37

Offer to take charge of Children's Church or the nursery for a month.

38

Spend one day in the church kitchen—baking Christmas goodies. Deliver the baked goods to shut-ins, orphanages, rest homes, etc.

39

Have your members invite lonely people to their homes for Christmas dinner.

40

Sponsor an Outgrown Clothes Exchange in your church. Invite church members and/or the public at large.

41

Organize a telephone blitz on Christmas Day. Call the friendless, shut-ins and lonely to wish them a Merry Christmas.

42

Give a copy of this book to a group without one.

Dare to be Creative—

How to Use the Arts

The Basics of Multimedia

by Edward McNulty

Ideas

These may come from the specific occasion that you're planning—such as a youth service for Easter, Christmas, or a retreat. You'll need to narrow this down in order to choose the audio and visual materials to express the theme. Write this out as a statement so that everything that goes into your show will be related and tied together.

Equipment

Don't let this scare you. You do not need $10,000 worth of gadgets. It's usually best to start out small with one slide projector and a tape recorder. Most churches have a filmstrip projector; check to see if this is the kind that has a slide adapter. The junior highs at one of my parishes put together a fast-paced slide show using such an unsophisticated projector.

Check with the members of your group or church. Almost every parish includes a parent who owns a slide projector, good single lens reflex (SLR) camera and home movie equipment. Often such folk are flattered to be asked to help out, probably never thinking that they or their equipment could be used at church. Other possibilities of places where you can borrow equipment—schools, Scout offices, hospitals,

agricultural extension offices, libraries. And for cheap equipment buys—don't overlook garage sales.

The audio

Okay, you have some assurance that the equipment will be on hand and a theme has been chosen—let's say ecology, "The call of God to care for his world." How can we express this in a way to move others? Let's start out fairly simply with a two-projector show of about 10 to 15 minutes.

Gather together your group with records and Bibles. As they, or a small committee, look through the records, write down the titles of possible songs. These may be secular or sacred. Look through the Scriptures to see if you find any useful passages.

Our junior highs began such a show with the theme from "2001: A Space Odyssey," a few verses from Genesis (chapter one), a folk song, and portions of Psalm 104 read over parts of Grafe's "Grand Canyon Suite."

The possibilities are endless, as there are thousands of records with good songs. You can also buy sound-effects records and recordings of famous speeches and

Multimedia is an exciting way to explore the meaning of the Gospel for today—and to share it with others. It is a demanding form of communication that can involve your whole youth group, or if time is not a crucial factor, just one or two persons. Multimedia can be used in worship, a way of kicking off a heavy rap at a retreat or fellowship meeting and for special celebrations such as Easter or Christmas.

If you have been to a large fair, church conference or many rock concerts, you probably have encountered multimedia in its more complex form. Five, ten or twenty projectors may have been bounding slides and movies off the walls or screens at the same time. We won't be discussing that big of a production. Unless you or your group has several thousand dollars to play with, such a complex production is out of reach. But you can put on one with from two to four projectors for very little cash. And this will be just as much fun and about as much as most audiences can handle.

Now maybe you haven't run into multimedia yet, so let me pause a moment to describe it. Multimedia, as I am using the term, is the combination of a sound track, usually on tape, with two or more slide, movie, filmstrip or other projectors, all going at the same time. It's a very exciting mixture, as you can imagine. Some folk have trouble watching it because of the ever-changing images. Thus it's very important that a multimedia show be carefully thought out, planned and executed. Otherwise, you simply pile confusion on top of confusion. In other words, you need to know what you're doing—you can't just throw together a bunch of slides, show a movie and play a few songs and call it multimedia. The effective thing about this form is the ability to show several things at once—and thus create all sorts of feelings and reactions in the viewer as he looks for relationships between the images—such as stark contrasts between scenes of love and hate, war and peace, poverty and affluence.

Multimedia looks complicated at first, but when it's broken down into its component parts, it isn't so awesome. One person can put together such a show, if he's willing to spend 40 to 150 hours working on it—which is why it's better for a group to tackle such a project! Following this are some suggestions on each part—the equipment, the idea or theme, the audio tape, the slides, movies—and where to get the supplies.

events. Check out the bargain bins at discount and dime stores (I once found Martin Luther King's "I Have A Dream" album for 35 cents!).

You should use as large a reel-to-reel tape recorder as possible to record the soundtrack. Most cassettes are not powerful enough for good sound, nor can you edit a cassette tape as easily as the reel type. Get someone who knows hi-fi equipment to help you on this, especially so that you can tape your records directly from your record player. More shows have been ruined by poorly prepared soundtracks than anything else, so work hard at this. If you are using a large auditorium, always find out about the P.A. system; usually you can plug your tape player into this for good results.

Once you have chosen your songs or voice tracks and taped them, prepare a script. This should have the audio—the words and other cues—on the left side of the page, and the visual cues on the right. These latter will include instructions as to lighting, when to turn on/off your equipment, and the number of slide(s) to be shown. Many of my shows are cued according to the words of the songs, so I underline the word when a slide should be changed and write the number of the slide at the right.

Slides

These will come from a variety of sources. Some you will shoot with your own cameras—Instamatics or whatever you can get. Our youth met one Sunday afternoon, piled into three cars and drove around our city to look for suitable scenes. We shot factories and their smoking chimneys, litter, junkyard scenes, as well as flowers, trees and lovely hills. One person knelt down to focus upon a "Stop" sign with a polluting factory in the background.

If you have an SLR camera, you can easily copy pictures and ads from magazines. This will really widen your horizons, as you can then have slides of war and violence, historic events, the life of Christ, etc., etc. Even if you have only an Instamatic, you can buy a portrait lens that will allow you to copy large posters or Sunday school pictures from three feet.

Another slide source—old filmstrips. Many churches have these lying around unused. You can cut them up—be very careful and mount them in slide frames which you buy at a photo supply store. Ask for "half-frame" slide mounts. This is a good way to pick up some pictures of Christ, church mission projects and all sorts of other scenes contained in otherwise useless, outdated filmstrips.

The Basics of Multimedia CONT.

Still another source—the commercial slides sold by some camera shops. These are usually travel and nature slides. Scenes of huge buildings or snowcapped mountains are available, usually at reasonable prices. An especially good source for slides is Blackhawk Films. Their free catalogue lists all the usual travel and nature slides plus sets on the "Life of Christ."

Last of all, you can make slides without a camera. You may have learned of the cheap method using magazines, clear contact paper and water. The "lift off" method is described in the pages following this chapter.

Another homemade slide that's fun—Kodak's Ektagraphic Write-On slide. Available in boxes of 100, these can be drawn or written upon with pens, pencils and good quality felt-tipped markers.

I start gathering slides as soon as I have an idea for a show. Then when the script is done I sort through them to see which to keep and which to discard. Use a slide sorter for this—either a commercial one or one you can make by putting a lightbulb in a box over which you tape a piece of frosted glass. Work on one song at a time, choosing slides that interpret the words—either in a contrasting or supporting way. At this point number the slides with a pencil, rather than a pen, in case changes need to be made later on.

Once you have chosen and arranged the slides and marked the script, load them into trays and run through them with your tape. Probably you will find places where they move too fast, or other places, especially during the introductions to songs or bridge music, where you need more slides. Mark these places on your script as you go so that you can re-arrange your sequence. A good rule of thumb is that a slide should be held on the screen for about four or five seconds. This, of course, will vary with the sound and the mood you're trying to convey.

Movies

Once you've done one or two projector slide shows, you're ready for a more complex production. You can shoot your own movies with an 8mm or super 8mm camera. If you do this be sure to shoot some slides also of the same scenes. This will create a stunning effect when your audience sees the same scene repeated in both slides and movie film. Your best combination is to show the movie in the middle accompanied by two sets of slides, one on either side of the movie. For this you will need one movie and two slide projectors. I've also done some shows with four projectors—two slide projectors in the center flanked by 16mm and Super 8mm projectors.

Blackhawk Films also sells some tremendous 8mm and super 8mm films—adventures, newsreels, even a "Life of Christ." These can be cut and spliced together with your own films for a fascinating addition to your media mix. Their NASA films are especially beautiful.

Do you live near a TV station? If so, you might have a gold mine of raw media material available. Ask your minister to contact the station—or, joy of joys, ask a friend who works at the station—to see if they will give you their used TV commercials. These are thrown away—yes, burned!—when they are outdated. They come on little spools of 16mm film containing magnificent scenes—cities, people, faces, animals, cars and cities and mountains. You can either splice them together as they are or cut out just the scenes you want to go with your show. Some stations won't give these away, but many will, once they learn that you plan to use them in church education.

For both 8mm and 16mm film editing you will need a splicer and splice tapes. Probably you know someone who has a home movie editor and splicer. It would be nice to have a viewer for 16mm films also, but these are expensive, so you will probably have to get by as I did for years—unwind the film next to a window, hold it up and look at it through a magnifying glass to see what scenes are usable. This is crude but it works. To figure out how long a time each scene lasts, remember that 16mm film speeds through the projector at 24 frames a second—thus if you have a scene of 84 frames, you have one lasting about 3½ seconds on the screen.

Screens

Light colored, blank walls work better for multimedia than several small, confining screens. That way you can make your images large, overlapping or arranged above one another if you choose. If your walls are too dark or littered, try using several sheets. However, you might want to use a beaded screen for your 8mm or super 8mm projector, if the bulb isn't too bright. If you must use screens, get the biggest you can find, even if you have to go clear across town to borrow some. Another possibility—buy a weather balloon from an army surplus store or Edmund Scientific Corp., inflate it (to seven or eight feet) and project your show onto it. Tie the balloon with a heavy cord weighted down by a book or brick and place it on a large round wastebasket in the middle of your group. They will remember that show for a long time.

Resources

Gadgets, Gimmicks and Grace, by Edward McNulty, Abbey Press.

Blackhawk Films, P.O. Box 3990, Davenport, IA 52808.

Edmund Scientific Co., Barrington, NJ 08007. Free catalogue.

Visual Parables, c/o First Presbyterian Church, S. Portage St., Westfield, NY 14787. Rents multimedia kits.

Making Slides Without a Camera

by Edward McNulty

The "lift off" process of making slides is so simple that even children can learn it. (If I start working on slides when ours are up, I can expect our five-year-old to ask "Can I make some slides?") Materials needed:

1. Cardboard slide frames available at a camera store. Ask for the 127 or 135 size. ("Size" refers to the opening; the outer dimension is 2" x 2" for both, thus fitting all standard size projectors.) These slides are available in boxes of 100. If your camera store develops slide film, you can arrange to buy a box very cheaply—I've found that the price varies from dealer to dealer.

2. Clear Contact paper, which you can buy under other brand names also at department and variety stores.

3. Slick paper magazines or catalogues such as newsmagazines, men's and women's publications.

4. A pan of water.

5. An iron and a smooth board.

Using the slide frame as a guide for size, select a small picture, ad or words that will fit within the opening of the frame. The 127 frame is the largest opening and thus the most useful for our purposes. Time and Newsweek are excellent sources for pictures since they use so many small ones with their articles. The major limitation of this method is seen at this point—the size of the picture. Whatever you want to turn into a slide must fit into the opening of the frame. The picture should have good color contrast and sharp outlines if it is to project well. Color pictures will work fine, though light pastel shades might appear somewhat washed out when enlarged.

After you have selected and cut out several pictures, cut the Contact paper into strips just a fraction of an inch larger than the frame opening. A series of dots or other markings on the glue side of the frame will indicate how far the transparency should overlap. The glue surfaces must come into contact all around, so trim the strip if it is too wide. Failure to do this properly could leave one side of the slide unglued, causing it to jam in the projector.

Making Slides Without a Camera CONT.

On each strip of Contact paper mark off the same width. Put two or three of the strips together and cut along these marks. You should have a stack of small squares slightly larger than the frame opening.

To peel the paper backing from the Contact paper, tear one of the edges slightly. The paper will tear but not the tougher plastic transparency itself. Touch only the edges, unless you want a large, personalized fingerprint in the middle of the slide. There is no way to remove this, so take care.

Carefully grasping the edge of the transparent square, hold it over the picture so as to place it just where you want it. This positioning must be done before the sticky side of the Contact paper and the picture come together. It is possible but very difficult to peel a badly positioned picture from the Contact paper. Very likely the picture will tear unless the removal is done slowly. When you have the postion you want, lower the Contact square to the picture.

The working surface for this next step should be perfectly smooth and hard. Start rubbing the transparency from the center out to the edges. Use your thumbnail for this (others prefer the bottom of a spoon). Apply considerable pressure so as to remove all the air pockets and tiny air bubbles. By holding the picture to the light so that there is a reflection, you can tell when the process is finished. These portions of the slide that look grayish or slightly mottled need further rubbing. The areas without air bubbles will appear very clear by contrast. This step is very important and worth spending extra time upon; at the workshops I find that more potentially good slides are ruined by eager beginners hurrying through this step than anything else.

When you are certain that you have rubbed out all of the air bubbles, immerse the slide in a pan of water. The temperature of the water doesn't make much difference, though some prefer warm water. Be sure that the slide is completely covered by water. Since it requires from five to ten minutes for the water to loosen the slick clay surface of the paper, thus "lifting off' the ink, go ahead and repeat the process with your other pictures. (I usually wait until I have from 20 to 50 pictures before making slides; this assembly line approach saves your most precious commodity—time.) As you place your ninth or tenth transparency in the water, your first ones should be ready to take out for the next step.

Often the original paper will float or peel right off the transparency. This will vary from magazine to magazine. Sometimes you must remove the paper by gently rolling or rubbing your finger over it so that the paper comes off in pieces. The ink will remain on the transparency as long as you do not scratch the surface, with your fingernail, for example.

Careful examination will reveal a grayish film on the sticky side of the transparency. This clay residue can be washed away under a faucet or in a bowl of clean water. Or you can dip your fingers into the water and wipe away the deposit; use a towel or lint-free rag both to clean off your fingers and to blot dry the transparency.

The next to the last step is to take another square of clear Contact paper, remove the backing, and place the two squares together, sticky side to sticky side. Again rub out all the air bubbles. You should now have a transparency smooth and well-protected on both sides. Something that works equally well is clear sandwich wrap (especially Saran Wrap—it seems to cut more easily); there will be enough glue left on the transparency to make the wrap stick on. Both methods will keep dust and fingerprints away from the sticky surface of the slide.

The final step in slide production involves your iron, heated to a medium-low temperature. Position the transparency in the frame keeping it within the guidelines (you will frequently have to trim excess material during this step). Fold the two sides of the frame together, and press firmly along the edges of the frame with the iron. For obvious reasons, do not iron the transparency itself! You are now ready for that first awesome view of the slide made with your own hands—a moment to remember.

The above process, complicated sounding perhaps, is simple, once you have tried it a few times. The "lift off" method is just that. The ink in slick paper productions is not actually printed on the paper but upon a thin coat of clay covering the paper. The water dissolves the clay, allowing the ink to be lifted off by the glue of the Contact paper. Whoever the unsung genius who first discovered this process deserves a place of honor in the hearts of all media folk.

The resulting slide will not be quite as clear as one made with a camera, except for words and line drawings. Clarity will depend upon the original printing process. The finer the dots making up the picture, the clearer the projected and enlarged image will be. Usually, the pictures in news magazines will be coarser then those taken from a publication such as the National Geographic. Often such pictures, mixed with clearer ones made with a camera, will add interesting variety to the production. Words, lines, drawings and cartoons will turn out the clearest of all.

Poster catalogues can provide you with colorful slides interpreting a theme or thought. Argus Communications, 7440 Natchez Ave., Niles, IL 60648 prints the most attractive and useful catalogue of all. Words of love, faith, hope, ecology and challenge are beautifully interpreted by the art. The reproductions, for the most part, are just the right size for slide making. Order some of their posters as well as their catalogue. Posted around the room before your presentation, these will intrigue your viewers when they see them appear in your multimedia show.

Banner-making

by Sandra Meredith McNulty

Has your youth group ever had a workshop to make banners for your church? In the last few years, there's been a resurgence of liturgical banners. And they have usually been created by youth groups.

But let me go one step further and ask if these banners were all you or the congregation had hoped they'd be. Are they being used right now in the sanctuary, narthex, halls, or entryways—or are they only hung in the senior high room? Are they stored carefully and brought out for special occasions and worship services?

If they are not utilized as you had hoped they would be, maybe the reason is because the "finished" product doesn't look finished. Probably the banners were done with burlap or felt. Perhaps the edges of the burlap are not trimmed neatly, so they have a few stringy pieces hanging here and there. Maybe cutouts of felt have pencil marks showing. And perhaps letters appear to be whacked out and pasted down. And to top this all off, the whole thing may be wrinkled. Perhaps that's why the congregation is not too thrilled to use the banners.

You may say, "I can't do any better—I'm not an artist!" or, "But it'd take forever to do it right." I've led workshops on banner-making with small children through adults in their 70s. And they are usually pleasantly surprised to find they can create something rather nice in a short time.

So, let's start with the "idea" for your banner. Where do you get it? Do you just decide you want to do something on "love," so you say, "Let's see—I think I'll draw a heart"? If you're very creative and can come up with a really good design in a short time this way— terrific! But most of us need a bit of help with ideas. Make use of poster catalogues such as those from Abbey Press or Sacred Design, Christmas cards, magazine pictures, etc. to give you ideas (but not to copy line for line). I've used everything from children's books to encyclopedias to get the correct lines for a camel or for something as seemingly simple as a palm branch.

Where people gather, banners can be used. Plan where you will use the banners *before* making them.

125

Banner-making CONT.

If they will be carried by a pole in a worship service processional, then placed in a flagpole stand at the front, they should be about five or six feet long.

If they will hang from balconies, be sure the banners are custom-sized for these spots—a too-little banner will be ineffective. Many balconies would need at least a set of two banners to look right. In one large church, I did a set of six enormous banners hanging from the balconies.

In another church fifth and sixth graders made small 8" x 11" banners of the disciples and friends of Christ. These were just the right size to hang around an entryway. (A book on Christian symbols was used for ideas. For example, 30 coins and a noose were shown on a black background for Judas.)

If you are using a long, low wall, a long banner (or maybe two banners instead of one) will fit the space better than a tall, narrow one.

Hang them from a tree in an outdoor service.

At an Easter sunrise service, many banners made by two participating congregations were carried from poles in a large processional going from one church to the other, several blocks away!

Before you start cutting out materials for the banner, always do a small sketch first on paper. Use felt-tip markers and colored paper to help choose the right colors. Normally, it's best to use no more than three or four main colors. An exception to this rule could be a banner with the theme, "The Earth Is the Lord's," in which you want so show a lot of different plants, animals, fish, etc., in a full array of colors.

One very common mistake is to have too many words, thereby turning your banner into a poster. Usually, the fewer words the better. If the banner is in a processional, remember that people will only have a few seconds to take it in—there's no way they'll be able to read the whole Twenty-Third Psalm.

Felt and burlap are the most common materials used—but of course, you can use anything that appeals to you. The advantages of both felt and burlap is that neither have to be hemmed. (Burlap edges should be trimmed neatly to keep from raveling.) Different materials will appeal to you for different reasons. A banner on "Fishers of Men" done in earth tones of blues, greens, and browns might be done in burlap; a regal "Rejoice, the Lord is King" would look great in rich purple, green and white felt and velvet with jewel trims. A "Joy Is Like the Rain" banner could be done in wet-look vinyl.

If your budget is limited, put out a plea to church members for materials. Secondhand stores and garage sales are good sources for cheap material; use large drapery and upholstery material. Fancy trims and beads are expensive to buy new; I've taken many old pieces of inexpensive (or free) jewelry apart for this, especially "pearl" necklaces. Yarn is one of the most useful trims. Outline letters with it, use it for hair,

even for sheep's wool. (For this, glue the cut and curled short white pieces of yarn close together.)

Take special care in making your letters. If you want your letters about five inches high, cut a long strip of your material exactly five inches high. Then you have only to outline each letter and cut, assured that they will all be the same height.

Almost anything from letters to figures will look better when outlined in a dark or bright, heavy yarn. It makes everything stand out and gives a finished look. Not outlining is one of the most common mistakes.

Don't limit yourself to the shape of a rectangle for banners. Here are several examples:

Most banners can be put together with glue. Elmer's Glue-All dries clear, and is washable. However, you may need to sew on big pearls, heavy trim, etc. One very large Easter banner I did looks like the yarn designs were done in fancy, complicated stitches. Actually, all the yarn was glued on—not sewed—a much easier and quicker job. For fancy French knots I simply made large knots of yarn, cut them off, and glued them onto the banner, making sure the ends were glued under so as not to show or come loose. (Some yarn designs will look better sewed.)

Be especially neat when gluing—a good banner can be ruined with splotches here and there of dried glue, or with pieces not carefully glued down at the edges. To avoid a lumpy look, use a few dots of glue on the back of each piece; and in some cases, especially with very thin materials, spread these dots with your fingers to keep them from showing through.

Remember these few points:

● Plan your banner for a specific function or service.

● Know where it will be used so the size will be correct.

● Do a small mock banner first with colored papers and felt-tip markers to select your colors. Make changes now before starting on the real thing.

● Don't fill the banner with too many words.

● Cut and glue *carefully*—make a pattern if necessary. Do not apply glue *over* banner—glue over newspapers and then smooth out and removed excess glue before placing on the background piece.

● Outline letters, etc. Yarn is very good for this. Make use of trims, feathers, shells for special effects and dimensions.

If you already have some banners and are not pleased with the results, get them out and see if you can fix them. Maybe all that is needed is to trim the edges, glue some parts down, and outline a few words or figures.

Meet with your pastor and see if you can do a good banner or two for a specific service. Follow these tips and you should have some liturgical art both you and the congregation will be proud to own and use.

2/28 - Visit to Nursing Home conversations with Mrs. Davis, Mr. Specs

group MAGAZINE SIDE

6/6 - Conversation with Mr. Smith, veteran of Normandy invasion

group MAGAZINE SIDE

12/14 - Various shopping center interviews on significance of Christmas

group MAGAZINE

GROUP Magazine, Box 481, Loveland, CO 80537 SIDE

Opening New Ministries with Cassette Tapes

by Dennis Benson

Some young friends of mine in a Kansas City church took a cassette recorder to a nearby home for the aged. Instead of singing for the elderly and giving them a piece of cake, the young listened with cassettes.

The response was startling. They saw the bored glaze leave people's eyes. Bent backs straightened and once withdrawn men and women gestured again with animation and excitement. The change came simply because their stories were being recorded.

There was something quite important to those words which were being captured for further sharing. Perhaps some of the folks realized that for the first time they were creating media material rather than just receiving it.

These high school youth found a couple of elderly people from their own church at that home for the aged. They asked them to give one-minute prayers of thanksgiving. At the following week's Thanksgiving Day service of worship, three of these prayers were played during the prayer time. It was a moving experience for the people at worship. It also communicated to the elders of the tribe in the nursing home that they still had something important to contribute even when their physical powers had declined.

You and I have a new tool for improving life around us.

The audio cassette is an entirely new medium of communication. Its handy size, its simplicity of operation, its minimal costs, and its variety of possibilities

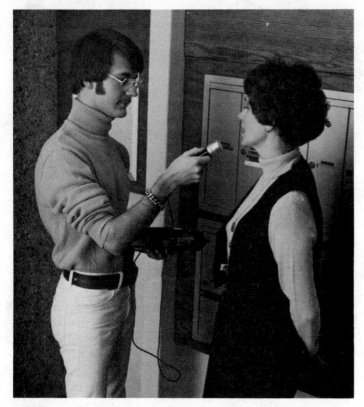

put the control of our media environment in the hands of the public as never before.

As with past inventions in communications, the electronic media and all their hardware are being pin-pointed for demonic possession at this time. Fiend films, violent television, and sexy recordings are coming under intense criticism by teachers and community leaders. If you've been reared on linear (written) sources of stimulation and learning, it is easy to see how the moving, singing, talking, feeling and spontaneity of the machine seem too free, too unpredictable, and too much fun. Many adults are particularly concerned because the tube, stereo speaker, and screen are so seductive. It must be dangerous to be entertained whenever you want.

Much of this suspicion and hostility has been deserved. There have been bushels of garbage running out of our media machines into our heads for a long time. However, I have found that the girl who didn't accept my invitation to the dance or the Rod Stewart LP which is scratched cannot be blamed in and of themselves for doing and being different than I desired. Instead, I have learned something which many of you may already know: *YOU and I do have control over the human and media environment around us!*

However, some of the TV and music critics are right. There is a temptation to believe that most media input is there to help us forget whatever problems, persons, or theology we should be dealing with. For some, media intake has become a drug. Our entertainment becomes

our master and we become the slaves.

Happily, this is not the way most of my young friends are interacting with medialand. Let's probe further just this one little member of the electronic family to discover how much grace and love we can create using an unhexed approach to media.

The audio cassette is not just another form of tape recorder. In fact, I believe that recording was reinvented by the Phillips folk a little more than a decade ago when they transformed the huge, two-handed, open-reel recorder into a palm-of-the-hand mini-world of intimacy and mobility. A virtual portable feast was dished out for us. The cost and operation complexity were minimized while the versatility was maximized.

Just feel that clean machine! The cassette can be snuggled up against your hip, dangled from your hand, or dropped into a purse. In the neat compact machines, we don't have the media freak's mob of buttons, dials and knobs. Just a switch or slider. The cassette tape is simple and offers a cool hour or so of possibility.

Manufacturers of media equipment are often also under the spell of a media hex when it comes to making use of what they create. They tend to use the format and material of the previous equipment as program material for the newest product. For example, radio became theatre without pictures, and television becomes radio with pictures. It is not surprising that cassette tapes are centered on material derived from its predecessors—from recordings, music and from reel-to-reel recorders, lectures.

The secret to turning the cassette into a means of genuine communication and human exchange is rooted in the person who uses the machine. The whole electronic web does not live on its own. There is nothing magical about what comes out of the tube. We are responsible for what we do with what we receive.

A student friend of mine, for example, was faced with the pain that his grandfather was dying. Tom didn't know how to deal with this situation. He found that this dear man was delighted to spend hours with his grandson as Tom tape recorded stories from his grandfather's life. This became a way of leaving behind the roots of who he was. At one point, his grandfather said that the sessions around the mike gave special meaning to his death.

Or take the example of a church school class of senior highs who took cassette recorders and interviewed adults in their congregation, asking them their opinions on the human and divine natures of Christ. The youth came back with every heresy in the history of the church! What a great discussion followed!

Interviewing is the area of greatest possibility for this most available of all media instruments. Such a statement reveals my belief in the gifts of God working through each of us. During the course of 7000 interviews, I have discovered more about my faith, my needs and my gifts than by any other means. I have

10 Tips for Taping Interviews

1 Check your power (good spiritual advice also). Use AC whenever you can.

2 Clean your recording/playback head(s) often with alcohol. Use a cotton swab.

3 Buy good tape (in the two-dollar-or-more price range for C-60). Cheap stuff is tempting, but is made from re-cycled ping-pong balls (not really!).

4 Watch out for sound demons in the recording area (I have recorded more flushing toilets in dressing rooms than anyone else).

5 Watch your hand. There is a uni-versal tendency to provide biofeedback concerning your nerves via the mike in your hand. It will make your recordings sound like the soundtrack from "Earth-quake."

6 Push the mike into the face of the interviewee. Then hold it to one side of the mouth (to keep the Old Faithful blasts of breath from wiping out the recording).

7 Look the person in the eyes. If they are watching the mike with fear, you are not providing a person-to-person rela-tionship with him/her.

8 Beware of the cute little remote control switch. When engaged, it keeps your battery working. It also can con-fuse you. Just don't use it.

9 If you are in the wind or faced by a "windy" person, use a foam rubber wind screen (costs under a dollar at radio stores).

10 Carry the tape recorder every-where! Force yourself to plunge into an interview.

learned more on the streets, in homes, at hospitals, and at airports, interviewing people than in any classroom. The music in the cadence and accents and tone of voice as humans put their stories into words is truly a vehicle of grace and hope.

Don't be fooled by the myth that claims that no one can possibly be comfortable in front of a mike. We have found that an interviewee is only uptight when the interviewer is uptight. If you are afraid to hold the mike, the person with whom you talk will also be afraid.

If you really care about what the other person has to say, both of you will be more relaxed. The interview happens when a real human encourages another to share the deepest dimensions of existence. Sadly, most folks are not used to this kind of affirmation. Most people are slow to speak into a mike because they don't think that they have anything important to share. It is this media myth which turns communicating human beings into consumers of other people's ideas. You will have to affirm and encourage to bring out the story gifts of others. Once a person experiences the heady quality of sharing with another who cares, you won't be able to turn him/her off.

I spent a great time with a group of young people who were visiting Philadelphia for a week. They went into the streets with their recorders. It was amazing what they found. People sang for them the songs of life, hope and sorrow. People cried as they told things which they had told no one else. One man thanked two of the interviewers for listening to his feelings about the death of his wife through cancer. "I was lonely. Now you carry part of my burden. It will somehow be easier for me."

What do you talk about in the streets with your mike? Your goal is to let people share what they are thinking and who they are. I find that there are basi-cally three steps to entering into a person's life with a cassette recorder.

First, the contract is the moment of connection when you make contact with another person. People are frightened by stories about the government and other people bugging their lives. The contract becomes the introduction when you introduce yourself, tell why you are doing this ("talking to interesting people"), and assure them that their name will not be used. If you don't cover this first step, you will not get a comfort-able exchange.

The second step is the encounter itself. The body of the interview is the most difficult of the relationship. We are called to listen. This is an overwhelming task. Listening means that we are *hearing what is being* said. It is so easy to worry about what *we* will say next that we are not really following the other person's story or comments.

One friend was confronted by three bus drivers who would not respond to his questions. He finally decided to ask a creative query. "If you were a cannibal, who would you eat?" Perhaps you don't want to go that far.

Opening New Ministries with Cassette Tapes CONT.

However, be free to explore questions which have no right or wrong answers. "If you had 15 minutes to live, what would you do?" "If you were invisible, where would you go?" There is no way a person can respond without revealing a whole world of feelings. The interviewee is telling us what he/she wants us to know. Doors are opened for us to follow. Therefore, follow-up questions add to the flow of the interview and add conviction that you're hearing what's being said.

I think that this step is particularly hard for young people. Normally, you often feel forced to give adults (teachers, etc.) the kinds of answers they want. It is different in our kind of story telling, for YOU are in control! This may be one of the few moments of empowerment that you have had. You can afford to listen and probe areas suggested by this trusting person.

Interviewing is the moment of crunch for a lot of people. It all comes pressing home about who you are. You stand quite open before another person. This stranger can turn you down or not respond at all. If he/she doesn't trust the way you look at them or how your body communicates, the stranger won't talk. This means that you are the message. As you nod your head, focus your gaze, and let your mouth shape in reaction to what is being said, you are communicating.

People will tell you more in company with your mike than they will tell you without it. It seems that we are called to be the Word more than saying it.

The third step to the interview is the conclusion. This process of getting out of your conversation is quite important. You will need to affirm the person for talking. He/she will want to know if the story contribution was helpful. You will want to share what you believe: it is good to be in communion with another.

You often see persons recording speeches. What might be much more interesting would be to interview the speaker. I have never been turned down. In fact, I have found about 300 rock performers who have kindly let me interview them (John Lennon, Alice Cooper, Pink Floyd, Jim Croce, Gary Wright, etc.). Why don't you talk to the music and sports stars visiting your city about their real selves?

And why not give new meaning to the summer trip your youth group may be planning by adding the media dimension? Bring along enough cassette recorders so that each pair of people has one. Then when you go to that big city, camp, or mission field, collect the stories of the people there. John Washburn calls this process, done in the context of a travel environment, "taming." Tame your experience by interviewing.

If all of this still sounds a bit magical, exercise your machine, capturing the story of your own grandparents. Ask about their youth and life. Edit the finished tape and make copies for the family at Christmas. It will really be an amazing experience.

There will be moments when the use of the machine will scare. I still am a bit nervous when I confront a stranger on the street. Personal encounters are always risky. So is love. But, in the hands of caring folk like you, the audio cassette becomes an opportunity for a special kind of human interchange.

Have fun with your portable feast.

How Cassettes Can Shape a Youth Ministry

Does your youth program need help? Why not put cassette tape recorders to work? How? Well, if a church's youth ministry is to be effective, you, its youth, should have some voice in the shaping of the contents, the direction, and the form of that program. And how do you get your youthful input to improve your church's youth ministry?

One idea is to start with a group of five or six interested young people and supportive adults. Equip them all with cassette tape recorders. Have them interview every youth in the church and some significant adults. Take ten to twelve weeks to find out where people are. What are their interests and their problems? What are their expectations for themselves, for their church, and for the Christian faith? Then go into the community and talk with kids not in the church.

I guarantee that after three months of listening, your initiating group will know how to shape a youth ministry for your church. But the sad thing is that many churches never listen to their young constituents. So do your homework well.

When you use a tape recorder, it forces you to listen and to feel that you really want to hear what she/he has to say. Plus, you've already made your major statement about youth ministry. It's with youth, not to youth.

Puppetry

by Dale VonSeggen

Hi! My name is Lucy. I'm a puppet. I like being a puppet. Why? Let me tell you. Since a year ago, when I was created out of some pieces of foam rubber, fake fur, and fabric, I've really had an exciting time!

First, I went on a long trip in a box on a truck, along with several other puppet friends, to a church in Colorado. You should have seen the excitement when my new owners opened my box! They practically tore my arm off in their enthusiasm!

The first few weeks in my new home were a bit embarrassing. The church where I lived was just starting something they called a "puppet ministry." I wasn't sure I'd fit in, because I'd never even been to college, let alone seminary. There were about 12 teenagers in this puppet ministry, and they were just learning to work with characters like me.

Puppetry CONT.

Sometimes when I was supposed to be talking, they forgot to move my mouth. Other times, I couldn't see the audience at all, because they had me either looking at the ceiling or sinking down behind the curtain. Once, they even threw me on the floor, and my face got all dirty. But I survived all this, and after a few months, the young people who made us "work" became better and better at helping us sing songs and act out plays.

We performed in children's church, shopping malls, and every month we performed in a Saturday morning program called "Kids in Denver Saturday." It was a lot of fun, even though we had to practice long hours.

When summer came, we hardly had time to rest! We went on tour with the youth choir to Wyoming, South Dakota, and Nebraska, and spent two weeks at a Navajo Indian reservation in Arizona with a youth missions team. Our friends who "operated" us were excited that we could go with them on trips. Another highlight of our summer was performing at the National Christian Youth Congress. The people there really liked us.

In August, our people friends boxed us up again and took us on tour to the Kansas City area for five days. There we performed in several churches, and spent one whole day doing "Backyard Bible Clubs."

Things have settled down a little now. We still practice every Tuesday night, and I get to go to children's church about every other Sunday to sing and play a part in a play.

I really enjoy being a puppet. I get to teach boys and girls and adults about Jesus, and about how Christians should live, and it makes me feel good when I see people smiling. I can't think of a better way to communicate Bible stories, songs, and drama than by using puppets like my friends and me.

What is a puppet ministry?

A "puppet ministry" consists of a group of individuals, usually teenagers, who are interested in using puppets to minister to others, and an adult director who teaches puppetry skills to the puppeteers. The puppet team usually practices once a week for one to two hours, and performs in children's church, class socials, worship services, Sunday school departmental openings, shopping malls, and wherever else the opportunity arises.

The puppet ministry may consist of two or three puppeteers and a couple of puppets, or it may expand to large groups of 18 to 24 puppeteers with several stages, lots of puppets, several adult sponsors, and sound and lighting systems. Some churches use junior highers as puppeteers, while others use senior highers, young adults, or even senior adults. Almost all churches involved in a puppet ministry use the moving-mouth hand puppet, as opposed to marionettes or puppets with mouths that do not open and close.

Getting started

Necessary ingredients for a successful church puppet ministry are a competent director, dedicated puppeteers, puppets, and script materials and songs for the puppets to perform.

The director should be an individual knowledgeable in the proper methods of puppet manipulation. Persons can become competent in these techniques through attending puppet workshops, reading books on puppetry, and by watching other puppeteers perform, live or on television.

The director should be part teacher, part disciplinarian, part artist, part guidance counselor, part drill sergeant, and totally convinced that puppets can be a powerful tool of education and ministry.

The puppeteers should view their involvement with the puppets as a ministry, and must be faithful in attendance at practices and performances. The age of the puppeteer is not as important as his dedication, but persons with wide age differences should not be on the same puppet team. Extreme age differences will cause problems in areas of physical size, social interests, and maturity levels.

The puppeteers should be encouraged to mesh together into a unit, all with the same purpose and goal. Many puppet groups choose a name for themselves, such as "God's Handful," "F Troop," "Sonshine Gang," "Truckin' for Jesus," "Puppet Power and Light Co.," and "Zacchaeus and Co."

The puppets are a big investment, and the puppet director should plan carefully to make available money go as far as possible. Most puppet authorities recommend that top quality puppets be purchased from a reputable company, although some churches have talented designers and seamstresses capable of making their own puppets.

"People" puppets should be acquired first as opposed to animal puppets or monster puppets. People puppets are more adaptable to Bible stories, Christian living stories, and other available script materials than the other two types.

The puppets should be colorful, durable, and similar in size. The most important factor in judging the quality of a puppet is the construction of the mouth. The mouth should open and close easily and completely, and should fit the hand snugly. The construction of the mouth should allow the lower jaw of the puppet to move down and up without excessive movement of the top part of the head.

Such features as changeable wigs, changeable facial features, and removable clothing also are desirable.

The two basic types of people puppets are the rod-arm puppet and the human-arm puppet. The rod-arm puppet has a wire rod attached to the wrist of the puppet, and the puppeteer uses this rod to move the puppet's arm—to gesture, to point, or to do whatever action or motion is required by the script. The human-arm puppet requires the puppeteer to put a glove on his hand and to put his arm through the puppet's sleeve. The hand actions are then performed by the puppeteer's hand and arm. To operate both the puppet's hands and mouth, two puppeteers must work together, coordinating their movements on one puppet. There are advantages to both types of puppet, and the experienced puppet team will have several of each.

Script materials and tapes are extremely important factors in an effective puppet ministry. Many puppet scripts, tapes, and songs written especially for the church puppet ministry are available from commercial suppliers, and some puppeteers write their own materials.

Many puppet groups find that performing songs is the easiest way to begin. There are lots of children's albums and contemporary gospel songs that are very adaptable to puppets. Sometimes "speeding up" a 33⅓ RPM record to 45 RPM gives the song a "puppet quality" that makes the song fit puppets better.

Performances are done either live, using microphones, or by using tapes and synchronizing the movement of the puppets with the tape. Most puppet groups use cassette tapes almost exclusively, but there is a definite place for live segments in a team's repertoire.

Some type of sound amplification will be necessary, and this can be anything from a simple cassette player to a sophisticated tape deck, amplifier, speakers, and headset microphones.

A lighting system also adds a great deal to the overall effect of the performance. Many groups use colored and white floodlights, spotlights, strobes, and blacklight. In addition to lighting, such things as props and prop racks, multi-level stages, and rear-projection screens are used by many teams.

Resources, materials, and organizations

Many companies and individuals are presently marketing puppets and puppetry materials for the church puppet ministry. Two of the companies with a wide variety of puppets and materials are: Puppet Productions, Box 82008, San Diego, CA 92138; Puppets From One Way Street, Box 2398, Littleton, CO 80161.

Puppet Productions has many good tapes available, with Bible Truths 3, 4 and 5 being the best ones. They also have an excellent series of substance abuse and health puppet plays entitled, "Alcohol on Trial," "This Was Your Life, Smokey Hackincoff" and "Keep Off the Grass." For weekly children's church use, their "Children's Programming Collection" is an excellent series of Bible story plays and applications.

Puppets From One Way Street has a useful series of seasonal puppet plays and tapes, with one play written for each of the months of the year. They also carry many different records and cassettes of puppet songs and dialogs. One Way Street also sells materials on ventriloquism and ventriloquism routines.

Both companies have catalogs available on request

Do's and Don'ts for Puppet Ministry

DO'S

- Remember at all times that you are "ministering," not just entertaining.
- Communicate your purpose and policies clearly to puppeteers and parents.
- Demand punctuality and faithfulness for practices and performances.
- Allow adequate practice time before your scheduled performance dates.
- Keep everyone informed regarding future practice and performance dates.
- Emphasize proper care and storage of your puppets.
- Be imaginative in the costuming of your puppets.
- Be open to criticism at all times.
- Stress the memorizing of your material.
- Emphasize proper mechanics of puppet manipulation—entering and exiting, lip synchronization, eye contact, and positioning.
- Make your stage as light and portable as possible. The most common stage type uses a 1½" PVC plastic pipe frame or a folding wood frame.

DON'TS

- practice or perform the same material so long that it gets dull and stale.
- allow puppets to hit, bite or use derogatory language.
- allow puppeteers to take the church's puppets home to practice.
- be satisfied with mediocrity. Strive for improvement and excellence.
- allow visitors to attend puppet practice.
- buy cheap curtain material. Invest in a good quality velour or polyester which cannot be seen through and doesn't wrinkle.
- allow your congregation to brand puppetry as being only for children. Youth and adults will enjoy good puppetry, too.

and Puppet Productions has a monthly newsletter filled with helpful ideas and scripts.

Some Christian book stores are beginning to stock puppet script books, instructional books, and puppets.

In addition to materials written specifically for puppets, there are records and tapes available which are very adaptable for use with puppets. Included in this category are:

1. Humorous skits by the Jeremiah People, who offer several records and tapes with useable songs and skits.
2. Humorous routines by the Christian comedy group Isaac Air Freight. They have two albums out: "Fun in the Son" and "In the Air, On the Air."
3. A comedy album by Squires and Zimmerman entitled "Pillars of the Assembly."
4. Musical numbers from albums of contemporary artists, such as the Archers, Imperials, Evie, and others.
5. General children's musicals, such as "Music Machine," "Bullfrogs and Butterflies," "Nathaniel the Grublet" and "Sir Oliver's Song" by a contemporary gospel group named Candle.
6. Seasonal musicals, such as "Mary Had a Little Lamb" (Christmas), and "And His Fleece Was White As Snow" (Easter), both written by Dan Barker.

Here are some addresses of organizations you may find helpful in your church puppet ministry:

Fellowship of Christian Magicians, Box 651, Marne, MI 49435. This organization is comprised of Christian magicians, puppeteers, ventriloquists, artists and clowns. They publish a monthly newsletter, and conduct a five-day convention in Winona Lake, Indiana, each July.

Fellowship of Christian Puppeteers, 16 Albro Avenue, Troy, NY 12180. This is an organization that publishes a newsletter of scripts and sources and holds regional conventions.

Clowns of America, Box 3906, Baltimore, MD 21222. This is a secular clown organization that publishes a monthly periodical and holds regional and national clown conventions.

Evangelizing Today's Child, Box 348, Warrenton, MO 63383. This is a monthly magazine that is an excellent resource book.

The puppet team concept is an exciting way of involving your group in areas of ministry that can produce lasting results, both in your lives and in the lives of those in your audiences.

"Ladies and gentlemen, children of all ages, welcome to the greatest..."

Clowning in the Church

by William Paepke

Hold it. Hold it. Clowns in the church? That's ridiculous. In fact it's a sacrilege. Isn't anything sacred any more? Are you suggesting that the Holy One of God was a clown? This is just going too far. I can't believe it. It's sheer blasphemy.

Now you hold it. I'm not suggesting for a minute that Jesus Christ was or is a clown. He is the Lord of Lords and the King of Kings. But he was a big attraction. He loved a party. He was entertaining. He could draw a crowd. And he loved children. He even told a few jokes (Matthew 7:3-5; 19:24). He loved a parade. He was the butt of jokes and ridicule. He was the laughingstock of Jerusalem. I am suggesting that clowning in the church may be a valid and meaningful symbol for people in our crazy mixed up world.

Clowning in the church may be a way to be all things to all men that by any means we might save some. The circus setting may provide children of all ages with a new opportunity to praise the Lord.

Consider for a moment the image of the merry-go-round. Without Jesus your life is like a runaway or broken down merry-go-round. Without Jesus at the center of your spinning world you have a constant source of power and a certain sense of direction.

Consider the imagery of the high trapeze. We all love to fly. Yet there are times when we can't, or we won't, or we look bad, or we may even fall. Why? We fail to fly because we don't trust our catcher. We look bad or even fall because we don't keep our eye on the catcher. A good catcher can make even a poor flier look good. Can you see the parallel? Jesus is our catcher. Every Christian is a flier. Jesus catches us, straightens us out, and sends us back into our flight pattern. He makes us look good. So trust him. Keep your eyes focused on him. Now do you see it?

There is a whole library full or parables in the imagery of the circus and the clown. Sink your teeth into them. Play with them. Act them out. Just picture it in your mind and then in your life. Communicate the

Clowning in the Church CONT.

Good News of Jesus Christ. If he could use sparrows with all of their diseases, and hair with its microscopic beauty, and camels with their unique odor, we can surely do something with Bozo, or Bertha, or Lea, or the Binaldis.

What's this dude, Jesus, all about, anyway? Well, he invites you and me to put our sadness in the slammer and to embark on a journey of joy. He came that we might have life, i.e., life in all its abundance.

Jesus is the joy of my life. So is my five-year-old son, Karl. When I think back on my fifth year of life, I remember the exhileration of going to the circus. It had to be the most exciting moment in my new life. All of the memories came back as Karl and I make our annual pilgrimage to the Shrine Circus. I can very easily recall the sights, the sounds, and the smells, the color and pageantry of the opening parade, the roll of the drum, the rainbow effect of the helium-filled balloons, the crack of the whip in the cage, the captivating voice of the ringmaster, the laughter, the applause, the overwhelming aroma of the elephants' afterburn, the popcorn, and the sweet taste of the cotton candy. It's all there right on the edge of my memory, a rich field waiting to be plowed.

Emily Dickinson described her experience this way, "Friday I tasted life. It was a vast morsel. A circus passed the house—still I feel the red in my mind though the drums are out."

What a rich set of symbols! We can mine this rich experience for a great treasure. We can harness these circus symbols to pull heavy meaning in the worship and witness life of the church.

By the way, have you ever described a worship experience, even in a retreat setting, as "a vast morsel"? Perhaps the many ancient symbols we use today in our worship are all too often archaic and empty shoes of the truth. By the time we finish explaining the meaning of the Chi Rho or the Ichthus for the seventeenth time, we need an alarm clock to pick up the worship tempo. We need and we have new symbols with a contemporary touch to communicate the ageless truth that Jesus Christ is for you.

The clown is a contemporary symbol with great possibilities for communication in the church and in the world. A clown is a real human being who gives of himself to make people laugh. A clown exposes his clumsiness and stupidity for all to see. He is not afraid to admit his frailty. He confesses his failures before mankind.

Jesus Christ gave much more than any clown can ever give, but he did give of himself that we might live and laugh and celebrate. That's a clown for you. A clown can offer a thousand different tricks, but he is really a representative of every man. Willie the Hobo, Emmett Kelly's tramp character, is probably the best known example.

Kelly describes Willie like this: "I am a sad and ragged little guy who is very serious about everything he attempts—no matter how futile or foolish it appears to be. I am the hobo who found out the hard way that the deck is stacked, the dice frozen, the race fixed and the wheel crooked, but there is always present that one tiny, forlorn spark of hope still glimmering in his soul which makes him keep on trying.

"All I can say beyond that is that there must be a lot of people in this world who feel that way and that, fortunately, they come to the circus. In my tramp clown character, folks who are down on their luck, have had disappointments and have maybe been pushed around by circumstances beyond their control, see a caricature of themselves. By laughing at me, they really laugh at themselves, and realizing that they have done this gives them a sort of spiritual second wind for going back into the battle."

Can you see why many people identify with Willie? Perhaps our goal in worship should be to give our people "a sort of spiritual wind for going back into the battle."

In the midst of death there is life in the God-man Jesus Christ. In the depths of despair there is hope because Jesus Christ has been raised from the dead. He is alive and well. How can we best express this our faith to our brothers and sisters around us? One possible way is by using the rich and exciting imagery of the clown and the circus world.

Now I would be the first to admit that it won't work with everyone in every situation. What does? A couple of years ago we designed a youth service for the dedication of a new church building. When it came time for the grand processional, we almost dropped our crucifix made with helium-filled balloons. The audience was probably 75 percent silver gray. Shortly after the service one aged and angry man, who had not even attended the service, descended upon us with vengeance. "What have you done to our beautiful church? You've made it a pigsty! You haven't heard the end of this." Undoubtedly he was referring to the confetti on the carpet.

I explained to him that it was good clean confetti and that we would clean up every bit of it. I had personally supervised the shredding of the paper in our paper shredder at the college. Well, it took us four hours to clean up the confetti. We finally had to pick it up piece by piece with our fingers. A word to the wise is sufficient: Don't use confetti on carpets.

Well, the old man has been mad ever since. Some of us have lost forever the little child in us.

My advice is to start where the people are. Maybe the best they can appreciate at first is a simple magic act.

Make sure you clear all the channels of authority. . . before you blow up the balloons. By the way, welding suppliers are your best source for helium. Insurance agents often have an ample supply of free balloons.

Let the people know what is coming. The element of

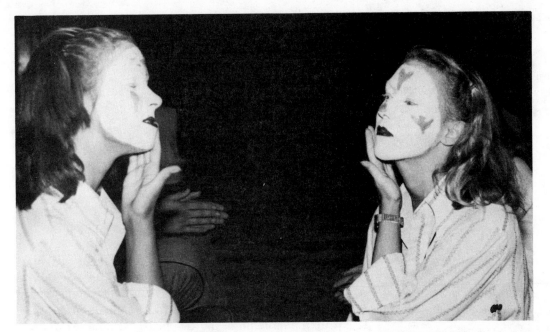

surprise is valid and important, but people whose nostrils are inflamed will find it difficult to drink in the rich meaning on your clowning. It really depends on the table of worship experience that you have in your church. It is best to be able to tie into something they already know or a similar experience.

Go slowly. Save the reckless abandon for your touch football games. Maybe you'll want to practice by putting on your face, suiting up, and going down to the local shopping center. Join a waiting line of customers at the cash register. When they have paid for their merchandise, offer to carry it out to their car for them. Grocery stores are great for this. Older folks really appreciate your help.

Maybe you can even get a small troupe of clowns together to help raise money for MDA or MS or the United Way. It is best to have permission whenever and wherever you do your clowning. Businessmen are usually very happy to have such an attraction working in their store. It's good for business. Just remember that you are on stage whenever you are in costume. Look for every opportunity to do good.

In some churches clowning will even work in the Sunday morning prime time worship service. But it must be polished and well-prepared. We must offer our very best to Jesus and his people. Look what he gave us.

Anyone can be a clown. There is a clown inside everyone. Jesus has called you to strip away all the masks, to apply the full white face as a symbol of your dying with Him, and to create a new you with your own unique color and expression (2 Corinthians 5:11-20).

Emmett Kelly started out as a poor Kansas farm boy who drew cartoons and worked to become a top flight trapeze artist. Along the way to stardom as Willie the Hobo, Kelly had to work at many ordinary and routine jobs just to keep food in the cupboard.

I'm not suggesting that you can become another Emmett Kelly (although you can), but am saying ordinary people can be clowns. People like you and me. We can lead other people to laugh at the absurd nature of man. We can initiate the victory dance as we make our pilgrimage to heaven. We can as God's people celebrate the victory of Jesus Christ over death.

Preparing a full blown circus worship service is hard work, but it's exciting and fun. There are really two questions to ask. First what do you want to communicate (message)? This means Bible study. What is God saying to you? Pick out a portion of scripture and study it until you really know and feel what God is saying to you. In my personal life and on the college scene where I work, we've found relational Bible study in small groups to be the most effective means to this end. Karl Olsson suggests a four step approach to relational Bible study:

1. Make the Bible story your story.
2. Identify with a character in the story.
3. Find the Gospel in the story.
4. Name the story.

Olsson's approach is simple, but it works for us. Try it. Dig. Get into God's word. Whatever method of Bible study works best for you, use it.

The second question is how you can communicate God's message to your audience(method)? Here is where you need to be developing your clown skills. Establish a character. Maybe you want to use a biblical character. The Rev. Michael L. Meier, campus pastor at Oregon State University, is Salaam the Clown (Numbers 22). Who are you? Take a look at yourself. Get in touch. Once you have it, then the fun begins. Develop your own unique face. You can use a full white face or perhaps only a partial white face.

Clown white can be obtained from or through most drama departments or theatrical supply stores. We use Noxzema under the clown white. It makes it easier to clean off. We also set our faces by powdering over the clown white with plain old Johnson's Baby Powder.

Clowning in the Church CONT.

You can use an old athletic sock or brush for each color. Cold creme works well to clean off your face. You'll just have to experiment for yourself. It's even fun to fail at this task.

Maybe mom has an old wig that she no longer wears. Discount stores sometimes sell wild colored wigs for a song.

There is even a pattern for clown outfits that you can pick up at any fabric shop. The local Salvation Army Thrift Store is a veritable gold mine for would-be clowns.

Your face and costume are crucial. Be unique. God made only one like you. After he saw you, he destroyed the mold. So be you. . . an original by Jesus.

Now you need to develop your routines. Balloons and clowns were created on the same day. Fill your pockets Kids love balloons. It's a ball to fill each balloon with a special message. Write a heavy thought or super Bible passage on a scrap of paper. Stuff it in the balloon. Blow up the balloon for a little one. He will have an extra pleasure to pick him up when the balloon pops.

The following service was prepared by myself and about 15 college kids at the invitation of Pastor Dick Hardel, who now does his clowning at St. Petersburg, Florida. Dick was the director of the Now Village discovery experience at the All Lutheran Youth/Adult gathering in the Superdome in New Orleans. We asked each of our kids to prepare a routine and character under the general theme, "Life in Christ Is a Circus." We then had auditions where we all sat in judgment of each other.

We did the service three times. The first service was a bomb. We were ready to go home. We stayed and prayed. Then we got the scissors out. We really cut ourselves to pieces. After we edited about half of the routines, we did the second service. It was a smashing success. We're still praising the Lord for the experience.

The service took place inside a circus tent 37 feet in diameter. About 150 people sat around on straw bales. The stage was simply a small platform (6' x 8' x 12") which was positioned next to a side wall. The lighting system was two heat lamps clamped to the two upright poles. The sound system included two microphones and a small amplifier. For music we used a piano and a cassette tape recording of general circus type music. Most public libraries have circus music records in the children's department.

Warm-up/Set-up

EXPLANATION: Two clowns, each with a Frisbee, play catch with the audience. The cleaning lady (Carol Burnett type) clears off the table/altar on stage which has been the site of a recent meal. Set-up includes a homemade candelabra made from 2' x 4's, a bottle of wine, and a loaf of bread.

SYMBOLISM: The preparation—the cleaning lady is a powerful symbol of the Holy Spirit; she cleans off God's landing strip to make room for Jesus.

Announcement

EXPLANATION: The angel clown, Gabby, alerts the people that something beautiful is about to be born (Luke 1:30-31). She always carries a bundle in a sheet.

SYMBOLISM: Traditionally angels, God's messengers, were there when babies were born and people were in need.

Parade of performers

EXPLANATION: Everyone joins in, skipping to the music, juggling, cartwheeling, pogosticking, skateboarding.

SYMBOLISM: The processional—God's people are a pilgrim people, always on the move.

Fire-eater

EXPLANATION: Schedley, the Stupendice, a magician of sorts, eats fire. Pour a couple ounces of Galliano in a saucer. Light it with a match. Dip your finger into the Galliano and quickly insert your finger in your mouth. Don't try to light the candles with your finger. In fact it's best to

wet your finger before dipping into the flaming Galliano.

SYMBOLISM: The invocation—God's people can be fired up with his Spirit even today.

Construction project

EXPLANATION: Charley, the carpenter clown, enters with lumber, saw, hammer, square, etc., but he only creates chaos.

SYMBOLISM: Confession—you can't build the city alone.

"The Elephant and the Flea"

EXPLANATION: Everyone sings with piano and clowns, "Boom, boom, ain't it great to be crazy!" (This song is used spontaneously throughout the service whenever the tempo lags.)

SYMBOLISM: More confession with a hint of release and celebration.

Making up a clown

EXPLANATION: Mathilda, the midget clown, with some help from the arms of a friend who hides behind her in her sweatshirt, shows us how to make up our clown faces. The arms of the person in front protrude below the sweater. Put a pair of tennis shoes on her hands and keep them on the makeup table too.

SYMBOLISM: Almost an absolution—you're starting to become the new creation (II Corinthians 5:17).

Willie the Hobo

EXPLANATION: Willie fails to blow up his balloon, then he succeeds but fails because he pops it. So he buries it. Then

Share God's promises that way.

An old rusty nail is also a powerful symbol. Most carpenters will give them to you for nothing. Just pick out some old sourpuss in the audience and walk right up to him and gently plant a nail in his hand. But while you have his hand, examine it. Look for callouses and scars and dirt under the fingernails. Then make the sign of the cross in his palm and shake his hand firmly. This routine melts the most hardened clown haters. Get your caring act together.

Gather your props. Practice on a mirror or on the members of your family.

Silence is a powerful medium. Even Shakespeare knew that. "Let clowns speak no more than is set down for them." Most of our clowns are silent. In silence, you are forced to look for opportunities to demonstrate your concern for others. The only time silence doesn't work is when you're in a public place where there is too much competitive noise. Then you may be forced to talk to make your point. Normally we use a ringmaster to introduce and interpret wherever necessary.

Lighting is also a very useful tool. A simple spotlight is really helpful for focusing on a given act. Depending on the size of your audience and the natural light in the room, you can sometimes get by with just an extra good flashlight. For larger audiences you may have to tap your local college or high school drama departments.

Whenever we do a clown worship service, we program into it as much audience participation as possible. Again, the lack of involvement in most Sunday morning worships is a real weakness. We've used everything from a 300-member rope-pull to an open mike time when people from the audience shared the most embarrassing moments in their lives.

The clown is inside you. Let God's Spirit move you. Let the circus begin. Jesus Christ is alive and well. That calls for a celebration. Can you think of a better way to celebrate than to have a circus? Just remember, everybody loves a circus. Don't forget to invite me.

"Ladies and gentlemen, children of all ages, welcome to the greatest Savior on earth, Jesus Christ!"

---

he fails to crack his peanut shell, but he succeeds by stomping on it. Failure again.
SYMBOLISM: More confession—Willie is a symbol of every man; we all fail daily to be all that he has called us to be, but he still invites us.

Delivery time
EXPLANATION: Gabby, the angel clown, returns with a bundle all wrapped up in a blanket, and finally she lays it on a young lady (relax, it's only a balloon).
SYMBOLISM: Are you expecting? His return? (Matthew 24:42).

A continuing project
EXPLANATION: Charley fails again, but he tries hard.
SYMBOLISM: More confession.

A pyramid
EXPLANATION: Gertrude invites nine adults and one youngster to help build a human pyramid, but it's really the church complete with a steeple.
SYMBOLISM: The church is people tied together by Jesus Christ (I Corinthians 12).

Smashing success
EXPLANATION: Schmedley returns to demonstrate the eternal lasting quality of man's technology by smashing an unbreakable cup.
SYMBOLISM: Don't put your faith in man's technology (Psalm 147:10-11).

An animal act
EXPLANATION: Lorna, the only female gorilla trainer in the world, finally tames Gronk because she has the right

equipment—a hard hat, a garbage can lid, an umbrella, and a life jacket.
SYMBOLISM: An interpretation of Ephesians 6:13-20; to do God's work, you need his equipment.

Willie fishing
EXPLANATION: Willie fails to catch a goldfish because he has the wrong bait, a grasshopper twice as long as the fish, and then he fails to catch him by hand because the bowl is too small.
SYMBOLISM: When you fish for men, Christ is the only bait that works (I Corinthians 2:2).

A pie eating contest
EXPLANATION: Four clowns, angry with the judges decision that the contest ends in a draw, give the judges some pie in the eye. The judges are willing volunteers from the audience.
SYMBOLISM: An interpretation of Matthew 7:1.

Project complete
EXPLANATION: Charley finds a blueprint in the Bible and builds a cross.
SYMBOLISM: I Timothy 3:16.

A discovery
EXPLANATION: The cleaning lady with mop and bucket cleans up a couple stray boards and discovers a cross which she props up against the table.
SYMBOLISM: The Gospel—John 16:13-14.

The cross
EXPLANATION: The spotlights focus on the cross as each performer brings to the foot of the cross a symbol of his life and work.
SYMBOLISM: The offering—Galatians 6:14.

Everybody's act
EXPLANATION: All present sing, "Father, I adore you, lay my life before you, how I love you (Jesus, Spirit)."
SYMBOLISM: Praise.

Shoe polishing
EXPLANATION: The cleaning lady moves thru the audience dusting off shoe after shoe. The clowns all follow suit and encourage audience to do the same to each other. Introductions are made. People are free to interact as the Spirit guides.
SYMBOLISM: The Passing of the Peace —John 13:1-15.

Announcement
EXPLANATION: Gabby invites all to let the circus begin in them (Ephesians 2:8-10), and she brings one last bundle, a watermelon, to a worshipper.
SYMBOLISM: The Benediction.

Parade of performers
EXPLANATION: The people are led out by the performers, especially the juggler and the clown spinning the ball on the tip of his finger, if possible in a snake dance out into the street and the world.
SYMBOLISM: Go (Acts 1:7-8).

An Interview with a Clown

GROUP: What is clown ministry?

SHAFFER: Clown ministry is an attempt to incarnate the historic religious symbol of the clown and inject it into the life of the church. The clown is probably the most unique way of understanding the role of servant that Jesus describes in the New Testament. In fact, the very word "clown" comes from the Anglo-Saxon word "clod," which is really a lump of the earth. And no matter how you interpret it, it always comes out the same way—God loved the clod.

The word "clod" is the lowly country bumpkin, the person who has no power, the one who does the commonest, lowliest form of work. This is almost synonymous with the New Testament word *doulos*, which, among all the Greek words for servant, is the lowest form of servant. It's almost akin to slave, a person without power who does all the lowest kinds of work. When Christ was in the upper room the night before he was crucified, he called upon his disciples to become servants as he took the basin and towel and washed their feet.

I understand clown ministry as a rather broad-based way of being servants of Jesus Christ in the world. It is more than just dressing up as a clown and shaking hands with someone. I don't think the simple action alone is as important as why the person underneath the makeup is doing it.

GROUP: How did you get started in clown ministry?

SHAFFER: It was a gradual thing with me. In the early 1960s I discovered that the word "clown" meant clod. I had to smile because being a farm boy I knew what it meant to be called a clod. That's a putdown word. But at the same time I remembered that people you really like, you describe as being "down to earth." It's the same thing, yet one is a downer and the other is an upper.

From then on, it just happened. I never set out to start a program. I introduced it to my congregation in 1969. To my knowledge, this was the first totally non-speaking service led by a clown, including holy communion, that was ever done in history. It was very well received by most people and from then on I just kept getting invitations. I began to inject myself more and more into some research of the clown. I began to say,

Youth groups around the country are donning clown costumes and setting out into hospitals, rest homes and shopping centers with the joy of Christ. To explore the colorful world of clown ministry, GROUP interviewed noted clown-pastor Floyd Shaffer. He's a Lutheran minister and the recognized pioneer of clown ministry.

"Hey, there's more here than meets the eye." I guess I would say my clowning grew out of a biblical theology, a pretty solid biblical theology.

GROUP: Why should we use the clown in worship?

SHAFFER: I think we should use the clown in worship for one of the major reasons that the clown exists—to remind us who we are. Up until the 12th century the clown was used on many occasions in worship to interrupt worship to remind people not to take their worship for granted. I don't care what denomination you may be in, those times come when worship becomes taken for granted. And the clown comes in with bizarre actions or using humor or sarcasm, and yet the central point is never lost.

I think that the clown is kind of a reminder of who we are and what we are to be about. It's not something we need a steady diet of, but I think it acts in a prophetic role in the church today. The clown reminds us of our humanity in the way that God intended us to be human.

A clown is never seen to be a performer. Never. A clown is intended to create an environment for the circus to happen. As you relate this to the church you begin to say, "You know, this is the task of Christians—to create an environment in their community and the world, so that people can learn to know of God's grace and respond to it." We are environment creators.

The opposite of the environment creator is the performer. The performer is the one who stands up front with a nice big smile and uses all the cliches and directs people from a standpoint of power rather than servanthood.

The clown says the most powerful person in the world is the one who can give away his power. This is what God did when he incarnated himself in Jesus Christ. This is what Jesus Christ did when he became obedient to death on the cross. This is what Christians ought to be about.

GROUP: Many people would say that a worship service led by a clown is irreverent. What do you say to such people?

SHAFFER: I remind them that the way I look upon the clown is not to be equated with what average Americans think about clowns. They think of certain television clowns or certain clowns in the comic books. They see him as a character or a puppet or a pretend person. Many people assume that a clown is somebody who dresses up and walks in a parade on the 4th of July and squirts water pistols. I don't think you're a clown just because you put on a costume and makeup, any more than you're a surgeon if you put on a green gown and a mask. I think the clown is a thoroughly honorable and highly powerful historic symbol.

GROUP: What's the significance of the costume and the makeup?

SHAFFER: It has to do with putting on a new personhood. The makeup, the white face in every race and culture is a symbol of the death mask. Even though there are many clown types, they all use white in some fashion. The white is the symbol of death and the colors become the symbol of new life.

The costume says, "Once you're dead to things, you know you're free to do all kinds of outlandish things." The clown characterization then becomes one that laughs at death. It says, "You can't kill me. I've already died." For the Christian clown, I think this is a reaffirmation of Easter. If you're dead to self and alive to Jesus Christ, when you put on that costume you're a whole new creation.

GROUP: In what ways can a youth group use clown ministry?

SHAFFER: I think you can use it to grow in your own understanding of your faith and life and theology. In practical ways, you can use it in nursing homes, in physical rehabilitation, in vacation church schools, in Sunday school.

Don't try to shove it into church worship right away. But after you get experience and after you really kind of know what you're doing, talk it over with your pastor. Perhaps the pastor can read the gospel for the day and you can reenact it as a clown. This permits people to see the word of God as well as hear it.

GROUP: Explain a little bit about what a group could do in a nursing home.

An Interview with a Clown

CONT.

SHAFFER: Typically, they'll go into nursing homes without words. One of the most important things we can do is touch people. I discovered that many young people do not feel comfortable in touching other people. But I believe that God knows that to love people you need to be able to hold them. I think that's one reason why God came in the form of a baby—a person you could hold.

If Jesus Christ dwells in human beings, youth groups that go to nursing homes should be able to see that these are people of great worth. We should feel comfortable about touching them and caring for them and experiencing what it means to translate the faith we talk about into action.

Take the commands of Jesus when he sent people forth by twos. Go and be caring, loving people. He didn't give them a blueprint, but he did give them love.

Clowning in Australia

The lady was about 40 years old. She was staring blankly into the boutique window.

"Er-um, we'd like you to have this," stammered 16-year-old Allan, timidly approaching the lady, relieved that his blushing was well-hidden by clown makeup.

At first, the lady just looked. Then she shyly took the little blue card in Allan's hand. "And this is for you, too" piped Allison, also in clown costume. Now the lady was holding a gift-wrapped plum. Her sad face smiled.

"Does it cost something?" she whispered.

"Oh no," Allan smiled. "It's a gift with love from the Church of Christ a few blocks away to celebrate Mother's Day. We thought we would come here to add some joy and to say welcome."

Tears filled her eyes. She stared at the little blue card, and then read the words aloud, "Keep hoping." Then Allan could hear her repeating quietly, "I will, I will."

"God bless you," Allan said shyly. He quickly placed his hand on the woman's shoulder. Then he and Allison moved on.

This incident is one of many witnessed by Pauline Hubner and Stan Stewart. The two often worked together—organizing clown outreaches in Australian shopping malls.

Here's their strategy. A local church contacts the management of a nearby shopping mall and proposes a half-hour stage show, followed by another half hour of good deeds by the clowns' "courtesy squad." The stage show features the clowns doing dance routines, drama and singing. The presentation is usually themed around a holiday, such as Christmas, Easter or Mother's Day.

After the show the clowns leave the stage and become the courtesy squad. Their job is to give out symbolic gifts (cake, balloons, gift cards, etc.), carry packages and open doors for shoppers. Their purpose is to extend a warm and caring attitude on behalf of the church.

Moving through the shopping center in pairs, the clowns make a subtle impact with their simple love, saying, "We're from Smithville Lutheran Church and this is for you, just to say we care."

Pauline said, "The message we would like to get across to the community is that the Christian life is one that can be brimming with excitement and vitality. Some within and outside the church seem to give the impression that to accept the Christian faith is to say 'no' to life."

Clowning in Texas

Nothing seemed to bring any reaction from the badly burned 8-year-old girl in Galveston (Texas) Burn Center. But then came the clowns. The little girl perked up for the first time since the fire. Her parents were overjoyed.

The clowns were young people from Highland Park United Methodist Church in Dallas. Visiting facilities such as the Galveston Burn Center is a regular thing for this active group. Since their clown ministry began in 1977, these young people have taken their special message of joy and love to hospitals, convalescent homes, retirement homes, rest homes, centers for handicapped people, and shopping centers.

These clowns offer a varied program—singing, magic shows, a "scrubb band," puppet shows and a clown dance routine. They've been well received wherever they've traveled.

They recently presented their first clown-led worship service at their church. And that too was well received.

Leaders at the church say the young people have gained much from the clowning experience. "They've learned to communicate love and bring happiness to people in all kinds of different settings," said one leader. "They've seen the importance of giving one's self to others. They know the personal rewards of seeing others smile and laugh."

GROUP: If a group becomes interested in clown ministry, what should it do first?

SHAFFER: Get your theology together. Get background on clown work. Research it out. Don't be afraid to study—not for a long period of time, but spend a couple of hours of introduction in some kind of clown ministry.

Second, understand what Jesus meant when he said, "Become as a child." Understand what the qualities of a child are in terms of trust, play, imagination and creativity.

And one of the most important things for youth who want to go into clowning is to learn to like themselves. I think that once you like yourself you can feel comfortable whether you're in makeup or out of makeup.

GROUP: Are there any danger areas in clown ministry—things that require special care or discretion?

SHAFFER: Sure. Never force yourself into another person's "space." Let them invite you into it. The clown creates an environment. You should try to draw people to you, not force yourself to them.

Second, I think a person ought to understand the whole nature of comedy. If you ever profane something by pulling it down there always ought to be the up-raising event which lifts a person higher than when you started. A clown's humor should never be the put-down kind of humor.

Third, understand the difference between childlikeness and childishness. For instance, worship ought to be dignified, but if you carry it too far it gets dull. Worship ought to be childlike because we use parent language for God; we call God our Father. But if you go too far in that direction, you get childish and silly. When you're *performing* you get *silly*. When you're a clown and *creating an environment* you're *childlike*.

GROUP: What resources can you recommend to those who would like to get started in clown ministry?

SHAFFER: There is a five-cassette series done by myself and Dennis Benson that is available. It includes a program that could be used for a weekend or for six consecutive weeks of two-hour sessions. It includes theology, an introductory worship service, 30 minutes of original jazz music, instructions for make-up, a bibliography, and some balloons for the training session. It's available from Contemporary Drama Service, Box 457, Downers Grove, IL 60515.

GROUP: Anything else you'd like to add?

SHAFFER: Enjoy it. Let it happen. Let the Spirit move through it. I believe God has a sense of humor. He laughs and delights. Do something intentionally foolish for Christ's sake each day.

Mime

by Michael Moynahan

It is happening in major cities. You can see people stricken with it on college campuses. It has infiltrated countless churches and youth groups. It has the power to make people laugh and cry. Its practitioners have been equally applauded and pelted. It was made popular in this country by one of its greatest performers, Marcel Marceau. It is mime.

Your group can use mime as a powerful communication tool in meetings or worship services.

One Easter Marceau brought his mimetic magic to Berkeley, California. Once again he cast a spell on all who attended. We were legion. Young and old, men and women, teachers and students, dancers, musicians, aspiring mimes, all huddled together in one room. Not everyone spoke the same language, and yet there were no communication problems. For two hours the master worked without a single word. We understood everything.

We laughed. We cried. We sighed. We applauded. We experienced more life and humanity in those two brief hours than we could have imagined. We witnessed success and failure, the tragic and the comic faces of life, God and people, joy and sorrow, beginnings and endings, life and death. At the end we stood as one body and shouted our approval and extended our applause. When he left we were changed.

What is the peculiar attraction and power of mime today? If you examine the phenomenon carefully, you will see that mime is not new to our society or our lives. Mime is communication without words. It is a language not just in the mind, but more importantly, of the heart. How often have you found yourself expressing your joy or satisfaction with a smile? How many times have you communicated worry or anxiety with a wrinkled brow? All a mime need do to register scepticism is raise an eyebrow. A mime doesn't need to say, "I beg your pardon!"

Have you ever waved at someone from a distance and communicated? Have you ever raised a clenched fist in anger or frustration and received a response? Have you ever noticed how we communicate who we are and what we are feeling by the way we walk? There are times we walk lightly as if we were walking on thin air. Then there are those times we can almost visualize humongously heavy burdens on people's shoulders. We communicate with our actions as well as our words. As a matter of fact, our actions speak volumes more than our words.

We are all, at heart, mimes. We are born imitators. Some of us learn to perfect these skills better than others. But the skills are there for all of us and found effective and rewarding when tried.

Why is mime appropriate for studying and proclaiming the Word of God? If one can speak of a goal in mime, it is to reveal and bring into the light what was before hidden and in the dark. The accomplished mime can make the invisible visible. The mimist can help us see the value, the power and the beauty of the ordinary by holding that reality up to us in extraordinary ways. We have lost our ability to see, to contemplate, to wonder and marvel at the magnificence of creation, at God's Word breaking into our world at every moment and all around us. Mime and its ministers can help us recover "good eyes" and this ability to see.

Four types

There are four types of mimes appropriate for use in group gatherings and worship. They are the silent mime, the narrative mime, the musical mime and the spin-off mime.

The silent mime is just that. There are no words spoken. There is no music used. After a piece of scripture is proclaimed, one or more mimists enact the scriptural story using no words. Their meaning and communication will be loud and clear. Silent mime can help make the scriptural story come alive and strengthen its impact on us.

Narrative mime involves a spoken text and mimed action. As someone proclaims the scriptural story, mimists act it out. The parable of the unforgiving debtor is an excellent example of how this type of mime can be used effectively. The humor, the sadness and obvious contradictory attitudes are brought out as one person or many people mime the action while the story is told. It comes alive.

Musical mime uses background music to help establish the mood and communicate the theme. Music is another powerful dramatic tool of communication. There is a wealth of music, classical and modern, to help you capture, create and translate for your group and congregation the feelings of success and failure, crisis, sadness, melancholy and joy that are found in scripture. An example of how this type of mime could be used effectively can be seen in the passion of Jesus Christ. How many times have you heard this story? We know most of the details. What a powerful experience,

then, to see this story mimed with some appropriate mood music! In this way we let this story of love speak to our minds and our hearts. Through musical mime you may experience the passion of Jesus in a new and powerfully moving way.

A spin-off is one that takes the theme, the message or kernel of a particular piece of scripture and then contemporizes its meaning for a particular congregation.

How do you go about creating spin-off mimes? The place to begin is with a group of planners brainstorming and sharing their reflections. After reading a particular piece of scripture, such as Jesus calming the storm at sea, toss around some questions and ideas. From these the mime will grow. What are some of the contemporary storms we find ourselves in? How do we, like the disciples, feel abandoned? What are the ways that Jesus quiets our fears? How do we know he is present? How does Jesus challenge our faith? It is a constant challenge to translate imaginatively the Good News into everyday life situations. It is also an excellent opportunity to contemporarily proclaim that the Word of God is still just that—Good News.

The Berkeley Liturgical Drama Guild has developed a process for creating liturgical mimes. It may prove helpful to you, too. First of all, gather together in a spirit of faith and expectation. Secondly, listen attentively to the Word of God you are working with. Pray quietly with this Word. Then share your prayer together. Thirdly, spend some time sharing your reflec-

tions. What do other people's reflections spark in you? What images or words of the scripture really strike you? Why? Fourthly, decide on whether your reflections and the particular occasion you are preparing for dictate that you do a silent, narrative, musical or spin-off mime. Fifthly, script or choreograph the mime. Have different people try to walk or move or express in a variety of ways the characters they represent. Learn more from your doing of the mime. Sixthly, practice and perform the mime that you've created. Does it accomplish what you wanted it to do? Does it communicate the Good News? Seventhly, evaluate the finished product after doing it. How did people who were not in on the process react to the mime? What did they experience through the mime? What did you and the planners learn from this whole process? When you do it again, what would you keep the same and what would you change?

DOs and DON'Ts

Here are some practical DOs and DON'Ts for working with mime. Always strive to be simple, but never simplistic. Mime is not sign language. Explore and discover how simply and powerfully you can communicate with a glance, a gesture, a turn.

Strive to be clear in your mimes. Don't be allegorical. Leave room for symbolic meaning in your mimes. This is meaning on many levels. Let each person make his/her own applications. Don't spell everything out in great detail. However, do be clear. If you are uncertain

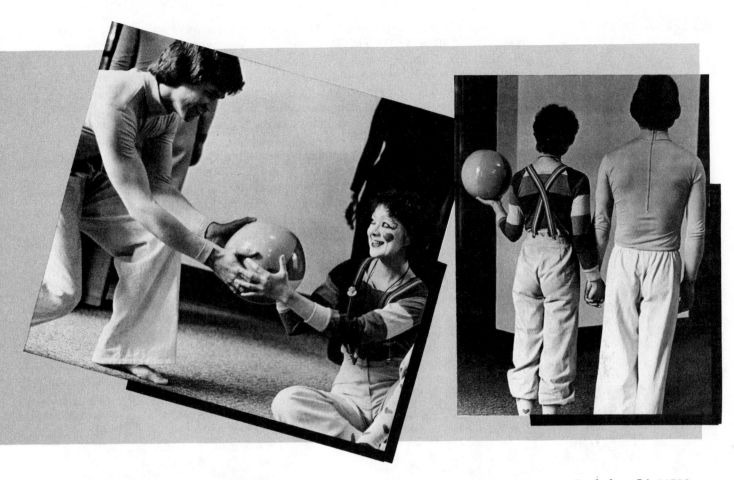

what your mime communicates, it will not be any clearer to the beholder. Good mimes like good symbols and ritual actions do not require explanations. If they do, go back to the drawing board.

Always strive to be brief in your mimes. Too many words can put your group or congregation to sleep. If your mime is too intricate or involved you can also lose the audience. Jesus' own stories were short and to the point. Strive to achieve these same qualities in your mime presentations.

Don't be ashamed if you find or deliberately draw out humor in your mimes. To bring out some of the obvious humor in the scriptures might help us to experience that Word for the first time.

Whenever you intend to perform a mime for your group or congregation, be sure to practice, practice, practice. The Word of God and the people we serve deserve this. Rehearsal is simply respect and reverence for what we are doing and those for whom we are doing it.

Resources

The scriptures should be your number one source of material. Your own experiences should be the second. Your ability and desire to share your faith with a group of people should be your third. The Berkeley Liturgical Drama Guild offers a number of mime scripts and articles related to scriptural mime. These are excellent mimes that have worked for other congregations. For more complete information write: Berkeley Liturgical Drama Guild, 1735 LeRoy Ave., Berkeley, CA 94709.

St. Anthony Messenger Filmstrips has a collection of four mime filmstrips done by the Fountain Square Fools. Each of the filmstrips deals with a parable of Jesus. These are extremely well-made and appropriate for meetings or worships. Inquiries can be directed to: St. Anthony Messenger Press, 1615 Republic St., Cincinnati, OH 45210.

Technical details

Some mimes prefer to use makeup. This is usually clown white pancake makeup. A black eyebrow pencil can accentuate your eyes and delineate the outline of the facial mask. This makeup is not necessary but can be helpful in certain situations.

Whenever possible avoid props. Mime them.

Good mimes don't need a great deal of costuming. Here as elsewhere, if you need it, use it. Otherwise, avoid complications and distractions. Let the mime proclaim or speak for itself. If you have a good mime, that is enough. If you have a poor mime, all the makeup and costumes in the world will not make it better.

Exploring the mimetic potential of scripture can be enjoyable and educational. It can lead us to new depths and dimensions of God's Word. It is an adventure. It is an invitation to come and see, to discover more of what the Good News is all about. It is a challenge to proclaim that Word as powerfully and effectively as possible.

The smiling man bops along the street with radio in one hand and a toy microphone in the other. His singing is amplified to those within a 20-foot range. Joy fills his face as he plays at being on the radio. You probably saw this TV ad in the past few years. Apparently the company who makes the toy microphones believes that many youth and adults are anxious to share this fantasy of being on the radio.

There was a time when I also had such dreams. When I was nine years old the base of a small lamp was my imaginary mike. I have discovered since that day that you don't have to play radio—you can actually be on the radio! This may seem like an amazing claim to most folks. Yet, I have trained 12-year-olds and senior citizens to produce and place radio programs. There is nothing magical about being on this medium or creating a show. It just takes work.

Your youth group can produce radio programming over your local station. Imagine touching the lives of thousands using your creativity and dedication!

Getting Your Group into Radio

by Dennis Benson

The medium

Radio has never reached more people and made more money than it does today. Most homes have more radios than rooms. I even have FM and AM in my headgear for jogging!

Radio is basically a music medium for most Americans. The music industry is totally dependent on airwaves to get those new sounds before us. Radio play is the key to sales.

Radio is a companion. It is the chewing gum of the mind. We can wear it in every mood and setting. Each station tries to discover just what its target audience wants.

Your journey into radio must start with the nature of the station and its listeners. Jesus provides an excellent model for communication. If we read the New Testament carefully, we are struck by the many different ways Jesus presents the Good News to his listeners. We watch him debate, tell stories, touch and even give objects to people in order that they might know his message. He did this because he knew that each person is open to a different way of receiving the message. So, it's important for us to plunge into mass media with sensitivity.

A media ministry task group within your youth organization should first focus on a particular station and learn what it is doing to reach its audience. Draw a circle and listen for an hour as you make a program "clock." Make a line from the center to the edge of the drawing with each new unit or input. It will become clear that there is an intentionality to the station's approach. You could take four popular songs and put them into three different kinds of "clocks" or formats and have three different kinds of experiences. Each station will attract different age groups and lifesyles.

It is also important to note the context in which the radio medium exists. Currently, the government licenses a local station for a three-year period. The station must serve the interests of the community. Each station seems to have three basic interests: 1) keeping its license; 2) getting the biggest share of its target audience possible; and 3) making money. These concerns are all connected, but they don't stand in the way of our goals.

Religious adults tend to shy away from radio and television. Even the most enlightened people seem to point out how bad everything is on the transistor or tube. They are right about a lot of bad stuff, but they are missing the whole point of Christian criticism. I don't believe that Christians are ever restricted to being the negative critics of the world. Even the Old Testament prophets placed their charges of sin in the context of an option. They pointed to what the wayward people could become.

The message

After we have learned about the medium and the realities surrounding radio, we must look into ourselves. What are we trying to communicate? Dick Gilbert, media visionary, helps us at this point by suggesting that there are two kinds of communication undertaken by the people of faith.

Sometimes the church is called to communicate to the world through mass media *about the church*. We know these kinds of programs. Locally, they tend to be broadcast versions of worship services, clergy talk shows, etc. There is an important place for the use of the church's language and history with the media audience. This style usually results in reaching those who have some church background. It also means that we use the formats of the church, which do not work well with some of the prime time "clocks" or formats. This is why these programs are aired on Sunday morning or late at night.

Dick also reminds us that there is a time for the church to communicate to the world *about the world*. This "new wineskin" approach is tricky and quite risky. It is the road least explored by the church. Our audience for this approach is the person who may not be familiar or comfortable with the language, settings and time patterns of the church. It does mean that the secular radio or TV person will be most responsive to those trying to reach this larger audience. I labor in this category.

What can the medium and the message really accomplish even if it does work? Radio doesn't save people. Only God saves us. I believe that the fullness of authentic Christian rebirth and nurture takes place only in the community of believers. The biggest danger facing religious folk using mass media is that they will assume that faith can be manifested through a wired relationship. It can't.

This means that our goal of bringing medium and message together is quite modest. It could be called pre-evangelism. We are seeking to give people a taste of what it is like being in Christ. The fruits of the faith can be sampled through radio and television, but the real feast can be fully experienced only with the people of God. We are then just sowing seeds when we undertake the kind of radio ministry I am suggesting. We are also trying to reach those who are not being reached by the existing programs.

On the air

Let's focus on a model that will work for your youth group. I would suggest that six or ten adults and young people make a covenant to explore this kind of ministry.

The adult advisor or youth pastor should get to know the program director (PD) at the local radio station of interest. After a couple encounters, the adult should admit to the PD that he or she really doesn't know much about radio. The advisor can ask the PD if it would be possible to hang out one night a week at the station to learn more. In just a few weeks the adult will learn most of the basics.

Then plan a weekend retreat for the covenant media group. Discuss the concerns outlined above, including the format "clock." Then go out as teams with good cassette tape recorders, extension mikes and good tapes. Do street interviews.

Each team should focus on one open-ended question. For instance, you might ask one of the following: "What is right?" or "If you had 15 minutes to live, how would you spend the time?" or "If you were God looking down on this community, what would make you sad (happy)?" Get about 20 people to respond.

The teams should then return to your retreat setting with the tapes. The cassette material should be transferred (via cables) to a reel-to-reel or open reel machine. It is now possible to physically edit the material by using an edit block and a razor blade.

Assemble the answers by repeating the question three or four times in the midst of the interview segments. You will be amazed by the impact of this montage of responses. Use 10 or 15 comments. The last one can tip the whole segment to make people think. You are building a 60-second spot by using street interviews. You might add an opening and close (or the station could produce one that can be used over and over).

After creating five or six of these spots, arrange a meeting with the local program director befriended by the adult. Play your spots for him or her. Offer to produce five of these a week for the station. Your only demand is that they be played at prime times.

The PD will immediately grasp the advantages of this proposal. Listeners talking on the radio will help the station fulfill the current FCC requirements to serve the community. Your spots will not cost money for the station. They will be short enough to fit into commercial clusters and won't lose listeners.

The time used for your spots is public affairs time. You do not pay the station for this time.

Of course, I am setting you up for a lot of work. Each spot will probably take a team two or three hours to produce. However, your youth group will be touching the lives of thousands.

You don't have to play at being on the radio. You don't have to take a back seat to others because you are young. Your group can make this exciting radio outreach happen. The only real question facing you now is, "Do I want to work this hard to touch the lost and dying?" I guess this is the question facing each of us when Christ calls us. I pray that you will respond faithfully.

45

Youth Group Candid Camera

by Thom Schultz

"**O**kay, stop snickering," whispers the kid in the big cardboard box. "Here comes a perfect specimen." His movie camera peeks out through a little hole in the box.

The two girls instantly turn on their sternest of faces. One tightens the white belt on her nurse uniform. The other arranges the two folding chairs around the small table in the middle of the downtown sidewalk.

The "specimen" approaches. "Ma'am, excuse me. We're nurses with the county health department. If you'll be seated for just a moment, we'll examine you for athlete's foot."

The lady sits, removes her shoes and socks, and watches patiently as the "nurses" smear the bottom of her pale foot with crunchy peanut butter.

"That stuff smells something like peanut butter," says the lady.

The "nurses" somehow resist the roar of laughter that's battling to explode within them.

"No, ma'am, this is a special compound that turns a terrible black if you are afflicted with athlete's foot," says one of the 'nurses.' "It works quicker if you vigorously slap your leg."

The woman begins earnestly batting her leg with both hands.

Still in his innocent-looking box a few yards away, the cameraman finally erupts into laughter and yells, "Cut! Beautiful!"

A bit of human nature is captured on film.

For several weekends, these young people have been lurking in boxes, in trees, and under cars, photographing local people in the act of being themselves. The results are often hilarious—as evidenced by the gales of laughter heard at the auditorium on the night of the big local Candid Camera Show.

This project, based on the recurring Allen Funt television series, makes a profitable, fun, and very funny fund raising activity for a creative youth group.

Producing a local Candid Camera show is quite a large project. Film must be shot and edited. Tickets

must be printed and sold. Advertising should be sold for the printed program. And the show must be presented to the audience.

The set-ups

One of the first things your Candid Camera staff must do is create a list of potentially funny set-ups. Some set-ups require a great deal of advance preparation. Others are very simple and involve little more than effectively hiding the camera. Keep in mind that your set-ups will necessarily be restricted by your limitations of budget and equipment. Avoid gags requiring sound recording unless you have access to a good sound motion picture camera.

In your brainstorming sessions, don't discard an idea merely on the basis of its simplicity. We've found our simple set-ups to be among the funniest. For example, try this one: Hide the camera in a van or another location where the view of the sidewalk is unobstructed. Dress one of your staffers in shabby clothes and have him stand on the sidewalk and ask

passersby: "You gotta quarter?" Most of your "victims" will say no. Then your grubby staffer says, "Oh, then here's one," as he hands the passerby a quarter and quickly walks the other direction. This gag gets a zesty variety of responses. One lady we filmed disgustedly threw the quarter in the gutter. Another lady caught up with our "panhandler" and asked if his mother knew what he was doing.

Another similar easy set-up utilizes common kitchen utensils. Watch the great reactions of your sidewalk "victims" when they're handed a rolling pin by a scurrying Candid Camera staffer. Egg beaters, graters, and lemon squeezers also work well in the hand-off.

Some of your set-ups may require specific "costumes." And you may be a bit surprised at the automatic respect many people have for any type of uniform. For example, try dressing a couple of your guys in white coveralls. Send them onto the sidewalk with a huge imaginary pane of glass. You'll see people jump out into the street to avoid the "glass men" and the pane that's really not there.

Another "glass man" set-up that receives great response is also simple to execute. Select a downtown shop that has a transom window above a door. Place several lengths of masking tape on the window to give the appearance of breakage. Tie a rope to the handle on the window frame. Your "glass men" on the sidewalk below hold on to the other end of the rope.

When a passerby approaches the "glass men" ask the "victim" to hold on to the rope and stretch it tight while they "run to the truck for a new pane of glass." The "glass men" disappear and the "victim" is left standing—stretching a rope across the sidewalk. After a few moments, one of your Candid Camera girls walks up with a basket of damp clothes. The reactions of the "victims" are priceless as the girl proceeds to clothespin the shirts, socks and underwear to the rope.

One of our "victims," a policeman, nervously glanced about after our girl walked away leaving him holding a clothesline across a busy downtown sidewalk. This inventive officer stretched the rope to a parked car at the curb and tied it to the front bumper. Then, with a slight smile, he continued on his beat, leaving the wash hanging to dry over the sidewalk.

One tremendously successful gag requires a $20 bill. Select a spot where there's plenty of pedestrian traffic. The entrance of a supermarket is a good choice. Park one of your staffer's cars so that one of the tires rests firmly atop one-half of a $20 bill. The other half should be easily seen by the passersby.

Then disappear and watch the fun! You'll see people attempting to lift the car, roll it, remove the tire, and some even abscond with half of the $20 bill.

If your pedestrians seem to pass by the bill without noticing it, you may wish to place another innocent-looking object beside it to attract attention. A pop can or an old glove will usually work.

Another delightfully messy set-up similar to the peanut-butter-foot-fungus routine involves raw eggs. Situate one of your girls in front of a supermarket with a small table and a sign that says, "New, Improved Brook Farms Gourmet Eggs." She'll need a supply of eggs and an ordinary hammer. She stops shoppers and delivers her sales pitch about the eggs. She beckons the shoppers to feel the "fine texture of the eggshell." Then, with great self-confidence, she picks up the hammer and shatters the egg in the "victim's" hand— and soberly continues her sales pitch. Some "victims" leap into the air. Some run away. Some, perhaps the funniest, stand patiently and listen to the remainder of the pitch—all the time watching the goo of the broken egg oozing between their fingers.

These are just a small sampling of the funny set-ups that produce excellent film for a local Candid Camera show.

You'll find it a great boon for ticket sales if you can manage to catch a few prominent citizens on film. Hide your cameras in front of city hall and make the mayor one of your "victims." Do likewise with the police chief and other notables.

Tickets will really sell to the kids at your school if you can boast that you caught a couple of teachers in funny situations. You may wish to film several gags in and around the school.

Remember that, legally, you must obtain the written permission of all of your "victims" before they appear on the screen at your show. Print a short form stating your purpose and the line: "I hereby authorize the (youth group) to use this film of me at a public showing." Don't use the film of anyone refusing to sign your release. Minors must receive the written permission of their parents.

Near your set-ups always station one of your girls with a clipboard and several releases. As soon as the camera stops, send her to catch the "victim," and obtain the necessary signature. She should also give the "victim" a card indicating the date and place of the show. Your "victims" will provide you with your easiest ticket sales.

Equipment

The most important piece of equipment needed for this project is a good motion picture camera. If at all possible, use a 16mm camera, and preferably one with a zoom lens. The 16mm size format will allow the projection of a much larger, clearer image than the more popular 8mm sizes.

Most churches own a 16mm projector. If yours doesn't, a projector can be borrowed from another church or rented from an audio-visual firm.

Film will be your greatest expense. But this cost can be reduced by using black and white film, and buying it from a specialty house such as Superior Bulk Film Co., 442-450 N. Wells St. Chicago, IL 60610. This company will also process your film.

A 100-foot roll of 16mm film will yield almost three minutes of footage. So, if you buy 30 rolls, you'll finish with approximately 90 minutes of film. If half of it is usable, your program will be adequate. Be thrifty with your film. Film only set-ups that garner funny results.

You'll also need film editing equipment. This includes a viewer, a film splicer and a pair of rewinds. Splice tapes will make your job of editing easier.

Include only the truly funny sequences in your finished film. Insert lengths of black film between each different set-up. Your projectionist will stop the film at each of these spots to allow the show narrator to introduce and explain the next set-up.

For your show, select an auditorium that is large enough for your anticipated crowd. And be sure it is equipped with a large screen and an adequate public address system.

Publicity

Allow enough time after all of your film is shot to publicize the big show. Premature publicity before the shooting is completed may tip off some of your "victims" to the possibility of a lurking hidden camera.

The local newspapers will likely generously print stories about the show. It's a good idea to invite a press photographer along on some of your filming sessions, or have one of your own staffers snap a few still pictures for press releases.

Any advertising you choose to do should stress that your show features local people and local places.

Distribute attractive posters two weeks before the show date.

Spread the word through your church newsletter and Sunday bulletins. Ask other churches in the area to do the same.

A printed program for distribution at the show can provide your group with additional income. Organize an advertising committee and send the members to local merchants to solicit advertising for the program. Establish your advertising rates after consulting a printer on the costs of printing. Collect no money from your advertisers until the program is printed.

Distribute a number of tickets to each of your members. Strive for a big advance sale of tickets. Also advertise that tickets will be available at the door on the evening of the show. We've found it successful to place "50 cents off" coupons at our participating advertising merchants' stores. These coupons are then redeemable at the door.

Show night

Your youth host for the evening should be very well-acquainted with the Candid Camera film. He should have a prepared set of notes. A carefully worded introduction and witty comments before and during the screening of each gag can increase the laughter at your show tenfold.

You may also wish to invite a local "celebrity" to co-host the program. A popular radio or TV personality can draw many people to your show. And a musical group to play before the film portion of the show will add a very nice touch.

You may find your Candid Camera show an activity that you'll want to repeat year after year. If you do a good job, your audience should grow in size each time.

Thinking Big—

How to Use Publicity and Plan Big Projects

46

Ever sent some information about your group's next great event to your local newspaper, then watched the news appear as an obscure sentence or two on the last page? Or maybe never appear at all?

Fundamentals of Publicity

by Thom Schultz

Knowing and heeding a few simple ground rules will enable your group to prepare publicity material that will be used by the media.

Whether you're promoting a fund raiser, publicizing a special meeting or worship service, or building interest for a special event, you need the media to get the word to the public.

Good publicity saves you advertising dollars, is better read than advertising copy, and provides the media with usable news.

Your goal should be to produce publicity material that will be used by the media without excessive editing. The less rewriting the media have to do, the better. But don't feel badly if your news release that you labored with for hours doesn't appear exactly as you prepared it. Many in the media rewrite everything that crosses their desks.

When preparing a news release, remember always to include the "who, what, where, when, why and how" at the beginning. Never wait until the end of your release to "spring the surprise" of important information. News should be delivered in the fashion of an "inverted triangle," to use journalists' jargon. That is, the most important information appears at the beginning and least important details are found at the end. This allows the editor to use as much of the story as he has room for—knowing that wherever he's chosen to cut your story, he's hacked the less impor-

tant material.

Use short paragraphs. Two or three sentences are usually plenty.

Do not editorialize. Do not write, "The M.Y.F. is planning a great ice cream social with lots of delicious homemade ice cream and taste-tempting punch." The editor will cringe and your news release may wind up in the trash.

That same information should be written more like this: "The M.Y.F. has scheduled an ice cream social featuring homemade ice cream and an original-recipe red punch."

Words such as "delicious" are value judgments and have no place in most news stories.

You can, sometimes, sneak in a few boastful adjectives by using direct quotes. Here's a sample: "M.Y.F. President Dale Higgins said, 'We have the tastiest black walnut ice cream recipe in the world.' " Some editors will let you get away with such frill.

Always type your news releases. Editors hate handwriting—even when it's legible. Double-space your material, and type only on one side of the paper.

Begin typing half-way down on your first sheet. This allows space above for the editor to write a headline. Always number consecutive pages.

Never deliver a carbon copy or a Xerox copy to the newspaper or broadcast station. It's an insult to any editor to believe that the OTHER newspaper or broadcast station got the original copy. When an original

...y) and her
Glenn. The second
...loris Bright (left)
...lliott. On the night
...n the nigical Em-
...e risen Christ was
...isciples.

Couple to show slides

Les and Loraine Jorgensen will show the slides of their trip to South Africa at 7 p.m. Sunday in the fellowship hall of Immanuel Lutheran Church, 1101 Hilltop Drive, Loveland.

Friends and aquaintences are invited to attend.

Eden Valley Bible school set

Eden Valley Seventh-day Adventist Church has scheduled its yearly vacation Bible school for 2:30-5:30 p.m. June 22-26. Children and teens from 4 to 15 are invited.

Activities will include crafts, stories, an Adventure in Nature program and The Healthland Flyer. The Flyer is a model train constructed by Linda Tatum to teach the principles of good health. The Flyer stops at Cleanupville, Long Sleep Mountain, Exercise Woods, Breakfast Valley, Baked Potato Hills, and Quiet Meadows.

For further information or transportation, call 667-6911.

College singers to perform

Contemporary gospel and traditional Christian music will be performed by the Chancel Singers from Azusa Pacific College at 7:30 p.m. Friday in Calvary Christian Reformed Church, 3901 14th St. S.W., Loveland.

A spokesman for the church says the eight members of the choir combine their music with a strong testimony of faith in Jesus Christ.

---

typed release reaches the editor, he's impressed that you prepared the material especially for him. A Xeroxed copy signals to the editor that all the other media in town have the same release. And he may have no interest in your mass produced "news."

If you plan to use more than one newspaper or broadcast station, type a different release for each of them. It's a lot of work, but you'll have a much better chance of having your releases used.

Your stories for large metropolitan daily papers should usually be shorter and more concise than the stories you'd write for the smaller newspapers.

For most events, the best time to submit your releases is one week beforehand. Smaller, auxiliary stories could precede and follow the main story, if the local media are prone to use such material.

Studies have shown that readers give much more attention to photographs than to printed words. So, whenever you can, submit photos with your stories. Use black and white prints—not slides, color snapshots, or negatives.

Always include picture caption information with the photo. It's best to attach a slip of paper to the back of the photo that has the typed information about who or what appears in the picture.

You'll find that you will get better results from many of the newspapers and stations if you deliver your releases and photos to the editors in person. Many times that personal touch will be enough to make the editors want to help you.

Always put your name and phone number on your releases in case the editor has a question.

Newspapers and radio and television stations are not your only means of publicizing your events.

Posters in store windows can often help promote certain events. The posters should be attractively hand lettered. They'll attract more attention than most of the professionally printed posters.

Posters should be distributed two weeks prior to the event.

Of course, there's your church bulletin to use for promoting your activities. Try a brightly colored special insert inside your Sunday morning bulletin or newsletter.

You can also slip handbills under windshield wipers in your church parking lot or elsewhere.

Then, sometimes a sign in your church yard will often attract a lot of attention.

And, finally, sometimes you can attract the attention of the local media by "creating a news event" especially for the media. One group of young people recently wished to dramatize how polluted a nearby river was. The kids scooped out a few gallons of the dirty water and carried it to the state capitol. There they packaged the water in small plastic bags and handed the ugly packages to startled passersby.

The local TV stations had a heyday filming the reactions of the recipients of the filthy water.

And the young people made their point.

Keeping every member of your group informed and excited about group activities is sometimes very difficult. But a group newsletter can do this and a lot more.

A regularly issued group newsletter not only keeps your members informed about coming events, but it can review past events, introduce new members, publish opinions, encourage personal devotions, create humor and gain and involve more members.

The organization of your newsletter and its staff depends a great deal upon the personality and make-up of your group.

It's best to have an all-volunteer staff. The kids who really want to work on the newsletter will do much better jobs than those who are appointed.

How to Publish and Maintain a Group Newsletter

by Thom Schultz

Staff

You'll need an editor, reporters, a typist, an artist and a circulation manager.

The editor should be someone who has both ability and available time. It's usually the editor's job to make writing assignments to the various reporters. The assignments can be made at meetings, or postcards can be mailed to the reporters. Then, after receiving the written articles, the editor prepares them for printing.

The reporters can write on past or future group events or they can be assigned to write a particular column every issue. An aware editor can often involve some withdrawn group members by assigning them to write a story on a particular group event. The member then has to come to the function in order to write about it. This is a great way to involve some of the relatively inactive kids in your group.

The typist should be capable—skilled enough to do the typing in a reasonable amount of time.

Your artist need not be a Rembrandt—just someone who has an artistic flair and enjoys contributing.

The circulation manager handles the distribution of the newsletters: addressing, stamp-licking and mailing. This job is very important and should be undertaken by a very dependable member.

Content

The most important consideration, of course, is the content of your newsletter. The prime function of most newsletters is to announce upcoming group activities.

The newsletter should always promote, well in advance, all future activities, giving all necessary details of who, what, where, when, why and how. Good newsletter coverage can many times make the difference in the success or failure of various group functions.

Also, past activities should be covered well. This lets the kids who weren't there know what they missed. And, the kids who did attend will enjoy reading about the event.

Some newsletter features can be carried regularly in each issue. One of these that's always successful is a "Profile" series. Each issue your "Profile" writer interviews one of your members and writes a short sketch on the "famous" kid. "Profile" columns work especially well to acquaint your members to the new members joining the group.

You may wish to set aside space each issue for your youth director's "pearls of wisdom." This feature is usually well-read by all members.

Some newsletters carry a humorous "Dear Abby" type of column where members write in with monumental problems for your staff problem-solver. These are usually good for a few laughs.

Speaking of humor, always include a good dose of it in every issue. Everyone usually enjoys it and it guards against a "dry" newsletter that's sometimes too easy to overlook.

Some newsletters include a short passage from a modern translation Bible. Think up a catchy title if you choose to include Bible quotes in your newsletter.

Another regular feature used by one group is entitled "Praise Ye the Lord." Following the title, the writer inserts a list of things for which he or the group is thankful. The listings have ranged from "our leaders" to "paper plates."

Some of your reporters may wish to review books or movies. Some may wish to contribute their own original poetry or essays. And some may wish to write editorials.

You can also use newsletter space to publish registration blanks for upcoming camps, conferences and retreats. This works a lot better than the old line in the Sunday bulletin that says, "Registration forms available in the office."

A highly-read column in one group's newsletter is called "Group Scoop." It contains short items about group members. A sample: "Jerry Higgins finally got his car fixed. It doesn't burp anymore." The writer of a humorous column such as this should strive to use as many different names as possible.

Use of many local names has always been an effective tool of any publication to gain readership.

Printing and layout

Most group newsletters are probably printed by mimeograph process. If so, the 8½ x 14 inch paper works nicely for a newsletter. It's available in many colors and weights.

Before typing your mimeo stencil, divide the page vertically down the center. Either draw a line or leave ample blank space. Two narrower columns are much easier to read than one wide one.

While typing, leave spaces for hand-drawn headlines and simple illustrations. Artwork (no matter how amateur you may consider it to be) will add a great deal of eye appeal to your pages.

Another method for illustrating uses professional "clip art." These attractive little drawings are available in many themes, from "worship" to "winter fun." This art is available for both offset and mimeograph processes from Louis Neibauer Co., York Road and Township Line, Jenkintown, PA 19046.

If your newsletter is printed by the offset method, you may include photographs in your newsletter. Action photos will demand much more reader attention than "mug shots" or "group portraits."

Also, new scanner stencil-makers allow fairly good photo reproduction by mimeo process. If your church doesn't have one of these costly machines, many office supply stores will make a scanner-cut stencil for you at nominal cost.

Take special care to design a good logo for your newsletter. The logo, or title, should establish visual identity for your publication. It should be simple to read, attractive, and always appear the same.

Remember to leave a blank space at the bottom of one of your pages, where, if the newsletter is folded and stapled properly, you may apply your address labels and stamps.

Circulation

Who should receive your newsletter? Many groups make the mistake of placing only their active members on their mailing lists. In many ways, the inactive members and prospective members are your more important readers. These "no-show" absentee-types will usually read their mail—including your newsletter. The more they read about the great stuff the group is doing, the more tempted they'll be to become involved.

It's usually a good idea to make a personal call to these inactive kids after they've received a few issues of the newsletter. A sincere invitation often works after the uninvolved kid has had an opportunity to learn a little bit about your group through the newsletter.

Also send the newsletter to all the adults in the church who occasionally help sponsor youth events.

And don't forget to send copies to your local newspapers. They'll often look forward to news of your group for their religion pages. This is an easy way to get city-wide publicity for your events.

You can make your circulation manager's task a lot easier by mimeographing mailing labels. The labels can also be duplicated by Xerox process if you wish.

Your newsletters should be sent by first class mail, unless you plan to mail more than 200 copies per issue. If your mailing list exceeds 200 names, you may send the newsletters by bulk rate. And churches are eligible for very low bulk rates.

Frequency

How often should you publish? Probably at least once a month. Many groups publish their newsletters every two weeks. And some even publish weekly. Frequency of publication depends a great deal on the size of the group, the size of your newsletter staff, and the number of activities your group undertakes.

Financing

Producing a newsletter is really not too costly, but you will need to plan ahead for your financing. Consider the costs of paper, printing and postage.

Some groups charge a small subscription fee. This fee should be enough to cover the inactive members' costs also.

Funds may also come from your youth group treasury. Or, perhaps money is available from your church's general budget.

Perhaps a congregation member would simply like to donate the necessary funds for your newsletter ministry.

Title

Well, now all you need is a name for your newsletter. Try to come up with something more catchy than "M.F.Y. Newsletter." One group calls its newsletter "Godsquad." Another named its paper "Wednesday Gazette." Perhaps you could sponsor a contest to see who can come up with the best name. Award the winner with a broken typewriter.

Building Enthusiasm for the Group by Using the Mail

by Gary Richardson

O n her way home from a particularly dull day at school, Linda stops at the mailbox and browses through the day's mail. She flips quickly through the bills and a handful of plain-looking letters addressed to her parents.

But her eyes open wider when she gets to the piece of mail that looks like a hamburger, complete with artsy sesame seeds and a small bug that's sitting near her name and address.

"My youth group's at it again," she says, chuckling to herself.

Once inside the house, Sue dumps her books and the rest of the mail on a corner of the kitchen table and takes a closer look at the paper hamburger.

As she opens this piece of youth group "junk mail," the first thing she reads is a large headline. "Attack a Big Mac." She reads on.

The brochure introduces an upcoming youth group starve-a-thon weekend to raise money for a world hunger organization.

Three weeks later she receives a 24" x 36" calendar that gives crazy information (Pat Boone got his blue suede shoes dirty on this day in 1956) and birthdays of kids in the group, in addition to planned Bible studies and exciting activities.

In the months to come, she would receive a football helmet, a free dating guide and a brochure that informed her of a spring retreat.

She was impressed. In the past, she felt as though she were playing a game with her youth group where the object was to find out what was happening and when. And if she happened to miss the poster in the church hall telling of an upcoming event, it was tough cookies for her.

But her youth sponsors—even her Sunday school teachers—have discovered a communication gold mine, one that is dependable, cheap and readily available. They are using the mail to help unify and expand their ministry. And it is working.

Mail communicates

You know the importance of keeping in touch with your group members. You probably also know that without a consistent follow-up plan you'll lose contact with a large number of kids who don't come to your group often enough to stay informed.

Young people want to feel a part of what's happening and to feel wanted and needed. Without this feeling of identification, the specialness of your youth ministry is lost.

Young people love to get mail. While some may tune out announcements at the end of an evening Bible study, they won't toss an interesting-looking piece of mail addressed to them.

You can learn to become an expert at reaching your kids using the mail with a minimal amount of cost and effort. All it takes is time and a desire to reach your kids with a quality piece of literature.

You are what you mail

Just because the U.S. Post Office is an efficient and effective means of communicating with your young people doesn't mean that you can dash off a hand-written memo, mimeograph it, drop the two-minute creation into the mail and expect record-shattering results.

Whenever you use the mail, what the young person sees when he or she rips open the envelope reflects your attitude toward him and toward your whole ministry program. Whatever you develop and mail should be first class: neat, clean, concise and contemporary.

Whatever happened to the mimeographed letter?

The importance, length and timeliness of your message will help determine the format you use.

Consider the following types of mailings and some of their advantages and disadvantages:

Postcards—Need to get a simple message out to your group quickly? Postcards are the cheapest and easiest form of using the mail. If your group already has the basic information, a postcard can act as a reminder and give last-minute messages. Postcards aren't the most effective tools for building interest and giving detailed information.

Letters—Want to explain something in detail? Letters call for greater reader attention and can be used to communicate with parents or make an important point. Don't overuse.

Brochures—If you want to spread the word about a camp, a hike, a retreat or a special form of ministry and need to have a registration form returned, a nice brochure will do. A brochure includes more information than can be covered adequately in a postcard or letter. It's also much easier to be creative and catch attention with a brochure than with a letter or postcard.

Newsletters—Get some of your young people involved in writing, typing, pasting up and distributing a monthly, bi-monthly or quarterly newsletter. Newsletters are great for building communication channels to hard-to-reach kids. These in-depth creations generally take more time and concentrated effort than other types of mailings.

"Junk" mailers—Whatever you want to call them, many of your most important mailers will fit into this category. Short, creative announcements with different formats and sizes can build interest in Bible studies, coming events, weekly meetings—anything you want to promote.

Calendars—Here's a way to keep some of your on-again-off-again youth group kids informed of what your group has planned. Make your activity calendar large and nice enough so your members will want to post it somewhere in their homes. Have some artistic young people help you illustrate the activities. Fill the calendar with crazy information and add special information about youth group members (birthdays, basketball games, recitals, driver license exams, etc.).

Building Enthusiasm for the Group by Using the Mail CONT.

Kiss!!

NOW THAT WE HAVE YOUR ATTENTION, take this brief survey and see if you need to come to our meeting. (Shh, keep it quiet, it's about s-e-x.) Do any of these situations fit you?

—you needed a club on your last date
—your girl likes to date in groups—like 25!
—on your first date, you went to kiss her and missed
—you get turned on holding hands
—your date seems to have 12 hands
—your last date brought a book titled "42 Ways to Seduce Your Date" with him

Whether or not you fit into these categories, you'll not want to miss this meeting on

The Dating Game

TUESDAY, DECEMBER 16   7 P.M.
MARK KLEM'S HOUSE
(PARK ALONG THE STREET)   GOODIES PROVIDED

Where do I start?

You can come up with a quality piece of mail if you first think through the entire project before starting to write anything. For example, let's assume you want to design a piece to tell your youth group about an upcoming meeting on dating. Once you have a topic (in this case, dating) list everything that comes to mind that relates both to your topic and to the youth culture. Brainstorm in such areas as current movies, songs, TV shows and commercials, posters or different situations your kids may be facing.

Nothing at this point in the creative process is too stupid or too crazy to rule out.

After coming up with several ideas for different themes and formats to publicize your topic, choose the one that creatively communicates your message.

Once you've decided on a theme and format, think of different attention-getting headlines. One church came up with the following headlines for some of its activities: "Cornflakes and Pickles" (for a retreat on sexuality), "Booze" (for an evening with reformed alcoholics)

and "Star Burst" (options for summer youth ministry).

Be sure your mail piece gives all the necessary information (who, what, when, where, how and why), and what you want the reader to do next (come to, contact, call).

Before actually writing copy for your mailing, study ads in some popular youth magazines (try GROUP). Look at how simple and to-the-point the ads are, yet they generally contain lots of information.

Whatever you write, keep it short, simple and punchy. Always assume that your reader won't be interested in what you have to tell him.

After working through this creative process on the topic of dating, a potential mailing piece might read something like the illustration to the left.

Don't stop with just the written copy. There's more to consider.

Graphics hook the reader

While graphics—artwork, cartoons, fancy borders, cute letters—are one of the last things you consider in the creative process, it's the first thing your reader will see. An appealing piece of mail should have a border or some other graphic that helps highlight the message area. Important information, such as dates, times and place should be underlined, put in boxes or printed in bold type so it stands out from other parts of the copy.

No matter how amateurish it may be, any artwork is better than straight handwritten or typed copy. Don't let the lack of good artwork keep you from designing effective mail pieces. If you stop and think about it, there are several sources for art around you: illustrations from books, cartoons from magazines, old encyclopedias, magazine ads, old textbooks, posters, catalogs, junk mail, coloring books, the yellow pages in your phone book, children's storybooks, calendars (for numbers), comic books, line drawings from newspapers, cartoon-type greeting cards, placemats found in restaurants.

Another handy source for good quality artwork is professionally drawn "clip art." You'll need to specify whether your printing process is offset or mimeograph. Sources for this clip art are: Louis Neibauer Co., York Road and Township Line, Jenkintown, PA 19046, and Harry Volk Jr. Art Studio, 1401 North Main St., Pleasantville, NJ 08232.

You can also spruce up your mailings by using professional-looking rub-on letters. You can find these low-cost sheets of letters at most art supply stores. If not, you can get catalogs of different type styles from the following sources: Artype, Inc., 345 E. Terra Cotta Ave., Rt 7, Crystal Lake, IL 60014; Prestype, Inc., 194 Veterans Blvd., Carlstadt, NJ 07072; and Chartpak, One River Road, Leeds, MA 01053.

You might want to use full-color blank stationery with crazy sayings and artwork. All you do is add your message and photocopy or mimeograph it onto the letterhead.

Get a catalog with different letterhead ideas by writing to: The Drawing Board, Box 220505, Dallas, TX 75222.

Layout and printing

Most churches have some sort of mimeograph machine which works nicely for most needs. This mimeograph process allows you to use different types and weights of paper and different colors of ink.

While typing the stencil, remember to leave space for the artwork and larger headlines.

Many office supply stores carry scanner stencils and scanner stencil-makers that will work on your church's mimeograph machine. This process also takes some art and photos.

While the mimeo process is the most inexpensive and accessible source for your printing needs, it may not be the best. If you've used a mimeograph machine much, you know that the quality of printing is sometimes questionable. And you can't be as flexible in your use for formats and crazy styles.

The *offset* printing method gives high quality printing and allows greater flexibility in the use of fancy artwork and photographs. But this method also has its drawbacks. It's more expensive than mimeograph printing and isn't practical for small mailings.

If you choose to use the offset method, compare different printers, since estimates for printing jobs often vary widely from one printer to the next. (Don't forget to check with the "quick" printers in your area.)

Don't rule out the print shop in your high school or area vocational center. The instructor may be able to do quality offset printing for you at a much lower cost than most print shops. You just may have to wait longer for the finished product.

Photocopying (Xerox, IBM, Smith Corona, Brand X) is a great method if you need a small mailing printed quickly. Have a cute letterhead you want to use for a creative mailing? (See the address above in this chapter for purchasing preprinted sheets with creative artwork.) However, a large number of copies can get pretty expensive, and artwork and photos don't reproduce well using this method.

If you plan to mail the piece without using an envelope, keep in mind that the post office won't accept anything smaller than 3½" x 5".

More may cost you less

If you have around 150 people who should receive youth group mail, you can save money by sending your mail via bulk rate. Check with the post office about bulk mailing procedures and costs for non-profit organizations.

Have more than 150 pieces of mail, but less than the required 200 minimum for bulk mailing? Have your youth group members give you names of kids in the area who may be interested in receiving some youth group mail. Also consider sending youth group mail to your kids' parents and to church leaders for added exposure for your group at a nominal cost.

Print on crazy things

Don't limit your creativity to sheets of paper. Try some of these ideas:

- If you're traveling somewhere and plan on taking brown bag lunches, print information about the trip on the bags and send them to everyone.
- Print a message about an upcoming Mexican dinner on tortillas and then mail the tortillas in envelopes.
- Planning a hiking trip, bike trip or athletic event? Have a rubber stamp made that includes the basic information (date, time, place), stamp the message on part of an old white sock and mail the sock. Most office supply stores can make rubber stamps with three- or four-line messages inexpensively.

Who can forget a message that's printed on a pencil, calendar, ruler, T-shirt, comb, balloon, lollypop or wooden nickel? Advertising specialty houses print messages on almost anything. The only catch is a 100 to 150 minimum quantity order. Consider having a general youth group message (time and place of the regular youth group meeting, puppet group, singing group) printed on a quantity that will last for a year or so. One advertising speciality house is Atlas Pen and Pencil Corporation, 3040 N. 29th Avenue, Hollywood, FL 33022.

If you have a small youth group, you can buy as few as 10 engraved pens or pencils, bumperstickers with special messages and a three-line rubber stamp and pad from Miles Kimball, 41 East 8th Avenue, Oshkosh, WI 54901. Atlas Pen and Pencil Corporation (for address see the paragraph above) also offers low-quantity specials on engraved pens and pencils.

Some free tips

- Keep a list of what you mailed and when.
- Don't overuse the mail. Four or five pieces in a month is too much.
- Be sure the piece will fold the way you want it to before pasting down the artwork or adding the large type.

- Have two or three people read your mailing piece before you paste anything down. Ask them to tell you what the copy says.
- Vary the size and style of the mailing. Don't let the envelope always tell everyone that the piece is from the church.

CHAPTER 49

How to Plan a Successful Garage Sale

by Thom Schultz

Your group can earn hundreds or thousands of dollars simply by cleaning out your garages and attics and setting up a yard sale

My group has always called them "garbage" sales. I guess we've called them that because the stuff always looks amazingly like garbage. But, even more amazing, people pay good money for it!

My youth group has made anywhere from $100 to $1,500 on each garage sale. Some groups have made $2,000 and more on a single sale.

The key to a successful sale is good planning. Summer is usually the ideal season for a sale. Warm temperatures will generally bring flocks of bargain-hunters to your sale. Colder winter weather may force a sale to the basement or other indoor location. And it seems the garage sale shoppers feel less hesitant about browsing in someone's yard or garage than they do about venturing into a person's basement.

Selecting the site for your sale will be one of your first considerations. Your church may be a logical selection. But we've always found members' homes to be better sales headquarters. The ardent garage sale shoppers seem more attracted to a home address than to a church location.

In choosing a member's house to host the sale, you have a couple of things to consider. First, is it okay with the family to clutter the yard or garage with a jungle of second-hand goodies for a day or two? And, second, is the member's house in the right location for a sale? A house on a well-traveled city thoroughfare is, of course, a natural selection. Or, you may find that a house in one of the prestige areas of town may be ideal. Sometimes the mere "classy sound" of an address will bring out many more shoppers to your sale.

I might point out here that you may want to warn the people in your hosting house that they're bound to get a few questions from neighbors. It never fails—at least one little old lady from down the street will survey all the stuff in the front yard, saunter over, and say, "I didn't know you were moving out." Then—when you tell her you're not—she takes another look at the new neighborhood "junk yard" and says, "Oh, that's too bad," and waddles home, scowling.

As soon as you can, you should begin notifying all of your friends and everybody in your church about your upcoming garage sale. Make sure people all over town start going through their attics, basements and garages looking for items they no longer use or need. Put announcements in the local paper and the church bulletin urging "garbage" contributors to call one of your members. When they call, pick up the goods and take them to a central storage place.

What kinds of articles should you seek to sell at your sale? Just about everything.

Gather all of your old Mad magazines. The little neighborhood kids will snatch them up in a moment. Your collection of National Geographics will be easily

How to Plan a
Successful Garage Sale CONT.

sold to older shoppers at your sale.

Anything that might be considered antique will be very popular. A word of advice: if you believe that you have a truly valuable antique, visit an antique dealer first. You may be able to sell it to him for a lot more than you'd get at your sale.

Clothes are always popular. Ladies' and children's clothing sells best. And jeans—get all you can. Your first customers the morning of your sale will likely buy up your supply of jeans.

Odds and ends of every description are always good at a sale. Toys, kitchen utensils, jewelry, books, candle holders, tools, pictures, frames, lamps, purses and mirrors are all good items.

Handmade goodies are often popular. Some groups have even set up a table full of crafts especially prepared for the sale.

Glassware is always a big seller. Glasses, dishes, vases, pitchers, bowls, toothpick holders—anything made of glass—will attract the eye of your female shoppers the moment they step foot in the vicinity of your sale.

Small appliances will go quickly—provided they work. Few people are willing to spend money on a toaster that has a sign attached: "Needs New Cord." If that's all it needs, go ahead and install a new cord yourself. The toaster will sell much better, and you'll get a better price.

Furniture is always very popular. Matter of fact, you'll probably make your biggest money on your used book cases, tables, chairs and chests. We've even found success in buying used furniture from a dealer, then turning around and selling it for a greater price at our garage sale. This buying and reselling works—but only when you're very careful to pay a low enough price for the furniture.

Make sure that everything in your sale is price marked. Customers do not like the idea of asking the cashier the price of every item. Masking tape works quite well for tagging merchandise. Others have used little white stickers. Some items are better tagged by a small string tag.

For clothes, a small slip of paper can be stapled to the collar. Or, clothes can be arranged so that a sign can be posted reading: "All Clothing on This Table: $1."

Setting the price for your "treasures" will probably be one of your hardest tasks. Some have said that 1/4 of the item's original price is a good place to start. If you price an item a little too high, this allows you some bargaining room. Don't be afraid to take a reasonable offer for an item, especially if the item has not sold in the first few hours of your sale.

You may find yourself adjusting the price of an item downward after too many shoppers have turned away after seeing your original price tag.

One of the best ways to set reasonable prices is to make a garage sale tour before you start your own sale. Take note of what other garage sale entrepreneurs are charging for specific items.

Make sure you insert an ad in your newspaper's classified pages. Most papers have a garage sale section in the classifieds. Your ad should appear the day before the sale and every day your sale runs. Running an ad too early usually brings "early bird" shoppers who can be quite bothersome.

A good phrase to include in your ad might be something like this: "20 Family Garage Sale." This immediately alerts the readers that a large variety of goods will be for sale. If you have a few unique items, you may want to mention those. But don't waste a lot of advertising money listing common things such as "clothes, furniture, misc."

Use the names of the days of your sale instead of the dates. "Garage Sale, Saturday and Sunday" is much less confusing than "June 27 and 28."

Street signs are another good method of advertising. A clearly lettered sign down on the corner that reads

"Garage Sale, 234 Main St." will attract many passersby. Always use an arrow on the sign, too, to get the customers headed in the right direction.

Make sure your lettering is large enough to be read by passing motorists.

Make sure you remove your signs after the sale.

For your sale, you'll need a good many tables on which to display your merchandise. Perhaps your church has a number of the long, folding tables. These are ideal.

Dresses, suits and coats should be hung on hangers where they can be displayed adequately. Again, borrow from your church, if you can. The portable coat racks often found in church entrances work very well.

Preparing a try-on booth may be well worth your while. The booth can often prompt many more clothing sales if the customer can become convinced the clothes fit and look acceptable.

And, always have a few sacks and boxes around to pack up the purchases of your good customers.

Select a good spot for your cashier and furnish him or her with an ample supply of change.

You should now be ready to "throw open your doors" and begin selling. Arrange to have more kids operating the sale during the first few hours. Your biggest rush of shoppers will come during the first couple of hours after you open.

Many experienced garage sale proprietors have said their one-day sales net as much as two- or three-day ones.

We've found the second day always seems to bring in less than half as much as the first. But some customers return the second day for something they saw earlier and later decided they "couldn't live without."

If you choose to have an extended sale over two or three days, do not hold back items for later introduction to keep your sale "fresh." Remember—your best customers will visit your sale during the first couple of hours. Don't hide good merchandise from your "big spenders."

Don't be surprised if your sale is visited by an antique dealer, an auctioneer or the keeper of a second-hand shop. These pros keep a constant eye on the used goods market. There are even a few professional garage sale operators who shop other sales and take the best stuff back to their sales to sell at inflated prices. One of these guys once bought an orthopedic neck brace from one of our sales. We noticed the brace at his sale the next day. He was asking more than four times our price for it. Well, it didn't sell. And we all got a good laugh when he sheepishly returned it to us so we could sell it at our next sale. Whenever you can sell the same product twice, you're in good shape.

After your sale, remove all of the price tags from the unsold items and call your local Salvation Army, Goodwill or other good cause.

If your group is planning another sale soon, you may want to store some of the nicer items to attempt to sell again. And, if you do have another sale soon, select a different location for your second sale. Garage sale shoppers will not often return to the same address a month later—even if you promise more items.

One last idea—refreshments. Our group has made a few extra dollars selling lemonade at our sales. If you happen to select a sizzling day for your sale, you may find the lemonade selling faster than the "garbage."

CHAPTER 50

Your group can operate
a Christmas tree lot

A LOT OF TREES:

A Yuletide Fund Raiser

by Thom Schultz

In mid-summer, long before the falling snow, roasting chestnuts and glittering lights, your group should begin planning some of its Yuletide activities. One project many groups have found very successful is the operation of a Christmas tree lot.

The Christmas tree becomes a central part of almost every home in December. For Christians, the evergreen tree symbolizes life in the midst of what is the dead season for most other plants. Christ, too, is the life more powerful than death. His love is the expression of vitality and growth in our daily "winters."

The Christmas tree is a very special symbol of the true meaning of Christmas. Your youth group's Christmas tree lot can provide a good service to your congregation and community.

As a fund raising project, the operation of a tree lot is a big job. But it's also very profitable if handled efficiently. Your group can earn hundreds and even thousands of dollars with a month of hard work.

Organizing and operating a tree lot is also fun. Meeting the customers—many of them often interesting characters—is always a highlight, and a good op-

RAND KRUBACK

portunity to communicate your Christian love. The fellowship of working closely with other group members and their parents is another joy. And, everyone involved in the lot's operation comes away with a new understanding of the way business operates.

Preparation

After your group decides to tackle the job of becoming a local Christmas tree sales outlet, you should select some committees. Groups should be set up to find a source for trees, to select a sales lot location, to get the necessary licenses and permits, to organize publicity, and to prepare the work schedule.

A meeting with the parents should be called, where the mothers and fathers can learn about your group's plans and, hopefully, volunteer for work shifts at the lot. Adult supervision at the lot will save you a bunch of hassles. And, you may find many of the parents good business advisors and eager helpers.

Next, make sure you get all the necessary permits and licenses for operation of a tree lot in your community. Most states require a sales tax license, and many communities require various business permits. Check with your state and local offices.

Your next job is selecting a suitable sales lot. This is very important, so take careful consideration before deciding on a location. Seek a lot on a highly traveled street. Many of your customers will do business with you because you were easiest to find. Also, make sure electricity is available—usually tapped from a nearby power pole. Contact your city's electrical department or franchise for details about obtaining power.

A lot with an existing small building is ideal. An abandoned gas station makes a good tree lot.

Expect to pay $100 or more for rental of a good lot for December. Owners will often discount the rent or even donate the lot when you tell them who you are and what the profits will go toward.

A LOT OF TREES CONT.

Try to locate near a busy shopping area—perhaps a popular supermarket or shopping center. Some groups set up on a portion of a shopping center's parking lot. This can be very advantageous.

One of the first jobs is locating a tree wholesaler. Don't delay. Many tree distributors insist they have your order in June or July, at the latest. But, many others are happy to do business with you if you contact them later in the year.

Check your yellow pages listings under "Christmas Trees." Tree wholesalers are often listed there. Or, check with a local large nursery or florist. These people often buy Christmas trees, and they often can supply you with the name of their distributor.

The best Christmas trees usually come from tree plantations. There the trees are planted in rows, pruned regularly, correctly watered, and often are even treated with fire retardant. Many of the large tree plantations are in Montana and Minnesota. Some distributors cut their trees there and truck them to other states.

Locally grown wild trees are sometimes of good quality. Sometimes, though, they tend to dry out very quickly and pose a fire hazard in the home. And, they're usually not shaped as nicely as the plantation-grown trees. But you may have to deal with what's available in your area. Sometimes, a combination of plantation and wild trees is a good idea. Sometimes customers may request a locally-grown tree.

How many trees should you order? That's difficult to answer. Some groups sell a couple hundred trees each season, some sell thousands. Try to find out the number of trees sold by others in your area who have operated lots. Perhaps your wholesaler, if he's honest, can help with this information.

Try to find a tree distributor who will have some extra trees on hand later in the season. If you've ordered too few trees and you're starting to run out after the first week in December, call your distributor and order some more. Many distributors cannot handle those late supplementary orders, however. They, like you, don't ever want to be stuck with a big batch of trees the day after Christmas.

Also, see if your distributor can supply you with related products. Wreaths, boughs, and evergreen roping often are very big sellers.

Some groups have been successful at selling tree ornaments and tree stands—but these products are risky. The discount stores will always outprice you.

You'll need to arrange for some type of shelter at the lot. In cold climates, you'll need a place to warm up. In moderate climates, you're still going to need a place to keep your cash and tools, etc. An existing building on the lot you rent is usually best, but also usually more expensive than a vacant lot. The existing building often has its own heating system, rest room facilities, and secure, lockable doors.

But don't select a lot in a poor location simply because it has a building on it. If no building is on your lot, the next best bet is a small house trailer. Borrow one from a congregation member or rent one.

The attractiveness of your lot is very important. Many people will select your lot because "it looks best," or "looks like it has the best selection."

Design your lot so it has only one entrance. This makes it easier to watch for the customers as you sit huddled in your trailer or building.

Border the lot with trees. Put many rows inside, but not so many that you do not have enough trees to cover all the rows. Group the trees according to size and type. Put the shorter trees toward the street. That way a passerby can see into the lot better.

If your lot has a dirt or gravel surface, drive iron posts (the kind used for barbed wire fences, etc.) and stretch tough wire between the posts. The trees can then be leaned against the tightly stretched wire. On windy days, the trees may have to be tied to the wire with twine. Getting the posts out of frozen ground is a real problem. Sometimes car jacks have to be used to help remove the posts.

On paved lots, the iron posts can still be used. But make sure you get permission from the owner. Small holes remain in the pavement after the posts are removed. Other methods of displaying the trees include the use of giant sawhorses with eight-foot spans.

In the aisles of your lot, display a few of the better shaped trees on individual stands. These inexpensive stands can be made from two crossed pieces of 1" x 4" pine.

You'll need some tall poles on which to attach flood lights for your night shoppers. (A good portion of the business comes between 7 and 9 p.m.) These tall poles can be lashed to your iron posts. Lights can also be placed a top your trailer or building. Make sure your lot is well-lighted.

Signs are another important consideration. Make big ones from plywood. Use simple lettering, dark letters on white background. Put your youth group's name on the signs. Many shoppers would rather spend their money at your lot after they find out the cash will go to a good cause.

When pricing your trees, a good rule of thumb is to double your wholesale cost. But check with your competition to make sure your prices are not too far out of line. Also, sometimes doubling your cost needs a little revising. For instance, you may pay your distributor the same price for all trees from five to seven feet tall. But you should not charge the same price for a five-footer and a seven-footer.

Make sure the price of each tree is clearly indicated. One system involves the use of string tags, available at an office supply store. Simply make the tag and attach it to the top of the tree or on a high branch.

Some groups have used a color code system. Each tree has a piece of construction paper about the size of a bookmark stapled to the top of it. The color of the paper stands for a particular price. A large board located somewhere in the lot indicates what price each color stands for. This system eliminates writing out the price of each tree—but it does take some customer education.

Try to avoid haggling with the customers. Establish your prices and stick to them.

Lot operation

Perhaps you've been wondering how your group will be able to operate the lot when everybody has to go to school during the day. Many lots open at 3:30 or 4:00 in the afternoon on weekdays, and are very successful. The fact is, most people shop for trees in the evenings and on weekends, anyway. Simply post your hours at the entrance of your lot.

Your lot should be open for business shortly after Thanksgiving. Your biggest rush of business will occur about two weeks before Christmas. Your selling season may last until you sell out or until Christmas Eve, whichever comes first. The last few days preceding Christmas, you may have to discount the trees to move them. Any leftovers on Christmas Eve can usually be given to a local service agency for distribution to families who cannot afford trees.

Do not encourage delivery of the trees. That's a pain. But if a customer insists, you can usually afford to deliver a tree for $10 or so.

Some tree lots offer flocked or artificially frosted trees. Flocking is a business all its own. To do it right, it takes expensive equipment, a heated flocking booth, and running water. A great deal of care is needed in handling flocked trees. Delivery to the customer's home is almost essential to protect the fragile coating of flock. A flocked tree usually costs the customer at least double that of a natural tree.

Many tree lots make a practice of visiting local merchants early in the season to take orders for flocked trees for show windows.

Promotion

Start advertising your lot early in your church bulletin and newsletter. Posters can be placed in your church and other churches in the community.

You can line up advance sales of larger trees by visiting other churches and businesses in November.

Your best advertising will be your lot itself and the signs you've placed there. As people drive to work, etc., they'll notice your lot, if it's well set up, and remember it when they finally decide to buy their trees. That's one of the reasons you should be ready for business soon after Thanksgiving. If you can, put up your signs before Thanksgiving.

You may find limited newspaper advertising successful. Stress selection and quality of your trees. Also mention your group and its cause.

Write news releases describing your group, your cause, and your lot. Deliver the releases to the local newspapers and radio stations.

Canvass your neighborhoods with advertising flyers.

Some groups have found great success by dressing one of their members in a Santa Claus suit and sending him out in front of the lot to wave at passersby and talk with the kiddies. Put one of your female members in the suit for an interesting twist. Often the local newspapers will come to your lot for a feature story on your female Santa. That feature story is the best advertising you can get. And it's free.

Another promotional idea is the candy cane tree. Put small wrapped candy canes all over one of your small trees. The kiddies love it and their parents will thank you and, hopefully buy a tree from you.

One of the best all-time promotions is what some old-time tree lot operators call the "$29.95 Special." Take one of your trees that was damaged in shipping or otherwise made unsightly. Trim most of the branches off. Leave a straggly branch here and there, stripped of most of the needles. Hang a big ugly pine cone from one of the branches. Put a bird's nest on one of the limbs. Hang a lone ornament. Then put a nicely lettered sign on the tree that reads: "Today's Special, $29.95." Then stand back and watch the reaction of the customers. Some of them will snicker, some will laugh loudly, some will take the sign seriously. Most of the people will admire your sense of humor and will often feel freer to accept you as a friend. And that's important for your group and for your business.

A Christmas tree lot is a big project, but well worth it—for many reasons.

Buying and Recycling a Bus

by Gary Richardson

The first three steps lift you into a world of magic. They transform your means of travel from a used school bus to something that seems to have magical powers in breaking down barriers and making people friendlier.

No longer are you riding in a long metal tube that once hauled screaming little kids to and from school. No. You've just stepped up into a brightly painted bus that has shag carpeting, a powerful sound system and seats that face each other, some with tables between them for games or just plain talking. The seats even tilt back so you can snooze on overnight trips.

But the greatest thing is that you and your youth group friends have done almost all the work yourselves —the seats, the carpeting, the sound system, the luggage racks.

At first, it all seemed impossible. But little by little you realized that even though the project was hard, it wasn't impossible. And now that you and your group are heading out on another cross-country adventure, you can't remember what it was like not to have a bus. Throughout the fund raising, the painting, the fantastic trips, even the breakdowns, you've learned a lot about your relationships with other people—even when those "other" people are tired, irritable and have smelly feet. But you wouldn't trade those times for anything.

Actually, there's nothing magical about buying a used school bus and making it a valuable member of your group. The "magic" happens when your group spends time together on the road, through devotions, singing, even listening to someone's favorite cassette 42 times.

172

Take the youth group from Zion Lutheran Church in Thief River Falls, Minnesota, for instance: "A bus changed our group drastically," says Jim Mattson. "It gave our youth group wheels. Before the bus we had to hassle with lining up cars and finding responsible drivers. Now, if we want to go somewhere, the entire group goes together. Our group's interest in going places has picked up unbelievably. Suddenly, places we never even thought about are within our range."

Almost any place is within range when it comes to the anything-is-possible attitude of many youth groups. Groups have traveled on 6,000-mile mission trips to Central America, trekked to Alaska, and have hit probably every ski slope and amusement center in the United States and Canada—all in reconditioned school buses.

Burnie Burnside of Dubuque Church of the Nazarene in Dubuque, Iowa, also gives a lot of credit to his group's flashy Corvette-yellow bus: "Having a bus has pulled our ministry together. We have a great sound system in our bus. As we travel we sing along with the tapes of our favorite Christian groups. You know, singing and riding along together has done a lot for our group."

In fact, having a bus caused the youth group at Burnie's church to grow. "We used the bus to create what we call a 'Work 'n Witness' trip, which is one of the most successful things we do. We get in touch with churches in our denomination and line up a trip to a certain part of the country. Then we spend time at each church doing whatever needs to be done. We've done such things as painting, yard work and passing out literature in the community. Everyone has grown spiritually from those work and travel treks."

Togetherness. Mobility. Those are key youth group concepts. A youth group bus also adds another key concept to your group—unity. "Traveling by bus is fantastic!" says Bruce Lawson, from First Covenant Church in St. Paul, Minnseota. "Instead of being cramped in some small car, we move around and do different things as we travel in our bus. More importantly, whatever we do, we do it together. For us, having a bus makes getting there just as valuable as what we do when we get there."

The first thing

So what do you do if you want to put your group on wheels? First, decide how serious the rest of your group and your leaders are in wanting to get a bus. Count the costs. A bus takes upkeep and a great deal of periodic maintenance.

Next step: Talk with your pastor, church board or whoever helps decide on financial support.

More importantly, making your bus a total church project can improve your chances for getting a bus financed, keeping it running and getting it fixed up the way you like.

Buying a bus

You can pick up a good used school bus for $2,000-$3,500, depending on its age, mileage and overall condition. (A new bus costs around $33,000.) That may sound expensive for a used bus. But check the cost of transporting your group anywhere by car, charter bus, train or plane. (One group even bought a bus for a cross-country trip and sold it afterwards. They saved a couple thousand dollars.)

So how do you raise the extra money to buy and renovate a bus? Here are a few ideas:

Get the church to buy it. If you can get a couple influential church members to catch the bus fever, the church might want to invest in the bus and let your group fix it up. This is the most common way youth groups say they got their buses.

Spread the word. Let church members know you're looking for a bus. Someone who's unwilling to donate money to the general fund may be happy to buy a bus for the church.

Buy the bus yourself. Many youth groups have sponsored fund raising events, bought the bus themselves and given it to the church, with the church agreeing to maintain and use the bus wherever possible. You may be surprised at how effective some fund raising activities can be. One of the best sources for effective fund raising ideas is GROUP's **Try This One** books.

Buy a bus part. Decide how much money you need for a bus. Then use cardboard and construction paper to cut out miniature parts of the bus (seats, tires, windows, engine, floor, transmission, steps, and so on). Make up prices for each part and have people buy the different parts.

Where to find a bus

Once you get an idea of how much money you have to spend, start thinking in specifics. What size? (Keep in mind that a 60-passenger bus is designed for 60 "little" kids, which means about 40 teenagers.) What sorts of improvements do you plan on making? (Luggage racks, tilt-back seats, bunk beds and tables take away from seating space.) Is there someone in your church who'd love to be a "grease monkey for Christ"? If not, maybe you should have more fund raisers and go after a newer bus.

When you're ready, check out the following sources for buses:

Used car lots. Haggle. Check with the previous owner about maintenance problems.

Auctions. Watch the newspaper. Be prepared to out-bid used car lot or wholesale bus dealers. But you can afford to bid a little higher than the dealers, who have to worry about a profit margin for resale. "The key to an auction," says a veteran auctioneer, "is that the buses are sold in 'as is' condition. What you see is what you get. Inspect and test-drive the bus before the auction."

Buying and Recycling a Bus CONT.

Check the yellow pages. Look carefully under "Buses—Charter and Rental." Some charter bus companies have sales outlets for their used buses. There are also used bus dealers around the country. These dealers buy buses from different school systems and recondition them. There are no warranties.

Other churches. A few years ago churches were buying buses like crazy to build their Sunday school programs. But keeping a fleet of used buses running each week takes work and money. Some churches are rethinking their priorities.

What to look for in a bus

Okay, you're sold on getting a bus for your group. So with visions of super buses with bathrooms, sleeping compartments, showers and TV rooms in your mind you go looking for a bus. As you look for that super bus, there are several important guidelines for you to keep in mind.

First, if you're not an A-1, do-it-with-your-eyes-closed mechanic, find someone in your church or community who's qualified and take him with you as you go bus shopping.

Most bus owners stress that newer isn't always better and low mileage doesn't insure that you'll be home free from maintenance problems. "The key," according to one wholesale bus salesman, "is how well the bus has been taken care of. Check the bus' maintenance records for repairs and regular maintenance. A beat-up, rusty bus with torn seats and crud on the floor should tell you something about how well the previous owner took care of the vehicle."

Don't let the following list of what to look for in a bus overwhelm you. Take your time and make sure what you buy is the best you can find for the money. Here's what to look for:

Tires. Check the condition of the tires carefully, especially the front ones. Better to include a new set of tires in your negotiation than to take a chance of having a blowout.

Engine. There's really no way you can tell if an engine will be dependable. But a look at the bus' maintenance record can tell you if it's been rebuilt and what repair it's seen. Best to get an engine with, say, 60,000 miles on it that's been well maintained than a bus with 40,000 miles that's been driven hard and not maintained properly. Does the engine leak oil? Does it start easily?

Clutch. Does the clutch slip when you test drive the bus? As a rule of thumb, a clutch needs repair every 7,000 to 8,000 miles.

Brakes. They're critical to your safety. When was the last time they were maintenanced? Replacing badly worn brakes is expensive.

174

Once you've visually inspected the bus, take it for a test spin. Does it burn oil? Does the transmission sound okay?

Fixing up a bus

According to Bruce Lawson, whose youth group travels from St. Paul, Minnesota to northern Michigan on skiing trips, comfortable seats are one of the most important renovations you'll want to make. The more horizontal you can get the seats to tilt back, the better. (Keep in mind that adding tilt-back seats will cut down on the number of seats you can get in your bus.)

If you can't get reclining seats, consider installing some way for everyone to stretch out for some decent sleep. One group put padded plywood across the top of its luggage racks in the back of the bus. Another group removed two rows of seats and built wooden bunkbeds. Still another group bolted hinges to each side of the bus interior and attached 4' x 8' sheets of plywood to the hinges. They attached the aisle edge of the plywood to a chain, which was hooked to a bolt in the ceiling of the bus. The bed could be lifted out of everyone's way when no one was sleeping, or lowered to accommodate four sleepers on each side of the bus. Even when the plywood was lowered to hold sleepers, there was adequate headroom for riders.

One of the problems you'll face on a bus trip is where to put the luggage. One option is to bolt a luggage rack to the top of the bus. This allows more seating room in the bus itself. But it also has draw-

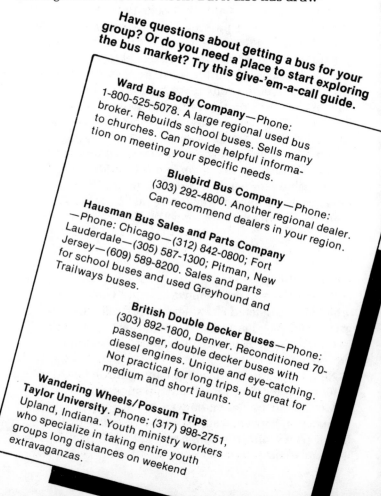

Have questions about getting a bus for your group? Or do you need a place to start exploring the bus market? Try this give-'em-a-call guide.

Ward Bus Body Company—Phone: 1-800-525-5078. A large regional used bus broker. Rebuilds school buses. Sells many to churches. Can provide helpful information on meeting your specific needs.

Bluebird Bus Company—Phone: (303) 292-4800. Another regional dealer. Can recommend dealers in your region.

Hausman Bus Sales and Parts Company—Phone: Chicago—(312) 842-0800; Fort Lauderdale—(305) 587-1300; Pitman, New Jersey—(609) 589-8200. Sales and parts for school buses and used Greyhound and Trailways buses.

British Double Decker Buses—Phone: (303) 892-1800, Denver. Reconditioned 70-passenger, double decker buses with diesel engines. Unique and eye-catching. Not practical for long trips, but great for medium and short jaunts.

Wandering Wheels/Possum Trips Taylor University. Phone: (317) 998-2751, Upland, Indiana. Youth ministry workers who specialize in taking entire youth groups long distances on weekend extravaganzas.

backs. All your gear will be exposed to the wind and weather (even under a heavy tarp). And packing, unpacking and repacking can be pretty time consuming and tricky. A group on a mission trip through Mexico City had to station a couple guys on the luggage rack to keep thieves from jumping onto the rack from second-story windows and unloading luggage as the bus navigated the narrow streets.

An alternative to the outdoor luggage rack is to remove the last three rows of seats and build a luggage rack using 2x4s and plywood.

One church group built a wooden luggage rack in the rear of the bus and added a nylon hanging rack above the seats down the length of the bus. They used eyebolts on each side of the bus interior and strung 1/8" nylon rope to make a webbing that held sleeping bags, jackets and other soft items.

Here are other ways of fixing up your rolling fun machine:

Get a good sound system. You'll never regret the purchase of a good cassette player and six or eight speakers to place at intervals throughout the bus. The youth bus at Hope Church in St. Louis has eight speakers: two facing the riders from the front of the bus and the rest spaced evenly throughout the bus.

CB radio. If you're traveling with more than one vehicle, a CB is a must. It's also a lot of fun.

Bean bags. You could remove several rows of seats in the rear of the bus, add carpeting or carpet samples and put bean bag chairs on the floor.

Carpeting. A group in Wisconsin carpeted their bus from floor to ceiling. The carpeting cut down on outside noise and added a touch of "class."

Paint. Since operating a bus that's "school bus yellow" is against the law in several states, one of the first things you'll need to do is paint the bus. Like almost anything else, prices for getting a bus painted vary radically. You can save money by sanding and taping the bus yourself. If you can get enough people involved the job is quick, easy and fun. Really. There may be people in your church who have the skills to paint your bus for free.

Come up with creative and innovative ways of painting your bus. One group added small figures of a dove, a butterfly and a fish along with the church name. Other ideas: paint the bus a bright orange. Then in blue letters across the side of the bus paint "SonKist." Or paint the bus a denim blue and add seams, zippers and pockets.

A group in Colorado held a design contest among its members. Each person in the group received mimeographed copies of a bus outline. Each person had access to different colored crayons. There were no rules for design or color. The ideas that were generated were posted in the church lobby and the whole church voted on the favorite design.

Kitchenette. Buses aren't sacred. From time to time, groups have added temporary sinks, storage cabinets and "built-in" Coleman stoves. Depending on the size

of the group, Don Miller's group from Hope Church in St. Louis used lumber to build a kitchenette and bunk beds. After the trip, the group dismantles the kitchen and replaces the seats.

On the road

It's always a good idea to plan for breakdowns. It never hurts to take along spare parts—things like a fuel pump, belts, hoses, etc. One group made a deal with the manager of a local auto parts store. Whenever the group went on a trip, they took spare parts from the store on a consignment basis. They only paid for the parts they used.

The magic is in the bus

Your bus can have a magical appeal to anyone who takes a trip. One way of creating that "magic" is by getting everyone involved in the process of travel.

Make sure everyone has a specific responsibility during the trip. Examples: An oil and water team (checks oil and water every time the bus stops); a window-washing team; a clean-out-the-bus team; a nose-counting team to make sure everyone's present before moving on; a luggage-loading team; a pop break team (to ice down your soda pop supply and ration it to the passengers); a music team (to take requests and make sure everyone's happy with the music).

The youth group at Thief River Falls, Minnesota, really gets involved in creating the magic. At the beginning of each planning year, the group selects a committee to help plan bus trips. Each high school year gets two representatives (two freshmen, two sophomores and so on). The leaders do most of the footwork, but nothing is definite, until the youth planning team makes the final decision.

This group also gets people involved with each other by having daily seat assignments. "That way, everyone has a chance to get to know everyone else in the group," says Jim Mattson, the group's leader. "And it works just great. Now, everyone in the group looks forward to sitting with someone new each day."

Breakdowns are beautiful

"I think someone in our group prays for breakdowns," says Rich Franklin, from Chicago. "And his prayers sometimes get answered. We've usually reached our destination on time though. A few times we've had to drive all night though."

"Breakdowns have a way of pulling everyone together," says Don Miller from St. Louis. "Some of the neatest times spiritually come when something happens to the bus and we're in the middle of nowhere."

Bruce Lawson agrees, "One of the funniest times came when we had two blowouts on a trip from Chicago. We were standing around feeling sorry for ourselves when one of our resident crazies started acting out TV commercials. Before long, everyone got in on the act. It was an experience I'll never forget."

Want some special memories? Get a bus!

How to Promote a Christian Concert

by Lane Zachary

Music attracts and communicates to young people like few other things. And just in recent years, churches and other Christian groups have realized the power of music to communicate the Christian message to young people.

Christian concerts are finding great success all over the country. They're being used to introduce Christ, to attract potential members to youth groups or churches, to strengthen the spiritual lives of Christians, and to offer an alternative to other kinds of less desirable entertainment.

With some knowledge and effort, your group can organize a Christian concert for the young people in your area.

First, let us establish that the youth audience is fickle. That's not to put young people down, but simply to realize a characteristic of the audience. But the youth audience by and large tends to be made up of last minute planners. They are not influenced nearly so much by weather and other factors as an adult audience, but there are some other dynamics at work. Let me illustrate: one winter we scheduled the group Andrus-Blackwood and Company into our youth concert series. The night before the concert we had hardly sold any tickets (even though we had done all the things we usually do to sell tickets). In addition to the lagging sale of tickets, it snowed the night before and nearly all day the day of the concert. We were very discouraged. But when the concert time came, we had an excellent crowd on hand.

Several months prior, with a concert artist of equal stature, with no snow, with better advance sales, we had a smaller audience. Who knows why?

However, I don't believe everything having to do with a gospel concert for youth is fickle. There are some basic principles of operation that are valid.

Long-term planning

A basic principle of living: we eliminate unnecessary stress in our lives by efficient planning. The youth concert is no different than the rest of life. If we plan well ahead of time, we eliminate much of the stress. In every concert there are last minute emergencies, but we can handle those if we have already planned the major factors of the concert. As a result, we are pressed only by those small emergencies as they come up naturally, without being harassed by knowing we could have done better.

Begin many months, perhaps as much as a year ahead, to plan your youth concert. I would suggest getting a group of interested youth and parents together. Share some of your visions with them. Challenge them to make this concert or concerts a matter of special prayer. All that we do will be done better with prayerful support.

Secondly, talk about possible formats for your concerts. Brainstorm as many details as possible and make sure the ideas are written down. Don't be afraid to dream big dreams. Our God is a mountain mover when our hearts are right with him.

After you have determined that the interest in the program and need for the ministry are sufficient to warrant moving ahead, begin to put together a concept of what you want to do. One of the major considerations early in the project is to balance auditorium size, advertising, performing attraction, and careful financial planning.

Scheduling

Who you schedule for the concert will depend on when and where the concert is to be and how hard you're willing to plan and work. Touring or local groups will be less expensive than a group flown in for a one night stand. An individual's or group's concert fee may range anywhere from $200 to $12,000 depending on how big the crowd is (auditorium size), how large the touring group is, how popular the group is, and how far the group has to travel to get to you.

If you want to get a big name group, you may want to schedule it while it is on tour. This will certainly limit your date possibilities but the terms will be more economical and the sound of the group will be tighter because of the consistency of scheduled concerts. In other words, you will probably want to schedule the concert around a person or a group rather than around a date. Trying to find quality artists to fit a date may cost more than it's worth.

Finding a good place for your concert is crucial. Successful youth concerts have been scheduled in nearly every setting—in churches, auditoriums, and open fields. The facility needs to be one that: 1) fits the concert "style" and is attractive; 2) is accessible to your audience; 3) has sufficient parking; 4) has decent acoustical characteristics. It may be more advantageous to sing on a hillside than in a gymnasium because of the acoustics.

If an outdoor setting is appropriate, care should be taken to check city sound ordinances, to prepare adequate parking and seating areas, to plan adequate sound and light systems for the concert, and to prepare lavatory facilities for your size crowd within close proximity to the concert site.

One of the finest settings I've ever seen for a concert was a field. The sun was setting in back of the performing group as the concert began. The silhouetting was gorgeous. Spots on the performers after dark made this warm summer night a superb experience. Great care was taken to make sure that the sun was down far enough to not shine in the eyes of the audience during the concert itself. However, we did get 45 minutes to an hour of natural light. The changing backdrop to the stage was absolutely breathtaking!

Be as creative as you can in planning the location and if you decide to go outdoors, be sure to schedule a backup auditorium in case of bad weather.

How to Promote a
Christian Concert CONT.

Performers

To a great extent, "big names" do not make much difference to the youth audience. A typical junior higher's "recognition level" of gospel performers (with a few exceptions) is nil. For your concert to be a success, you need to *build* an awareness through effective advertising.

It *does* matter who you get for the concert. Primarily, a group must be credible spiritually in their individual relationships with God and be able to communicate that relationship with a youth audience. If your intention is purely to entertain the crowd, there are many easier, cheaper ways to accomplish that. I'm assuming you want to make a spiritual impact on the lives of young people.

If you demand a big name personality or group such as Debby Boone or B.J. Thomas, you must be ready to pay handsomely for them. If you can get a large arena or stadium, this may be a valid project for you, but most of us would do better with a credible lesser known person or group that doesn't require enormous fees.

One must also realize that the groups that appeal to a young audience may not appeal to an adult audience. You may need to decide early that you cannot please both audiences. Spend time in your group discussing musical styles that are appealing to youth and then search for gospel talent with those sounds in mind.

With any group you hire, *sign a contract.* Make sure all related details such as money, arrival time, housing and so forth are spelled out on paper.

Support groups

At my church, as we plan a concert we also schedule support groups. A concert is most often effective with several features rather than one. The "name" group then becomes a climax or feature of the program rather than the entire program. There are few groups versatile enough to be capable of sustaining the interest of a youth audience for an hour and a half to two hours. Observe the "Midnight Special" format. TV programs such as this are formulated this way

because the audience has a rather short attention span. Whether we like the fact of an audience's short attention span or not has little to do with whether we should acknowledge it in our planning. Now, someone is bound to say, "Yeah, but Alice Cooper entertains people for long periods of time." While this is true, such variety of production capabilities is generally beyond the capacity of most gospel touring groups.

In our church, we use the support groups as warm-up (before the scheduled beginning time of the concert) and for the early part of the concert itself. Using support groups for 45 minutes to an hour and then allowing the artist(s) to do an hour or an hour and a half seems to work well. We generally schedule the feature artist in two shorter packages—again, to give the concert a sense of movement and direction rather than stagnation.

And the support group concept adds attendance to the concert. For every performer used in the concert, there are usually two to four family members and friends who come, who might not attend otherwise. This is also an excellent opportunity to give exposure to your local church groups (teen choir, college ensemble, etc.).

Advertisement, ticket sales

The first major consideration in advertising is to create a name for the concert-sponsoring organization. If you intend to use the church name, realize that there may be some limiting effects on your audience. In choosing a name, remember that your audience needs to tie it to more than one concert if, in fact, that is what you desire.

Your first major printing item is an attractive poster that can be tacked to posts, bulletin boards, walls and windows. Sometimes posters are produced by a group and are for sale from the agent handling the artist(s). In most cases, you will need to design and print these yourselves. Include on your poster: something to catch the eye, who is performing, where they are performing, when they are performing, and where tickets may be purchased.

A second printing project is a handbill that may be given out in quantities, used as handouts at bookstores or as stuffers in church bulletins, etc. Handbills could very well be a smaller version of the larger poster.

Unless you plan to support the concert by a free will offering, tickets will need to be printed. One ticket price with open seating is generally the easiest way to handle ticket sales and is easier on ushers at concert time. Tickets should include price, and answer the standard questions—who, what, when, where, and why. We've set our ticket price at $4 ($4.50 if purchased at the door.)

A fourth printing project to consider is a brochure for your series of concerts (if in fact you intend to do a series) or a program for the concert, which includes upcoming features. These would be handed out at concert time.

Ticket sales are a crucial part of your whole concert system. Unless you motivate people to get involved, you may have trouble getting an idea of attendance before the night of the concert. Ticket records must be kept carefully. We've found they should be centralized with one person. Consignments tend to be a hassle to follow up, with the exception of the Bible bookstores (which can be one of your major outlets for tickets).

When bookstores handle ticket sales for you and distribute handbills, you need to plan a 10 to 15 percent cut of proceeds for their services.

Some concert organizers attempt to cover their expenses through free-will offerings at the concerts. We've found this works very poorly, particularly with the youth audience. Young people do not tend to carry a lot of money and it's very difficult to motivate them to part with $4 or $5 for a free-will offering.

In advertising, great care should be given to planning your money expenditures. Advertising on radio seems to be a very profitable enterprise, particularly on gospel stations. Whenever you contact a station, have a news release prepared that includes some interesting details about the groups performing and details pertaining to the concert itself. Be ready to give a complimentary album or albums to the station, and be prepared to be interviewed.

Sometimes newspaper articles and advertising can be profitable, particularly in the religion section. You'll probably need black and white glossies of the group, complimentary tickets for the editors, and an attractive layout for the advertisement. Most newspapers can do layouts for you at additional cost.

Organization behind the scenes

Crowd control and security should be carefully evaluated. If allowed to wander, young people may get into areas of the building where you do not want them.

If the crowd is large and access to parking is limited, you may choose to hire off-duty policemen for vehicle control. Whether you use professionals or volunteers probably depends on the size of the problem. Have adequate flashlights and flares for the attendants.

You will need to plan for ticket takers at each door (two per door). Adult ticket takers seem to work out better than those from the audience's age group.

You may choose to print programs. Use the printed program to prepare your audience for the concert. Include biographical data on the feature groups, and perhaps information on the sponsoring organization.

Unless your audio system is adequate or the feature group is bringing its own equipment, you will need to contract with a reliable company for your sound needs.

If your artist(s) requires a piano, have it tuned the day of the concert.

Many groups like to do their own record sales in a foyer area, so you should have tables ready. And, you might make some money from handling the sales for them.

A secure place should be provided for overnight or weekend deposit of proceeds from the concert.

You may wish to prepare individuals who'll serve as counselors after the concert. Some concert organizers always end their concerts with an "invitation" or altar call. A separate, private room is usually prepared for counseling. We rarely give an invitation at our concerts. With youth attending our concerts from many area churches, we feel we must be quite careful. We use the concerts as an outreach, to stir spiritual interest.

Concert schedule

Anytime you present a concert, you need to plan a flexible concert schedule so all details are remembered. Here is a sample:

12:00 noon—Lance and Billy pick up Archers at airport

2:00 p.m.—Archers rehearsal in sanctuary and then to Howard Johnson's for change, meal & rest

6:00 p.m.—Microphone check (Les)

6:15 p.m.—Billy picks up Archers at motel

6:30 p.m.—Doors open

6:45 p.m.—Archers, Roger, Lane and pastor meet to discuss concert

7:00 p.m.—Participants meeting in the parlor (mandatory) for briefing and prayer

7:10 p.m.—Lance and band

7:30 p.m.—TACT (1 song)

7:35 p.m.—Lane does welcome and introduction of TACT and Les Stallings

7:38 p.m.—TACT (1 song)

7:42 p.m.—Les Stallings (2 songs)

7:50 p.m.—Lane introduces Archers

7:52 p.m.—Archers package #1

8:30 p.m.—YCS skit for Andrus-Blackwood (next YCS concert)

8:35 p.m.—Lane announces about tickets in foyer

8:38 p.m.—TACT (2 songs)

8:45 p.m.—TACT and Les (2 songs)

8:55 p.m.—Archers package #2

9:25 p.m.—Lane closes and dismisses

8:15 a.m. SUNDAY—Vince Beer picks up Archers at motel and takes to airport

Post-concert evaluation

Post-concert evaluations tend to center around money issues. Planning a concert with financial responsibility is valid, but let me encourage you to carefully evaluate all the above topics. When you evaluate the major areas of organization, do it point by point in conference with the persons in charge of each area. Secondhand or hearsay information is weak information for evaluation.

Now a final word to the faithful. After each concert, review why you are a sponsor of concerts. Be sure your reasons are personally, corporately and biblically valid. Thank God for your success, for he is the author of all good things.

179

Hitting the Road

How to Take a Group Trip

TAKIN' OFF:

How to Plan and Execute a Group Adventure

by Thom Schultz

Funny things happen when you take 25 kids from a little town in Kansas to the middle of New York City. And, funny things happen when you take 25 kids from inner Detroit to the uninhabited wilderness of northern Montana.

Funny things happen, all right, but beautiful things happen too. Some kids find themselves. Some kids find new, close friends within their group. And some kids find God.

Lots of things happen when a Christian youth group packs up and takes off on a trip.

More and more groups everywhere are discovering the value of traveling. Some groups revolve all of their programs around their summer trips. In the winter, the destination and purpose of the trip are announced. The group members get excited, tell their friends, and the group starts to grow. By the time spring rolls around, fund raising projects are underway. Summer brings final preparation and the trip itself. Then, after the trip, time is devoted to reviewing the fun and meaning of the trip—and conveying the message of the trip to the rest of the church, family and friends. And, soon it's time to start talking about the next trip—once again, attracting more new members.

Building membership isn't the only benefit to come from group trips. Many groups perform some service on the way—helping others through a work project or inspiring others through music or drama.

Undoubtedly the greatest good to come from a trip shows up in the members themselves. The group almost always draws closer together—grows into a caring community, a loving family. And, the trip should strengthen the members spiritually. Watchful groups will see God working like never before. And, some kids will meet Jesus Christ for the first time during the myriad of activities, people, places and feelings that make up a trip.

Types of trips

Every group trip should be designed to accomplish more than simply to provide a good time for the members.

Some groups find a need somewhere and set out to fill it. Needs are everywhere. Home repair and construction are needed in Appalachia. Love and time are needed by handicapped children in dozens of special institutions. Teaching and health care are needed by migrant farm workers' children in several states. Reconstruction is needed by victims of natural disasters. Home repair is needed on the nation's Indian reservations. Renewal is needed in the inner cities. Bricklaying is needed by scores of new little churches. Needs are everywhere.

Music and drama and comedy are used by many groups to fill a different kind of need. These groups rehearse for many months. Then they pile into buses and take their message of Christ and love to those who need to hear it.

Other groups don't use a script. They simply spread out in an area such as a beach or national park and quietly share the Good News of Christ with whomever they meet. Some groups travel to a selected spot to teach vacation Bible school to a bunch of little kids.

And some groups simply set out on an "odyssey with God"—designed to help the members grow closer together and closer to God. This may occur on a raft in the white water rapids of the Colorado River. It may occur in dune buggies in the desert. It may occur in the core of Washington, D.C. It may occur on a mountain in

northern California. It may occur in a canoe in the Minnesota wilderness.

Who goes?

Should a group trip be limited to the "good kids" who've been active in the church ever since their finger painting days in the nursery? Or, should a guy be allowed to go on the trip if he shows up at group meetings two weeks before your departure date? These are questions that need to be carefully considered by members and leaders.

Some groups fall into the trap of using the trip as simply a reward for the "goody-goodies." Chances are the "goody-goodies" are the ones who need the trip experience least. Trips need to be seen as growth experiences. And that means those kids who are most difficult to love are probably most in need of love. . . and in need of the things that can be given them during a trip.

It's also important that each trip participant feels a part of the planning and preparation for the trip. To accomplish this, everybody should be required to participate in the fund raising projects and the pre-trip group meetings. All potential trip participants should join the group and sign up for the trip before a specified date.

The adult sponsors for the trip should be carefully selected. These leaders should enjoy traveling, should not be disappointed with less than ritzy accommodations and food, should be physically strong enough to handle the trip, should be responsible, and, most importantly, must be mature Christians and must relate well with young people. Sometimes one of the trip participant's parents is suggested as a sponsor. This usually doesn't work too well, and it often places the son or daughter in an awkward position.

One sponsor for every five kids seems to be the best ratio. Both male and female sponsors are needed to handle the various situations and problems that may occur.

It's always a good gesture for the members to share the food, lodging and traveling costs of the sponsors.

Getting ready

First, the destination, length, and purpose of the trip should be determined. Then, gather all the information, pictures, movies and brochures available on the destination point. Have a special meeting with this material to fire up all the members.

Also, plan a special meeting for all the parents to make them aware of the plans, and to get their support.

A couple of weeks before the departure date, set a meeting for members and parents. Here, parents should sign release forms, if required by the church. Also, a sheet of information and rules for the trip should be passed out and carefully explained. The sheet should give information on the amount of baggage allowed, the clothes needed, insurance and health requirements, and conduct guidelines. Many groups require the parents to sign a form that makes them agree to pay for immediate return transportation if their kids become too much of a discipline problem for the leaders. Usually such drastic action is never needed, but it's important the members realize this option is open.

Also at this meeting, pass out copies of the trip itinerary—listing each day's activity and the location of the group each evening. Names, addresses and phone numbers of each motel, campground or host church should appear on the itinerary sheet. This gives parents the needed information in case of an emergency at home. Also, some parents send ahead letters and even boxes of cookies. Some lucky kids have real "gold mines" awaiting them at stops along the way.

Many months before the trip, a budget should be worked out in detail, and the fund raising projects should be planned and put on the calendar.

And, soon after the trip is announced the group should begin working on relationships. The trip will force everybody to live together, work together, play together, eat together and worship together. Without thorough preparation the trip can turn into a nightmare. Concentrate on building trust, acceptance, unity, cooperation and communication.

Raising money

Trips typically cost from a few hundred dollars up to tens of thousands of dollars, depending on the number of kids going and the type, distance and duration of the trip. Don't be immediately discouraged by a long and hefty list of expenses. Even a small group can earn

TAKIN' OFF cont.

thousands upon thousands of dollars with careful planning, enthusiasm and work.

There are several ways to finance a trip. The easiest involves adding up the costs, dividing the total by the number of members, and asking them to shell out their share. This method may be the easiest, but it's not the best. It automatically shuts out many kids who should go on the trip.

It is a good idea for each member to pay something, though. You'll get more out of the trip if you know some of your hard-earned bucks are in it. Many groups require a per person registration fee of $20 to $50.

The rest of the trip costs are generally covered by a series of fund raising projects. Standard fund raisers such as car washes, dinners, garage sales and slave auctions are still used by hundreds of groups to earn thousands of dollars. Other more creative fund raisers are also being used, very successfully. The keys to fund raising are careful planning and hard work.

Getting there

Transportation is one of the important aspects of the trip that requires careful decisions. Again, the size of the group and the type of trip will steer your decisions.

Small groups may choose to travel by private cars or vans. This will require good drivers and relief drivers, if much driving is planned any day.

Some groups use public transportation—the airlines, railroads and bus lines. These modes of transportation are generally more expensive than other choices. But bargains can be found in special fares. It is worth checking these fares with a travel agent.

Charter buses are often used. Expect to pay several hundred dollars per day for a Greyhound-type bus. These buses carry about 40 people, a lot of luggage and a bathroom.

A growing number of churches own their own buses. The church bus is usually the most economical form of transportation for groups. Most church buses are recycled school buses, which may sound very uncomfortable for long distance trips. This need not be so. Many groups have modified their buses—turning some seats to face each other, putting in small tables for card games, etc., building simple sleeping berths, installing air conditioning and stereo tape systems.

If your church doesn't own a bus, your group may wish to look into the possibility of buying one. School buses have a low resale value, putting them financially within reach of many groups. A good 40- or 48-passenger used school bus often sells for $2,500 to $3,500. Used Greyhound-type over-the-road buses are priced between $35,000 and $50,000. Check with a local used bus broker. Perhaps your group can buy a bus and give it to the church for general use.

No doubt some of the best times of a trip are experienced while on the road.

184

Many groups are turning from conventional forms of cross-country transportation to an older method—the bicycle. Bike tours can be an exciting alternative where great distances do not need to be covered.

Lodging

Lodging during the trip offers several choices. Some groups choose to spend most nights in churches along the route. Many churches welcome traveling youth groups. Usually a room is set aside for girls and another for boys. Then just drag in the sleeping bags and you have an instant hotel. Some churches will offer use of their kitchens, also. But remember, most churches do not have showers.

Other groups line up lodging in local churches families' homes along the way. The host families will usually furnish a meal or two, too. This form of lodging, however, requires a good deal of advance planning.

Camping out is another possibility. The country is now dotted with good campgrounds. Most offer showers. Many have laundromats. Some have swimming pools. Several campground directories are available, including a good one from AAA.

Local YMCAs offer another lodging alternative, usually quite inexpensive. Many Christian and secular colleges are also happy to rent out their dorm rooms during the summer.

Motels and hotels are used by some groups, especially when trip scheduling is tight. A number of motel chains have quite reasonable rates. Costs, four to a room, two double beds, are $5 to $7 per person per night. These motels usually offer pools and TV. Check with AAA or Mobil for good motel/hotel directories. Another source is the **National Directory of Budget Motels** (Pilot Books, 347 Fifth Ave., N.Y., NY 10016).

Food

Eating should be made an important part of trip planning. Without good meals, you're asking for fatigue and sickness—things that are very undesirable on the road.

Groups planning to camp out need to plan each meal well before departure. Buy all unperishable foods before leaving, and be sure to pack adequate camp stoves, fuel and a few good cooks.

Meals eaten in restaurants can be handled a couple of ways. Kids can simply pay for their own meals, or everyone's meals can be put on one bill, to be paid from the trip expense account. To use this method, a maximum spending amount per person should be announced beforehand. For instance, for lunch set a limit of $2.50 per person. Then everyone may order whatever he wishes, providing he doesn't exceed $2.50. If someone is especially hungry, and wishes to go over the specified amount, he should pay, from his own pocket, the amount over the set $2.50.

When pressed for time, speedy meals can be eaten on the bus. A huge sack of donuts and little cartons of milk make a pretty good rolling breakfast. Also, many groups have prepared sack lunches for each day's bus travel. This saves time and money.

Worship, Music, Misc.

In your trip planning, be sure to set aside time for daily worship. Special emphasis should be given to the worship time. This aspect of the trip should be elevated to the most meaningful, most memorable position in the entire trip experience.

Some groups prefer a first-thing-in-the-morning worship. Others prefer a last-thing-in-the-evening worship. Some do both. Some place the worship at a different time each day. Beware of the last-thing-in-the-evening time. Usually everybody is really pooped by this time of the day, and many kids may drift off to sleep during a prayer.

It's a good idea to form a worship committee before departure. This group of kids and leaders is then responsible for each day's worship. Some plans and worship outlines should be set before the trip. But, the worship committee should also meet daily while on the road to specifically design each worship, taking into consideration all of the day's happenings, experiences and feelings.

Trips offer a beautiful opportunity to "watch God work." Some groups include a "God-watching session" in each worship, where all the members are encouraged to relate experiences from the previous 24 hours where they've seen God at work. A typical response might be, "When we made that wrong turn yesterday, we were able to stop and help those newlyweds get their car unstuck from the mud. If we wouldn't have made the wrong turn, who knows how long they would have been stranded. I think God had something to do with that."

Music is a central part of worship, too. Be sure those with musical talent bring along their instruments—unless, of course, they happen to play something like a piano. Also be sure to pack some songbooks.

Members with a talent for writing should be enlisted to write a trip journal.

And, be sure to have at least one trip photographer who'll take plenty of pictures along the way. The photographer should remember to capture all the different facets of the trip. Don't get so wrapped up taking pictures of Mt. Rushmore that little things such as sleeping on the bus or eating in a tiny restaurant go unrecorded. Sometimes it's those little experiences of a trip that are really treasured, and should be preserved on film.

Upon your return, share the trip experience with the church, family and friends. A good way to accomplish this is through a simple multimedia presentation.

Traveling is considered by psychologists as a major life event—something that startles and alters our normal day-to-day living. Changes often come about from such experiences. The opportunity is here for your group to make lasting changes for the good in your members—through the experience of a group trip.

Summer Jobs Prevent Group Travel?

There's one common (and unfortunate) excuse we hear constantly from youth leaders who are frustrated in putting together a summer trip: "Well, you have to understand that my group is a little different from these other groups that take a trip every summer. You see, most of the kids in my group will have summer jobs. They couldn't possibly be involved in a summer trip."

Baloney.

Rest assured that your group is not at all "different" if your members have summer jobs. And, more importantly, these summer jobs in no way make your group trip plans "impossible."

It's natural for young people to think that taking off a week or two from their valuable summer jobs would be impossible. As a youth leader who sees great value in the benefits of group travel, it's your job to enlighten your young people about the realities of summer jobs.

Encourage your kids to talk with their employers about your group trip. Be sure they explain to the boss the purposes, benefits, highlights and details of the trip. If necessary, your youth can explain that they'll find replacement help for the time they'd like to take off.

Help your members understand that employers receive (even expect) requests like this every summer.

Offer to talk with the employer if the youth desires.

The vast majority of employers, if approached properly and if they understand the importance of the trip, will gladly give time off to the young employee.

Since I began organizing summer youth trips more than 10 years ago, only one employer has declined to let a kid off for a couple weeks.

Youth group travel is too important to allow a myth about summer employment deny your members of a life-changing experience. Your attitude toward the summer job issue will, more than anything else, determine which of your working members will reap the many benefits of your summer trip.

54

Twelve Money-saving Group Travel Tips

by Thom Schultz

Youth group travel is powerful youth ministry. There are few tools as effective as youth group travel to help create a life-changing impact on your members.

But it's no secret that a youth group trip can be quite costly. So, here are 12 useful ideas to help you trim your budget.

1

First-day sack lunch. Have everyone pack a sack lunch for your first day on the road. You'll save the cost of a restaurant meal. And you'll save some valuable time too.

2

Make motel reservations early. If you plan on staying in motels on your trip, reserve your space far in advance. The bargain rooms are often booked early. Many require a deposit, but it's usually refundable if you discover later that you must cancel.

3

Avoid metro areas. Motels in metropolitan areas are typically much higher priced than those in rural areas. Plan your itinerary so that you stop in more affordable areas.

4

Stay in churches. Arrange to bed down in churches along the way. Check with churches in your denomination. Or, use GROUP's **Youth Group Travel Directory**. It lists churches all over the country that offer their facilities to traveling youth groups. Simply contact the listed churches and make your reservations. There's little or no charge involved. And, many of the host churches will arrange for your group to meet with the host youth group for some fellowship.

5

Stay on college campuses. Many colleges and universities welcome groups, especially high school age groups to their campuses. The dorms are usually comfortable and ideally suited for youth group lodging. You'll pay as little as $2 per person per night. Plus, you can usually eat in the school cafeteria— a great bargain.

There are two guides that list campus lodging opportunities: **Mort's Guide to Low Cost Lodgings on College Campuses**, Box 630, Princeton, NJ 08540; and **The U.S. and Worldwide Travel Accomodations Guide**, available from Teachers Tax and Travel Service, 1303 E. Balboa Blvd., Newport Beach, CA 92661.

6

Shop charter services. If you're planning to charter a bus, don't assume that all charter outfits offer the same rates. Prices vary substantially. For example, in comparing four charter bus services in Minneapolis, we found prices varying more than $500. Our comparisons were based on a simple trip to Colorado in a 43-passenger bus.

7

Buy your own bus. You can often actually buy a used school bus for less than the cost of chartering a bus for a single trip. School buses can be fun and quite comfortable. Fix up your fun machine with carpet, tables, luggage racks, bunks, a galley, reclining seats, beanbag chairs, and air conditioning.

8

Use vans. They carry twice as many people as a car. Your savings in gas can often even pay to rent a van, rather than borrowing another family car. Look into renting a van from a local auto dealer, rather than a car rental agency. The car dealers often have much cheaper rates.

9

Drive straight through. This isn't recommended as a regular diet, but it'll save you money as a one-shot idea. Instead of stopping for the night, just keep driving (alternating drivers). In addition to saving the cost of a motel, you'll save a big block of time.

10

Arrange a discount meal. This is particularly useful for breakfast. Many motel and restaurant chains offer discount tour meals to traveling groups. With advance notification, the restaurant will prepare a batch of identical meals for your group. Everyone has to eat the same thing, but you'll save some bucks.

11

Plan a water-only day. Set aside a day when everyone agrees to drink just water with meals. You'll save all the money that would have been spent for Cokes, coffee and prune juice.

12

Two meals a day. Instead of breakfast, just stop at a supermarket and pick up some juice and rolls. Then plan to stop a little earlier for lunch and dinner. You'll save time and money.

How to Plan a

by Jack Timm

Backpack Trip

So there's a backpacking trip in your future! Congratulations! You are in for one of the most demanding yet potentially one of the greatest "natural high" experiences still available free in our commercialized world.

Did I hear someone groan, "But I'm not Jeremiah Johnson or Grizzly Adams or Eagle Scout Sam"? Relax. You don't have to be anybody but yourself to enjoy the wilderness. The pioneers didn't go to "pioneer school" before they set out across the mountains to found your hometown. One day they simply decided to do it. And they did. So will you.

Planning

Where to go? There are all kinds of choices from the nearby forest to a more distant mountain range, from someone's back forty to one of our nation's beautiful national parks. Dig out the travel guides or an atlas to find some of the highlights of your own state. Then locate them on a road map.

Once you've decided where you are going, get a topographical map of the place. The forest ranger station or a nearby sporting goods store ought to have them. Also ask for a trail map. Then learn how to read it. Seriously! You will have lots of valuable info folded up there in your hands, but it might just as well be written in Sanskrit if you haven't been properly introduced. So ask someone. . .like a member of the local "Orienteering" Club.

While you're at it ask that same person about compasses. You'll need one. One that you know how to use with confidence. (Orienteering is the sport of racing against time through the wilderness following a course drawn on a topo map with only the terrain, a compass, and occasional checkpoints as guides.)

Preparation

Preparation takes time. It is not just a matter of going out and purchasing your ticket for the summit of Mount Lafayette and then sitting back and letting someone else get you there. In backpacking, you're doing it—all of it. And if you don't, there are some things even the rest of your group cannot help you with once on the trail.

For instance: propulsion, the art of getting there on foot. Without doubt this is the most important consideration of the whole "getting ready" process. It is the one part that only you can do. It is the one part that, if you don't do it, can endanger all the other group members.

Work on your feet, the muscles that drive them, and the boots that protect them. There is no other way of getting from here to there in the wilderness except under your own power: walking, climbing, balancing on rocks over streams, crawling, sliding, jumping. . .for hours at a time. That takes muscle power. You already "own" it. It is just perhaps a bit soggy from lack of use.

Unless you are an all-round athlete, expect to spend at least a month of hard work getting the power system into shape. Once on the trail you'll appreciate every minute of that preparation, and you'll be able to enjoy so much more of the whole trip. Your school gym teacher ought to have some good suggestions on a program to fit your needs. I find jogging, deep knee bends, and push-ups are best for me.

Boots

Now for something to protect and give traction to those feet on the trail. Boots are the best choice—the only choice if you are going to be out for a week or more, or if you are hiking over the sharp rocks often found above timberline in the mountains. Choose a 6-inch high variety to protect the ankle bone. The canvas types don't give much protection, but are fine for walking in the rain.

On the other hand, those "mountaineering-type" boots that weigh a half-ton each and completely remove your feet from any enjoyment of the feel of the trail aren't for you either. (Anyway, they cost too much.)

In selecting your boots you are looking for comfort and protection. "El Cheapo" leather work shoes will usually do very nicely as long as they fit comfortably, have a substantial sole, are well broken in, and you have treated them with a few coats of boot oil.

Wear two pairs of socks—thin cotton inside, heavy wool-cotton outside, and fit your boots accordingly. The thin cotton socks wick your feet dry, the heavy ones cushion against the constant pounding.

High sneakers will work for short overnight trips not involving too much hiking, but don't push your feet too far in them or you will begin to get complaints.

Anything else on your feet is asking for trouble.

Clothing

Clothing was invented for protection against sharp jaggers, biting insects, burning sun, and freezing cold. Keep these purposes in mind and you will know what to wear on the trail.

Protection against sharp jaggers suggests that what you choose ought to be sturdy, able to take your sliding down a rock ledge without suddenly adding unwanted ventilation. Cotton twill is a good choice.

Protection against biting insects means reducing the

target area to a minimum. Long pants (cut full) and long sleeves are often necessary against the mosquitoes, black flies (in New England), or whatever your own special form of plague happens to be.

Protection from burning sun speaks about that part of the anatomy which sticks out all the time—the head. Cover it. A hat with overhanging brim all around is great. Any style. Some make dandy water buckets. Others have built-in ear flaps. I have one with an attachable bug net tucked away inside, and fishing gear hooked and draped on top.

Protection against freezing cold is a most serious concern to the wilderness traveler. If the weather turns bad there are no convenient roadside restaurants to hide in until it clears. You just hole up, or keep on truckin'. I prefer the layered approach—different layers with varying degrees of warmth available depending on the situation. Wear a T-shirt for hot going, a long sleeve button up cotton twill or flannel shirt next, then a long sleeve dacron-filled (or wool) inner jacket and finally a waterproofed nylon windbreaker with no lining but with a hidden-in-the-collar hood. That combination will keep you going and comfortable down to around freezing. Of course you wear the whole wardrobe only if you meet up with the worst.

Bathroom

For the bathroom you will need a toothbrush in a plastic bag, a half-used tube of toothpaste, a comb or hair brush, and a quarter roll of toilet paper. A motel-sized bar of soap in its own plastic bag, a handkerchief, and an old hand towel will take care of cleanups. Bring a couple of spring-type clothespins for hanging the wet towel and washcloth out on your pack to dry during the next day's hike, or hang them on the tent line at night. Throw in some large Band Aids, a tube of Chapstick for the lips, some safety pins, and a tiny package containing some strong thread and a needle. Girls, don't forget some emergency menstrual supplies.

All of your bathroom needs should be safely dumped into some kind of bag to keep them together and dry. It then goes into an outside pack pocket that you can reach easily while on the trail.

Backpack

Obviously then, you need something to carry all the extra stuff in when you are not using it. This is where the "backpacking" comes in. Everything you are not wearing, eating with, or sleeping in is carried on your own back in a nifty gadget called a backpack. Properly fitted and loaded it will enable you to carry an amazing pile of gear all day on the trail with relative ease.

You start with a frame, which often looks something like a short curved aluminum ladder. It should have padded shoulder straps and a fully padded hip belt. If

you are a clever sort with hand tools you can put your own together out of hardwood. Check the Scout Field Book for a construction diagram.

Note on equipment: Some of this can cost you quite a few coins, so, unless you have the original money tree, don't race off to the local friendly sporting goods store and buy up their super-beautiful frame, pack, and associated goodies until you have tried out similar equipment first to be sure it is the kind that best fits your needs. There is quite a variety of styles from which you must choose so beg, borrow, or rent first, then buy.

On the pack frame goes a tough waterproof bag into which goes everything else. This bag should fit the frame and should be lined with a plastic garbage bag before you start packing. (I haven't found a pack yet that doesn't leak in a downpour.)

If your pack has a number of outside pockets, great! All kinds of goodies in little plastic bags may be stashed there.

However, if you can't afford the fancy bag, don't fret. A plastic feed sack with the plastic garbage bag liner will work just as well. Use a diamond hitch to secure it to the frame. Remember, the frame carries the load; the bag or pack merely organizes it and keeps it dry.

There are, of course, other items you must carry in your pack besides clothing. "Home Sweet Home" on the trail will also include kitchen, bathroom, and bedroom—trail style, that is.

Kitchen

Your kitchen includes a simple metal plate with sides at least one inch high. It will be bowl and dinner plate for every meal. Add a metal soup spoon and a hot-drink plastic measuring cup and your place setting is complete. You group leader will provide all those cooking pots, #10 cans, stoves, and other paraphernalia needed to set up the kitchen.

The leader will also provide all the food (that's one of his major responsibilities) so don't drag along a bag of chips or cans of your favorite drink. Trail food matches the altered tastes and needs of wilderness travel. It is excellent, if you expect it to be. Trust your leader. The menu will be well planned and loaded with high energy foods, the kind you need to keep your machinery operating at peak efficiency.

Cut-ups

Another item to be left at home, contrary to everything you have ever heard, is that super-snazzy, keen edged, long handled cutting tool: ax, hatchet, hunting knife, machete, or whatever has caught your fancy weighs too much, is not needed, and is dangerous.

Even if you are fortunate enough to be going into a wilderness area that has not suffered from over-use and you are permitted to enjoy the luxury of a wood fire, the only wood you use for your fire should be those small, dead branches which are available on the ground. If you can't break the stick with your hand, it is too big for any fire you need to build. A good-cooking fire is small and concentrated. It should go out soon after the cooking is completed, and then be doused with water to put it to sleep.

Forget the roaring campfire bit. The fire is part of your kitchen, not stage dressing. Enjoy the darkness, the sounds of the forest, the dance of the stars. With a fire you miss much of that beauty for which you have worked so hard to get where you are to experience.

In fact, talking about cutting tools, I haven't even found much use for a pocket knife, but I suppose it is asking too much for you to leave yours at home. So put it in a pack pocket and forget where you put it. The trouble with knives is that they usually end up cutting things or people. After all, that is what they were designed to do. But in the wilderness, who needs cut fingers or carved campsites?

Bedroom

The bedroom is the chunkiest group of items you'll have to gather for the trip, and the most expensive. It includes the sleeping bag, insulating pad, and shelter.

Sleeping bags come in different weights, shapes, and fillings. If you are going winter camping and need the greatest warmth, the lightest weight, in the smallest package, then a goose down mummy bag is the choice. A down bag has the advantage of keeping you comfortable over a great temperature range. It will squeeze into an unbelievably small stuff bag. But it suffers from the "triple whammy" of being next-to-useless if it gets soaked, has to be commercially cleaned, and costs a bundle.

There are other choices. Dacron fiber is light, warm and inexpensive but it doesn't compress into quite as small a package as down. It is probably your best compromise choice. Other synthetic fibers, feathers, or foam rubber fillings are also available in bags. They cost about the same as Dacron.

A "luxury" item that quickly becomes a necessity in cold weather, on rocky ground, or wooden tent platforms is a sleeping pad. This foam rubber marvel fits under the sleeping bag and cushions those trail tired muscles against ugly mean designs from below. It doesn't cost much in weight or money. The only trouble is that the pad tends to be a bit bulky to pack.

All of the preceding goes into some kind of shelter for the night. The chances are good that you will have to carry your own. Shelter can be anything from a full tent with netting, rain fly, the works, to an old piece of building plastic draped over a rope or pole. Two things have to be kept in mind: you can be as wet and cold from below as from above, and take care to provide plenty of ventilation even in cold weather.

Some kind of waterproof moisture barrier must be put between you and the ground. It doesn't matter what: an old piece of plastic sheet, a plastic table cloth, an old shower curtain. Cut it to the size of your sleeping bag area. Rain gear will double for this purpose as long as it hasn't been rained on all day (which is when you need it most).

If you get cold during the night concentrate on where you are cold and put your jacket at the spot. Chances are it will be under your sleeping bag. Of course nothing will help you if you pitched your shelter on a low spot and the rain is quickly turning that soft bed into a soggy mess. Head for the nearest dry tent with your semi-dry sleeping bag. Bring along what is left of your sense of humor—you'll need it.

Ventilation is a sneaky thing in the shelter. Forget it and you will wake up to a wet tent—inside—even if it was a perfectly clear night. Condensation from your own respiration is the culprit. Don't underestimate it. It produces a very wet and cold sleeping bag.

Natives

Bugs are more obvious. Trying to sleep with the mosquitoes, gnats, "no-seeums" or black flies buzzing overhead and periodically extracting their sample of your blood can be downright disruptive. A good bug dope helps. For mosquitoes, look for a formula which contains a high percentage of meta-toluamide (50%). For black flies a tar-creosote concentration seems to work. I haven't found anything that works for "no-seeums." Even the finest tent netting can't keep them out. Fortunately, they seem to be around only at dusk.

When you turn in for the night be sure to take all edible goodies out of your pack (which is then propped against a tree near the tent and encased in an upside-down plastic garbage bag to keep it dry). Include these goodies in the communal food supply which is put in a net bag and hung from the end of a high branch away from the squirrels, raccoons, chipmunks, or bears who are always interested in a cafeteria of fresh food delivered right to their doorstep. These local residents will not hurt you, incidentally, unless you threaten them. You are however, intruding on their homeland, remember, and they set the rules. When in doubt, retreat or remove.

Take your flashlight into the tent with you, along with your notebook, pencil and pocket Bible. This is the time to reflect on the day and write down your thoughts. It is also a great time to get in close touch with many of the people who lived in the Bible...after all, most of their lives were lived in the outdoors, close to the natural revelation of God. Their writings reflect this closeness throughout. Once you are tuned in to it you will begin hearing new meaning from those old words.

And that, for me, is the purpose of any wilderness trail camping experience. On the trail with close friends, it is possible to get in touch with important parts of life that are all but submerged in the "civilizing" efforts of the modern community. On the trail each person is an entity, self-contained, and of great beauty. The less you intrude on that revelation, the greater will be the rewards of the experience.

CHAPTER 56

Experience a

by Don Rittenhouse

Scents of pine and wild flowers gush into your face as you pedal through the mountain valley. In the pasture beside you, a frisky calf trots along in pace with you.

You're on two wheels, pedaling with the rest of your group on your first bike hike. You can't believe how much of God's creation you've been missing while traveling by car or bus.

Traveling becomes more than "just getting there." It becomes a real happening as you feel the cool wind, smell the sage, hear the crows, taste the wild raspberries beside the road, see the delicate patchwork of the clouds, and talk with a stubble-bearded old-timer on the porch of a little country store.

Youth Group Bike Hike

When you stop for the day, your mind wells with memories as you toast a marshmallow over the crackling fire. A strange warmth cuddles you as you realize how close your group has become. You remember how the whole group waited patiently for you that morning as you adjusted your bike. You remember how the real athletic types in the group never grew irritated at the other guys and girls who are out of shape. In fact, they really encouraged the slower bikers, making a personal sacrifice to stay back with them.

You begin to understand what it means to be a part of the body of Christ.

Biking has opened a new world for your group.

"Pedal power" can be a great means of having a lot of fun while developing some valuable growth and maturity in your group. Taking a bike hike for a weekend, week or longer, has some real merit for a group that is interested in: 1) spending some time together; 2) having a lot of fun; 3) physical activity; 4) developing individual character; and 5) learning more about what it means to follow Christ.

The first step in your planning is to raise the interests of your group. If the bikers are excited about the trip you have a real "tailwind" for a great time. The group can take ownership in the experience and be involved with planning.

If you're on top of your planning, there will be time available to scout out the most appropriate route. This will insure proper facilities, rest areas, and knowledge of the road conditions.

Trip length

It is not wise to plan a hectic day. The distance biked has some valid rewards, but there is much more to a bike hike than bicycling. The mileage potential of every group varies with the age and abilities of each of the members. A good distance to bike would be 30 to 45 miles in one day.

If the hike is only a couple of days you will want to keep the distance shorter to allow enough time for other group activities such as games and sights to see.

In a longer hike it is easier to bike longer distances, since the bikers will be in better condition after two or three days in the "saddle."

At all costs, keep your biking enjoyable. Don't try to cover too many miles. Respect the needs of your members who may be out of shape.

The longer the hike the more intense is the interaction within the group. Persons learn to know and communicate with each other more effectively and intensely as they spend more time together.

The goals of the group determine what length of hike would be most appropriate. There may be some specific destination or a specific bike route that is particularly attractive. There are likely limits as to how much time your members will feel they can afford.

Experience a Youth Group Bike Hike CONT.

Another factor for some groups will be the cost of the experience. If the hike is coordinated by a biking organization, there might be a per day charge. Or, if you're organizing your own trip, the cost of food, bike parts, camping, and lodging need to be considered.

To claim all of the benefits, you'll want to spend at least two days together.

Itinerary

The route and itinerary should be carefully planned. Main highways are usually too heavily traveled for optimum safety. A good secondary road is usually most beneficial. Avoid (if at all possible) steep hills, especially those with curves. Attempt to work out your travel arrangements to avoid traveling through major towns during busy hours of the day. And stay away from large bodies of water, where winds may be difficult.

Pick your route in such a way that there will be rest facilities every 10 to 15 miles. This allows for restroom needs and possibly a chance for a snack.

The itinerary should be arranged so as to have a fewer number of miles the first day, to allow a chance for bikers to get accustomed to the bikes.

If there are special or unique sights in the area, it may be a good idea to plan on biking to them for recreation or a rest break.

Semi-frequent rest stops will help everyone remain energetic and excited about the journey together. These breaks could be spread out between 5- to 15-mile stretches, depending on the group and terrain.

Lodging

You should determine whether the group is interested in camping, sleeping indoors, or finding more exotic lodging, such as a hotel. The places where you spend your evenings will help to determine what type of activities will be suitable for an evening together.

Meals

Food is an element that requires careful thought for large groups. Menus should be planned to provide well-balanced meals that are fairly easy to prepare. Try to choose foods that will be easy to take along on the trip.

Many community buildings have kitchens available to groups. If camping, be prepared to cook over the open fire.

Lunches are usually prepared quickest if they don't involve any cooking.

Equipment

Ten-speed bicycles, because of their gearing and thin, high pressure tires, are best for bike hiking.

Be sure your tires are well-treaded and free of cracks. Also check for bent rims, which can drain your power.

If you're not using an accompanying vehicle to carry your baggage, equip your bikes with carrier bike bags.

The carrier is mounted over the rear wheel. Don't wear knapsacks. These can unbalance the cyclist and cause accidents.

Insure yourself against breakdown holdups by carrying the proper equipment with you. The length of the trip has little effect on equipment needs. You should be prepared for all circumstances on any size trip.

For easier bicycle maintenance, try to use similar types of bikes and wheel sizes. Carry the essentials to repair flats, malfunctioning derailleurs, etc.

Just as important as the equipment you take is a responsible person who understands bike mechanics enough to handle any minor and major bicycle failures.

You will need to determine how your equipment and belongings will be transported, on bike or in a vehicle that accompanies the group.

Spiritual growth

The elements of a bike hike listed thus far are the physical elements of hike organization. The part that brings forth growth and maturity comes through living together and the spiritual input and guidance. The ability for a group to be sensitive to each other's feelings is a real asset in affirming one another. Learning how to help each other reach the same common goal of your destination has lasting benefits.

You may wish to work together in smaller units to develop some group support. Spending time together on the bicycle is a chance to minister to persons who are stretched physically and emotionally. It is a chance for others to see your Christianity being lived out. The care shared in times of need is a real witness.

An evening of singing, sharing, and group activities will be helpful in bringing out the true value of the gospel as it becomes pertinent to the lives of bikers. Evening devotionals should be kept lively. If the bikers are involved and can identify and express themselves, the greatest growth will occur. Since you may be tired from a long day, avoid sleep-inducing, dull worships.

Biking organizations

There is much to be planned and many responsibilities in organizing an effective bike hike. Many groups have found it helpful to use the expertise of Christian biking organizations (e.g. Out Spokin', Box 370, Elkhart, IN 46515) in organizing their trips. The biking organizations may supply all equipment and facilities. Such elements as sag wagon with locker space, bike rentals, kitchens, and all biking and camping equipment relieve much of the work of local organizers. These organizations also have years of experience in developing a spiritual experience out of a fun and rewarding bike hike.

Biking Equipment

There are two important questions related to equipment. What equipment should be taken along? How will it be transported?

Will the hike be self-contained [all items carried on the cycle] or will there be a resource vehicle to carry sleeping bags, clothing, food and camping supplies? If the hike is planned in cooperation with a hiking organization, a sag wagon may accompany bikers with locker space, bike parts, etc. To bike self-contained necessitates racks on the bikes, and bike bags. If a vehicle or trailer is used, it should carry all camping gear, personal items, cooking equipment and food, as well as first aid supplies, parts and tools. The driver and vehicle should be available in emergency situations and at all rest stops, lunch breaks and evening stops.

The following is a basic essential list of tools and parts needed for bike hikes.

BARE MINIMUM SPARE PARTS
• extra tubes & tires to fit all wheel sizes
• extra chain
• extra brake and derailleur cables
• extra tire patches and cement
• thin bicycle spray lubricant
• one extra derailleur [front and rear] if 10-speeds are used
• extra wire for emergency
• 2" diameter hose clamps

TOOLS
• wrenches to fit all nuts and bolts
  7-16mm metric
  1/4"-5/8" standard
  alien [hex] wrenches if needed
• 2 different sizes of Phillips and regular screwdrivers
• vise grip
• pliers with wire cutter
• 12" and 6" adjustable wrenches
• spoke wrench
• chain removal tool
• at least one good tire pump

Safety Tips

There are many basic safety precautions to follow when biking. Most accidents are a result of carelessness or foolishness. So, here's a quick reminder of bike safety tips.

1. Obey all applicable traffic regulations, signs, signals and markings.
2. Observe all local ordinances pertaining to bicycles.
3. Keep right: drive with traffic, not against it.
4. Watch out for drain grates, soft shoulders and other road surface hazards.
5. Watch for car doors opening, and for cars pulling into traffic.
6. Don't carry passengers or packages that interfere with your vision or control.
7. Never hitch a ride on a truck or other vehicle.
8. Be extremely careful at intersections, especially when making a left turn.
9. Use hand signals to indicate turning or stopping.
10. Drive single file.
11. Drive a safe bike. Have it inspected to insure good mechanical condition.
12. Drive your bike defensively; watch out for the other guy.
13. Make sure all bikes have lights, reflectors and brightly colored flags for easy visibility.

___

You may also find it very helpful to have the mechanic demonstrate the proper use of a geared bicycle. It is surprising how many bike owners are not informed as to the effective shifting procedures [especially for 10-speeds].

Someone in your group should be trained in first aid to take care of all minor scrapes and bruises.

FLOATING:
Canoe Adventures for Your Group
by Rickey Short

Dig out your Daniel Boone coonskin cap. Your group is setting out on a wild expedition by canoe.

Who hasn't dreamed of putting on the buckskins and returning to that primitive time when people were close to nature? The spirit of exploration, challenge, and survival of the fittest.

Images of a Blackfoot Indian, or a frontier trapper, dance across your mind as your canoe slices the water. Twin fawns blink in the early light as the river reveals a silent beauty seen and experienced by few.

Group canoe trips are simple, inexpensive, and great for unity-building and growing closer to God. And every state in the union has rivers and lakes suitable for floating.

The cost? Perhaps less than a one-day trip to an amusement park. The benefits? A deeper sense of self-worth. A sense of accomplishment. A new appreciation of God's creation. The catalyst to help a group of assorted individuals become a caring, Christian community.

How to find a river to float

The best source of information about a river or lake is a friend who has floated some of the waters in your state or in a neighboring state. If you don't have any "river rat" friends you may write to your state department of parks and recreation requesting information on float rivers in your state. They will supply you with a list of float rivers and may be able to put you in contact with some of the canoe outfitters on those rivers.

Rivers are rated as to float difficulty by an international scale. A rating of 1, or class I, means that the river would be easy to negotiate for beginners. A class II river would have some easy stretches and some rapids of medium difficulty. Some class II rivers will have a section of class III which may have to be portaged (walked around) by inexperienced canoers. People who have accidents on rivers usually have overestimated their ability and underestimated the difficulty of the passage they are attempting to make. Class III rivers or long sections of class III should not be attempted unless your group has had experience in extremely difficult white water.

Most commercial float rivers have a current that moves about four miles per hour and are very suitable for youth groups.

If your group does not own canoes (about $600 each) a commercial outfitter can supply canoes, life vests, paddles, and transportation to your put-in point. Canoe rental is usually cheap and the headache of transportation back to your car from downriver is also solved.

Commercial outfitters may also rent items such as tents and sleeping bags if you need them. Usually, though, these items can be rounded up from friends, relatives or neighbors.

When you have all the brochures and information you can find, phone the outfitter who looks the most promising to you. Ask his advice on the river his camp serves. Be sure to find out the best time of the week to come. Ask about group discounts.

The best general advice on the length of trip to take: Don't get too ambitious. Seventy miles is a lot longer in a canoe than it is in a car.

Equipment to take

Canoe: If you plan to camp and intend to carry provisions, tents, etc., you will need canoes that are at least 17 feet long with a three-foot width span. A 17-foot canoe will carry two people and reasonable luggage without becoming unsafe or unresponsive in the water.

I have found that unpainted aluminum canoes tend to smudge your clothes. This could be a factor in the canoe you choose to rent or buy.

Paddle: The major factor you will be concerned with is the length of your paddle. The standard rule is that the paddle should reach from your toes to your nose when you are standing. A paddle that is too long is better than a paddle that is too short because of the leverage that it affords.

Ask the outfitter if you may carry a spare paddle, especially if you're intending to float several days. Tie the spare to one of the canoes. There is always the chance that you will lose a paddle or break one.

Tents: The four-man tent is ideal on a canoe trip. Larger tents are also fine. Use tents with sewn floors and mosquito netting. The sewn bottom is insurance against insects and snakes. Sleeping with a snake would be my idea of a negative experience!

Cooking equipment: The utensils you will need depend somewhat on the size of your group. If the individual type of cooking kit will not be adequate then a set of aluminum pots should be purchased. Aluminum pots weigh less than steel ones.

A propane or similar type stove should also be taken if you will be in an area where open fires are prohibited. A waterproof match container is a must.

Odds and ends: This list is not inclusive, but items such as Coleman lamps, rain gear, insect repellent, suntan lotion, and first aid kits should be packed. The size and the supplies found in the first aid kit should be based on how isolated you will be and the difficulty of getting help should an accident occur.

A 50-foot length of nylon rope is a useful item to tie down tents in a storm or to pull a canoe free that has wedged under a tree.

Each person also needs a ditty bag filled with personal grooming needs and changes of clothing.

How to pack: As much as possible, everything should be placed in waterproof containers. Food items in boxes can be removed and placed in plastic bags. Other items can be placed in large plastic trash sacks.

Food and water

The morale of your group will be affected by the quality of food served on your voyage. So plan to have the best! Unlike a backpacker, a canoer does not have to worry so much about packing weight, so fruit, meat, and vegetables can be planned into your menus. Dehydrated foods and canned goods can be taken if desired. Most canoers plan all of their meals in advance and then stick to some kind of ration plan.

FLOATING CONT.

I would recommend freezing all water you plan to carry with you. This will provide some ice even on the third day. River water and spring water should not be drunk unless assured safe. Boiling water for ten minutes will almost guarantee safe water. Ten drops of Clorox bleach in a quart of clear water will purify the water. The water should be left standing for 30 minutes and should have a slight odor and taste of Clorox. Five drops of iodine in a quart of clear water and a 30-minute wait will also purify water. Iodine is handy to use because it is found in many first aid kits.

Early American foods: For a real treat your group may elect to eat only wilderness food during its float trip. Breads such as bannock are easy to premix and may be baked in a skillet or even baked on a stick. Staples such as jerky are harder to prepare and can usually be bought in a grocery store. Pemmican is easy to prepare with modern dried fruit. These three pioneer foods should be sufficient, and they are loaded with nutrition and energy.

Bannock mix for one person: 1 cup flour, ¼ teaspoon salt, 1 teaspoon double-action baking powder, 2 table-spoons of powdered skim milk. Mix can be carried in a plastic bag until ready to use. Add cold water to make soft dough and make a cake about one inch thick. Brown in skillet on one side and turn over. Prop skillet at an angle so that the top of the bread receives heat. Bake about 15 minutes. Check by sticking bread with a toothpick or stick. If dough sticks to toothpick the bread needs more baking. Raisins, berries, or cinnamon may be added as desired.

Pemmican mix: In a food blender mix one cup each of dried peaches, dried apples, dried prunes, chopped peanuts, coconut and raisins. Add ½ cup each of margarine, honey and peanut butter. Mold into bar size and roll in white powdered sugar. Store in plastic bags in the freezer until you are ready to float.

The rustic sounds and natural setting of the river bank will provide a beautiful environment for spiritual growth. In the wilderness of God's creation there will be frequent opportunities for in-depth conversations and the application of biblical principles to lifestyle and behavior.

The early morning hours might begin with a period of reflective meditation and prayer. A vow of silence might be effective during this time period. Some members of the group could keep a journal or diary to share with the group later.

Prior to the trip, Psalm 19:14 could be discussed in order to prepare for the morning quiet time. How do we meditate? What are acceptable meditations?

During each day's events, group members should focus on the conversation and behavior of the group. How are members of the group reacting to each other and to the situations that arise? Are you living out Christian principles, or have you removed Christian beliefs from daily life? Are group members practicing the servant role in their interactions? (See Mark 10:42-45 and John 13:3-15.) Do conversations begin with, "Let me help. . . ," or do they start with, "Give me. . . ," "Pass me. . . ," "Carry my. . . ," and "Get me. . ."

If an afternoon discussion period is planned it could focus on similarities between this canoe trip and life. How are stress situations on the river like difficult times in our spiritual growth? Are there situations that can only be solved as we work together?

For a wide range of creative devotional experiences, different members could be assigned topics to present on the trip. Here are some ideas:

1. Musically talented members could be asked to write a song about the experiences and happenings along the way. This song could be presented the last night of the trip. Using a familiar chorus or tune the entire group could learn and sing "The Ballad of Our River Trip."

2. A River Jordan service could focus on crossing over some of the barriers of growth and life to better things. Spiritual crossing-over should be a central emphasis.

3. Creative river parables could be built: "If Jesus did not have wheat fields, fig trees, or mustard seeds, he might have picked up a . . . . and said. . . "

4. Prayer exercises could focus on different elements of God's creation—sounds, sights, the wind, people, and so on.

5. Campfire share times give opportunities for group members to tell how they have been growing spiritually on the trip, some of the warm memories they will be taking home, and how their view of and relationship with God has changed as a result of this trip.

On the last day each member might find a meaningful symbol of the trip to take home. This might be a small piece of driftwood, shaped rock, or shell. In a future meeting members bring their symbols of the trip and share with the rest of the group the symbol's meaning. For instance, a rock might symbolize a promise or a covenant.

These symbols will remain meaningful for years to come.

Getting along with the wildlife

The pesky mosquito abounds along waterways in the spring and can be bothersome enough to be classified as wildlife. Plenty of insect repellent should be carried and tents should be equipped with mosquito netting. Choose a campsite on an island or a point that can receive the benefit of any wind—this will also help discourage mosquitos.

Snakes may also be found around the water but they often disappear as soon as they know you are around. Care should be exercised on wilderness rivers to avoid an unpleasant accident. On rivers that receive a fair amount of canoe traffic, snakes do not seem to be much of a problem.

Complete your first aid kit with the addition of Snakebite Freeze, which can be purchased at a pharmacy or ordered from Amerex Laboratories, Box 32827, San Antonio, TX 78216. This treatment does not require cutting and has been recommended by several outdoor magazines in the last few years.

Skunks and raccoons do not present a problem as much as an inconvenience. The enduring charms of the skunk come from the rear part, and the tail goes up before any real action begins. Skunks are inquisitive, so do not get excited if one wanders into camp. Let him have his way and he will wander out in his own good time.

Raccoons can open almost anything, so food should be wrapped and tied to a tree limb. Nothing is so surprising after your first night on the river as to find all your jars opened and their contents gone when you wake up for breakfast.

River safety

Rapids and river bends can be hazardous. And stretches where the current flows into a toppled tree are dangerous, so approach them with care.

Kneeling in the bottom of the canoe lowers the center of gravity and lessens the chance of an upset in fast water. Staying on the inside of a bend where the current will not be so strong will also help you negotiate safely.

Should your canoe overturn do not allow yourself to get between it and a tree or large rock. If the current is sweeping you down stream always float feet first, using your arms for navigation. If you are carried into a tree or boulder by the current, your feet will absorb the shock better than your head.

If a canoe has turned sideways to the river current, leaning upriver will almost always turn it over. Exercise care to lean downriver even if you are about to bump a log or boulder.

Camping and float tips

Some rivers run through private land and permission must be secured before camping. I prefer to pitch camp about 5 p.m. and enjoy the late afternoon gathering wood, swimming, fishing, and just relaxing.

Sanitation and garbage disposal should be handled in approved methods.

It is difficult to float more than 15 miles with a group of canoes during a day. Locate your general camping area on your map and then take your time getting there. The quietness and the beauty of the river should not be rushed past. A river covered in fog with the shrill call of the native loon is an unforgettable moment.

Load and unload your canoe while it is fully afloat.

Be sure your canoe doesn't float off on you while you are asleep. Pull it well up on the land.

Interpersonal relationships on the river

In any activity where your group will spend long hours together in fun and work, there are bound to be some periods of tension. A canoe is operated by teamwork and does not float well when the occupants are feuding.

If the tension arises because the partners do not know how to steer the canoe, a little instruction will do a lot to help them restore harmony.

If the source of the tension arises from a personality, here's an opportunity to weld your group together. Campfire discussions and share times give people a chance to express their feelings and bring healing to your group.

Departure

Leaving the river to return to civilization is a sad experience. You toss a rock or two into the water and stare downriver, trying to pierce the trees where the river turns. And you resolve to return one day and see what is down there around the next bend.

Mystery Ramble

by Jan Hancock

As we got within a few miles of our next destination, the group began to guess that we were heading for Disney World, Florida. As a counselor, I had the unforgivable job of convincing 40 teenagers that we could not go to Disney World because they needed to save their spending money for our "real destination." In elaborate detail, I explained that it was necessary to push on past such an exciting retreat to reach the secret goal of our Mystery Ramble.

I watched their faces as they stared blankly at me in disbelief and began to release their frustrations through groans and grumbles. I methodically proceeded to take sandwich orders for lunch. "One turkey with mustard and a Coke." "One ham, no mayonnaise, and a Dr. Pepper." All the orders taken, the group was still grumbling in disbelief and discontent.

I began to wonder if I could complete my next appointed task. I was to stand before this busload of 40 tired and restless teenagers and make them believe we were having bus trouble which could delay us. I asked that they resume their seats and keep the noise level to a low roar in order that Mike, our bus driver, could hear the strange grinding noise coming from the motor.

Two miles down the road, as I notified the kids that the trouble was increasing, we began to coast to a stop 100 yards short of a motel parking lot. They pleaded to get off the bus. I jogged to the motel office and asked permission to send the group inside a few at a time to use the restrooms. Returning to the bus, I breathlessly explained the arrangement.

The kids began deboarding in groups of four and five, unaware that once inside they would find our youth director who had secretly flown here from Dallas.

Coming through the door, I watched excitement and confusion mesh into almost total chaos. Immediately, I was bombarded with such comments as, "Jan, we thought the bus trouble was legitimate! How did you all make it so convincing?" "Are we really going to Disney World after all?"

We did go to Disney World. Actually, it was in the plans all along. But the plans were known only to us leaders. For six months prior, our group looked forward to the summer trip. But none of the members had the slightest idea where the bus would go when it left our church parking lot.

The summer Mystery Ramble is becoming a tradition with our youth group. Every year now the kids begin early trying to guess the secret destination. They analyze everything the leaders say. We have to be very careful about the "leaks." During the months of planning, I often keep my office door closed and locked. And all correspondence about the trips is now sent to my home address.

In addition to Disney World, our first Mystery Ramble took us to New Orleans, Daytona Beach, Vicksburg and Shreveport.

One summer, our secret destination was Estes Park, Colorado, for the National Christian Youth Congress. We also visited the Air Force Academy at Colorado Springs, Pike's Peak and the Royal Gorge.

Both trips were seven-day excursions.

Housing, transportation, sight-seeing schedules, chaperones, menus, and work committees were all organized far in advance.

First, arrangements were made with churches in the various towns where we stopped to house the group. Each member brought a sleeping bag. We tried to find churches with shower and kitchen facilities, but a swimming pool substituted for a shower when necessary.

Second, the bus was chartered and the driver requested. I realized after two trips with teenagers that the choice of a bus driver was as important as the choice of chaperones. Both required the ability to play and work with youth while maintaining control. It was necessary that they be sensitive to the kids' needs and support the kids in their attempts to learn and grow. We were fortunate enough to have a driver and chaperones with these qualities.

Third, sight-seeing locations and schedules were secured early and with great secrecy. All deposits and payments were made by the church for the group with no mention of destinations to anyone other than our staff.

Fourth, menus were planned for all meals that we would cook. Breakfast was usually cereal, milk and juice at the church. When the schedule demanded, we provided donuts, juice and milk on the bus. Lunch consisted of sandwiches with chips, cookies and soft drinks. Dinner was generally cooked at the church or in a picnic area and was a bigger meal. We tried to provide at least three opportunities for the kids to eat out at their own expense.

Fifth, all youth were divided into work committees with an adult in charge of each. This gave each youth the responsibility of cooking, cleanup, worship, or unloading the bus. The adults worked with the youth to develop the most feasible system and to supervise the completion of the task.

Finally, a meeting was held of all parents and youth participating in the trip. Information is distributed concerning cost, appropriate clothing, personal items needed, emergency procedures, medical forms, and departure and return schedules. Parents' itineraries were distributed after our departure.

Last year, as we coasted to a stop on the side of a Colorado mountain, my mind flashed back to Florida. I once again stood before a group of 40 restless teenagers explaining our predicament. In detail, I told the group that it was necessary to deboard, to relieve some weight on the bus and walk over the next hill. Once cool, the lighter bus could manuever the hill without overheating. Forty young people began their hike, each grinning in disbelief and giggling. They could be heard making such comments as, "Does she expect us to fall for this again this year?"

Atop the hill, many of the group began visually searching the fields, the billboards, and the buildings, seeking a likely hiding place for our youth director. Little did they know that this time, our bus trouble was real and there was nobody hiding in the bushes to surprise them.

59 YOU SHOULDA BEEN THERE:

How to Produce a Mult

by Thom Schultz

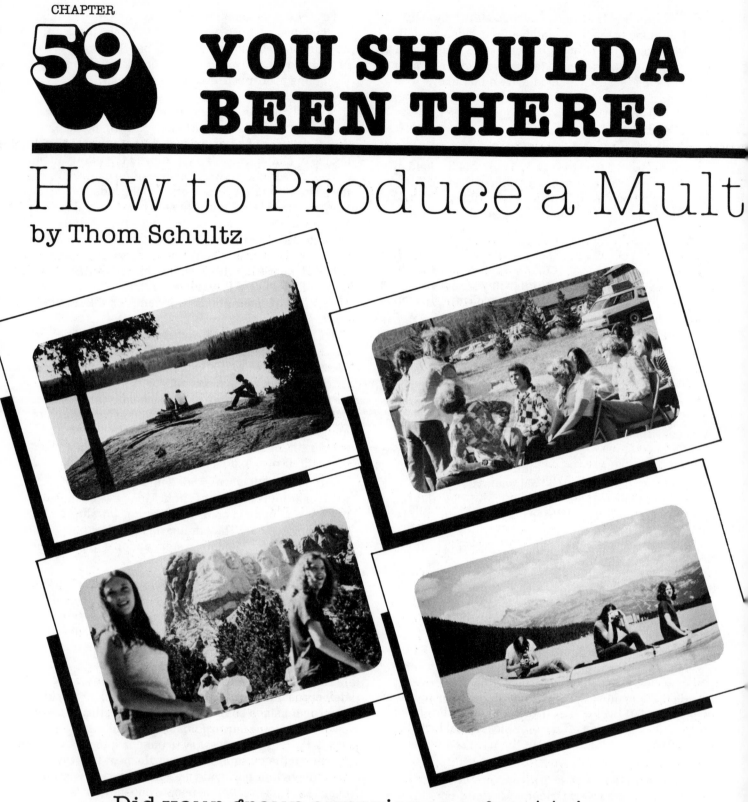

Did your group experience a great trip or camp this summer? You can share all the sights, thoughts, emotions and values of your group experience with your congregation, parents or another youth group. How? Multimedia!

media Show of Your Trip

A simple multimedia program can be extremely effective to communicate your group's activities to others. It's also great to show the program one year later to your own group to generate enthusiasm for your next trip or camp.

All you'll need are slides from your trip and a couple of tape recorders. All put together, you'll be taking your audience on an exciting trip of sights and actual comments from your members.

Be sure one of your members always takes plenty of slides on your trips and camps. Include all phases of group life in the photography. Don't ignore simple things like meals and riding along in a bus. Sometimes those simple times are the most memorable.

Then, after you return from your camp or trip, set up a time when all the members can talk individually with an interviewer. The interviewer can be either your leader or a member, but he should have some skill at interviewing. The interview time can be scheduled during, before or after your regular group meeting time, or you may wish to plan a special get-together for the taping.

Your interviewer should have a number of questions prepared to ask each member. The questions should be geared to the slides you have from the trip. Don't ask a question about the Empire State Building if your photographer forgot to photograph it. Some sample questions might be: "How did you like Disneyland?" and "What did you think of our work project with the migrant children?" and "What was it like traveling in the bus?" and "How did you like the worship we had near the lake?"

Also ask some general questions about the value of the trip or camp. Examples: "What did you get out of the trip?" and "How did you see God working in our group and in the trip?" Your interviewer should also feel free to ad lib some questions.

Avoid questions that could be answered with a "yes" or "no."

Take each member separately to a quiet spot for the taping session. Use a good tape recorder and microphone. Try not to spend more than four or five minutes with each member. This will make editing easier.

Now, play the tape, making note of good quotes from members. This job will be easier if you use a recorder with a footage counter. With that gadget, you just need to mark down the footage numbers of the good quotes, and they're simple to find later.

In editing, be sure to include at least one quote from each member. Don't leave anyone out.

After you've selected the best comments, arrange on paper the quotes and the slides. You needn't follow chronological order. For longer comments, you may plan to use four or five slides. Or, sometimes you may wish to hold on the same slide for one or two or three comments. But, as a general rule, plan to leave one slide on the screen for only a few seconds.

When you've placed your selected comments in their best order, you may want to write some additional narration. But hold this narration to a minimum. Use it to tie thoughts together, etc. Your audience is much more interested in the voices and comments of all your members.

Next, record your narrator's introduction. Or, you may want to begin with one of the actual comments from a member.

Then, proceed to put all the comments and other narration in the proper order on your master tape. You'll need two tape recorders. Cue up the selected quote on one machine. Set the other machine on record, put a mike to the speaker of the first recorder, and start both machines. If you have a member with talent in electronics, he can do a better job by using patch cords between machines.

Continue to master-record every comment and bit of narration in proper order. You may want to end the program with a little music.

Then, turn the master tape and slides over to one member who will spend the necessary time of familiarizing himself with the proper spots on the tape to change the slides on the screen. This must be well rehearsed.

Use a good tape player for your actual presentation. If it is not powerful enough, you may need to run it through an auxiliary public address system to get necessary volume.

This project takes some work, but is tremendously effective with audiences. Plus, it provides a permanent record of your group's great experiences together.

Fine Tuning for Experienced Leaders

60

What will you do if you catch a couple of kids with beer at your next retreat?

Problem Solving in Youth Groups

by Gary Richardson

I found myself out in the sub-zero night before I knew where I was and what was happening. I hadn't even stopped to tie my shoe laces.

"Jay's missing," were the two words that started me on my middle-of-the-night trek. The added phrase, "I think he's smoking dope," didn't help any.

This was Jay's first winter retreat with our group. From the start, I wasn't sure I liked his cocky, macho attitude.

I crunched across the frozen northern Wisconsin snow toward the lights in the recreation building. But my angry gait dragged to a slow walk as my mind started playing gruesome tricks. What if Jay was smoking pot? What if he was in there with a girl? What if. . .?

Then my thoughts turned toward me—and my responsiblities as a young leader. What would the other leaders think if I blew this situation? How would I react if Jay is smoking pot or involved with a girl? How should I handle it? Why did Jay have to be assigned to my cabin? Why did I suddenly feel so responsible for what was going on inside that building?

After what seemed like a frozen eternity, I reached the icicle-covered building. I couldn't smell any pot smoke as I slipped through the side door. Relief. But the voices told me Jay wasn't alone. A girl's voice. Laughter. My heart did a free fall and smashed into my belt buckle.

Suddenly the whole situation changed. I recognized one of the voices as that of the retreat speaker. He and his wife were murdering Jay and his girlfriend in a game of Rook. They were talking about one of the retreat's topics: dating relationships.

With still sweaty palms, I crunched back through the frozen snow toward my now cold sleeping bag. There had been no confrontation. No punishment. No action. I'd been reprieved—this time.

In the years since that experience, I've faced quite a few sticky problems. And I've seen other youth leaders

react in a thousand different ways when they were confronted with a tense situation. Those reactions range from seeing a leader fling one of his rebellious kids against a wall to hearing a leader, in his one-of-the-gang voices, tell some of his group members to keep quiet about the beer drinking and promise not to do it again.

Youth group problems are universal. No one is immune. Just when you think things are going smoothly you get zapped. Someone is drinking beer. Or you stumble across passionate lovers. Or three of your macho types "light up" in front of other group members. Or one of your group's cliques is two hours late in returning to the bus at an amusement park. There's no end to the creative hassles that happen when you're in charge.

An attitude check

Your attitude toward problem situations and the kids who get tangled up in them can often determine whether or not the end result is guilt, notoriety or spiritual growth.

Ask yourself these questions: What should the relationship be between a leader and young people who cause problems? How responsible do you feel for the behaviors of your young people? Do you feel that you can handle most problem situations yourself? Or do you feel comfortable letting other people help you deal with your problem kids? What's your pastor's attitude toward kids who cause problems? Your church's attitude? Your kids parents' attitude?

"The mark of a spiritually mature youth leader is his or her ability to focus on the youth, and not on himself when problems come," says Perry Downs, professor of youth ministry at Trinity College, Deerfield, Illinois. "Too many youth leaders put their feelings and their responsibility as leaders ahead of the youth with the problem. Many leaders are ruthless in dealing with a problem because they want everything to return to normal as quickly as possible. But they should be more concerned about talking with the young person and listening to why he did what he did. We need to look at those problems as a sign of pain; that something's not right."

While you can't handle any two problems or any two young people in exactly the same way, there are several principles that will apply to almost any situation you'll face. Here are a few:

• The world's future doesn't depend on how powerfully and decisively you react in a problem situation. Stay calm, take a few deep breaths. Sometimes it's even helpful to put everything on "hold" for a couple of minutes while you think things through. If so, tell the problem person you need a little time—then let him or her do some thinking and evaluating too. Realize that your relationship with the problem person after the incident is more important to his future behavior and spiritual growth than the problem itself.

soon as you've gathered your thoughts can prevent a guilt reaction from building up in the problem person. In some cases, a prompt reaction can put the brakes on a publicity flood, where the problem kids gain notoriety from others who hear about whatever happened.

• Don't make threats or give ultimatums unless you can follow through with them. One leader at his church's district retreat threatened to send two guys and three girls home if they went swimming instead of attending one of the seminars. They went swimming. And when the leader tried to make good his threat, he found his pastor unwilling to remove the kids. Everyone lost something from that experience: the kids, the leader, even the pastor.

• Communicate. Let everyone know the rules and what will happen if they're broken. Jim Mattson, of Fargo, North Dakota, sends copies of the group's rules and expectations to both kids and parents. "We set specific rules before we leave on a trip. I send a list of the rules to the parents to read, sign and return to me.

• If you're relatively new to youth work, you've probably noticed that "older" leaders seem to handle problems better than you. Of course, experience is a valuable asset. But more importantly, the people in his group have learned to trust and respect him or her. Caring enough to look beneath the surface of a problem to where a kid is hurting is a big chunk of the problem-solving process.

• It's better to deal with a problem while it's still fresh than to wait till later. Dealing with a problem as

Then I go over the rules with the group before we leave. If anything major happens on a trip, everyone knows the consequences. When there are minor problems we just stop whatever we're doing and talk through the situation."

Other groups have the parents sign a form stating they'll pay their child's return air or bus fare home in case the group's leader feels it necessary to do so. Most groups say they've never had to send someone home, though.

Problem Solving in Youth Groups CONT.

Bruce Lawson, from St. Paul, Minnesota, discusses the "why" of the rules and punishments with his group. "I've found that you can't always be cut-and-dried with the consequences," he says. "I've had great success in giving the person a second chance. A second chance puts the responsibility on the person who did the rule breaking, rather than always putting the pressure on me to react."

• Cut down on potential problems through careful planning. One group that spends several weeks on the road each summer in a singing ministry doesn't allow the girls to wear running shorts or halter tops. The guys aren't allowed to wear running shorts either. And shirts are required. "Those rules have almost eliminated the sexually-related hassles we used to have," the leader comments. "And the kids don't seem to mind the rules. In fact, I think most of the guys are relieved."

• Include other youth leaders in your problem-solving process. Talking about specific problems with other leaders can help you be more objective and keep your emotions and ego from getting too heavily involved. The added perspective can be a valuable asset in working with the young person to nurture his personal and spiritual growth.

When you have to act

Even though each problem and each young person is different, there is a valuable person-oriented process you can follow.

John Shaw, veteran youth leader, former mental health worker and present director of GROUP Magazine's National Christian Youth Congress and annual workcamps, outlines a basic process which facilitates personal and spiritual growth on the part of the person involved in the problem.

This process includes the person or persons involved in the problem, the leader, and potentially the people affected by the problem. This problem-solving process is designed to get at the causes of the problem, its effects and consequences by using listening, feedback and clarifying skills. At each step in the process the young person is at the center of attention.

Step 1: It's important to identify and clarify all aspects of the problem: its effects on the group, on individuals, on property and how it relates to the people who created it. For instance, it's important to know whether the problem arose because the kids were releasing anxiety, for attention, for notoriety, and so on.

Step 2: Identify what led to the problem. How did it come about? Did the events that led to the problem occur spontaneously? Or was the problem the result of prior planning and premeditation? Who else might have been involved that could have shaded the importance of the problem-causing action?

Step 3: Once you've identified the problem and what caused it, look at its consequences. Who is affected by the problem? (The whole group? The entire church, retreat or camp? Property?)

Ask questions so you know the problem people understand exactly the problem and its consequences. If you make assumptions about what the kids understand and feel, you may infer things that they don't intend.

Step 4: It's important to find out in their words what they see as potential solutions to the problem and its consequences. What things would they do to correct the problem?

Who else should you tell?

As far as relating the problem to the rest of the youth group, you need to make a value judgment after talking with the person or persons involved in the problem. What will airing the problem do to relationships within the group? within the church community?

Whether or not you should include parents in the process depends on the nature of the problem. The most effective guideline is to involve the parents if the young person feels they can be constructive to the outcome. On the other hand, a parent may be quick to administer punishment that's far out of proportion to what happened.

However, if you see the problem as continuing or serious, like pot smoking, drinking or vandalism, you may have to bring the parents in as a resource in order to get something constructive done. If so, tell the young person, "I'm asking your parents to become involved because I feel you need their help to deal with this problem effectively."

Regardless of who you include in the process, it's your responsibility to inform the church leadership about the problem before they hear of it from secondary (and usually unreliable) sources. Explain what happened and how you handled the situation.

Practice, practice, practice

Your problem-solving effectiveness will get pretty watered down if you wait till you have a crisis before working through this process with your young people. A practical way of preparing for potential problems is through using role plays. For example, choose a potential problem situation (slipping from a room at night on a retreat, drinking, disregarding group rules). Work through the "problem" with the entire group using the process outlined earlier.

Before you role play potential problems with your group, meet with other leaders and work on listening skills, feedback methods, question-asking skills and clarifying techniques. All are vital to getting at the root of what the young person feels, thinks and values.

Your careful consideration and planning for problem situations will pay off in the lives of your members. Seasoned youth workers have found that the greatest growth often arises not from smooth times but from those painful problem episodes.

You're at the annual Youth Workers' Awards Banquet. And your youth group kids have gone ahead with their threat. They've entered your name in The Popularity Contest in which the winners and the losers of the year are announced.

Just before the announcer names the most popular—and the least—you start having wild thoughts about what it means to be a popular youth leader.

THEY LOVE ME, THEY LOVE ME NOT:

Is There Something Wrong if Some of Your Members Don't Like You?

by Bill Stearns

Wild Thought #1: You're supposed to have warm, gushy feelings about every kid in your group.

This myth is based on a false concept that love—the cement of any real relationship—is a warm, gushy feeling. When you meet a kid, you either feel warm and gushy and you relate or you don't relate because you feel nothing. That's dumb.

My relationship with Harry was hardly warm and gushy. He'd always cause hassles in our discussion sessions by pretending to throw up or crawling under the chairs and tying shoelaces together. When things would quiet down he'd suddenly scream, "I never meant any harm by staying alive! I only meant it as a joke!" He made me look pretty bad as a leader.

Rather than discipline Harry in consistent, biblical love, I tried to humiliate him. I'd cut him to ribbons with wit such as, "If you can't sit still, Harry, the little boys' room is just down the hall." I wanted to make sure the rest of the kids realized that Harry was a turkey. To me, Harry was a condition, not a person. I

209

THEY LOVE ME, THEY LOVE ME NOT CONT.

treated him the way I felt about him.

Having less than gushy feelings about a kid is normal. Lots of kids will anger, sicken and humiliate you. But you don't have to respond according to those feelings.

Real relating, caring, and loving goes beyond feelings. The Bible teaches, "This is love, that we obey his commands" (2 John 6). So love isn't a warm, gushy feeling at all. Love isn't even a reaction to a feeling. It's a decision to treat a person the way God says— regardless of how we feel about him or her.

Within the biblical love that goes beyond feelings, you can care about that scab-faced freshman who thinks it's the ultimate to spit tobacco juice in your pencil holder. You can care about the girl who picks her nose and criticizes you constantly.

So relax. It doesn't matter if you don't feel warm and gushy and positive about every kid you meet. You can love him anyway.

Some sentence-completion exercises for you:
• Three kids I have bad feelings about:
• One of the ways I act out those negative feelings toward those kids is:
• Something I know God wants me to do for those kids regardless of how I feel is:

Wild Thought #2: Good youth leaders are naturally gifted.

Riley, staff member of a campus outreach organization, always knew how to be at ease with even a new mob of youth. He made it seem that relationships with kids happen magically.

I hated him. No, I'm lying. I just envied Riley. A lot.

The magic of relating seems to come easily to some youth workers. But for most of us, it takes effort. But there's the point. The skills necessary to relate to youth can be learned.

A young intern who worked with me always got so nervous around the youth group that he'd stutter. He couldn't look anybody in the eye in a conversation. His opening line when talking to a kid would always be, "I'm sorry, but. . . ." But he practiced speaking in front of a mirror and forced himself to spend time with kid after kid. It took time and effort, but he calmed down. He learned to speak more casually, to talk with the kids instead of at them. Today his "style" of interacting with youth is so relaxed, most observers think his kid-relating skills came naturally.

For others, relating is a matter of careful planning.

"I pick a monthly victim," says a midwestern youth pastor. "Usually a kid who's giving me trouble. Then I choose a verse to act out toward that kid. For example, 'Think of others as more important than yourself' (Philippians 2:3). I work at thinking of him as being

more important than me. The funny thing is, after that kind of effort, I usually start feeling better about the kid, too."

The formula for deepening your relational skills of caring for kids is simple: Practice God's commands toward others. Remember: "This is love, that we obey his commands" (2 John 6). Take the definition and practice it.

Consider a few of the following projects:
• Begin listening regularly to the kids' most popular radio station.
• Start a collection of yearbooks from your kids' schools. Look up their friends' pictures, memorize names and faces, find out who's in what clubs. Also subscribe to the school newspapers.
• Ask a friend—youth or adult—to name one negative thing about the way you come across to other people. Then ask another friend the same thing. And another after that. You'll get a fair idea of what you need to work on.
• Pick out an unlovable kid; pick out a loving command; then put the two together in a personal project of growing in relating.

Wild Thought #3: You can make kids relate to you.

Just because you are loving and caring doesn't guarantee loving actions and attitudes from the other person. Relating is a one-way street; a relationship is two-way.

Jim had emotional problems, and everyone seemed to avoid him. So I determined that at least I would care about him. And I did. I still do. But Jim never seemed to relate back to me. The last time I saw Jim was when his mother and I sat in a cold courtroom, the only friends at his murder trial.

Later Jim tried suicide. He stuffed his prison uniform with toilet paper and set himself afire. He said nobody cared. I reached, but he never let me touch him.

Write it down somewhere: *You're not responsible for the way a kid relates to you.* Taking on that responsibility is a 100 percent guaranteed, foolproof method of terminal frustration.

Kids, naturally, are inexperienced at relating properly to others. They're often totally bamfoozled at the thought of caring about somebody in spite of negative feelings, of working to relate to somebody who's not their style. And you might not be their style.

Relax; close your eyes as you think through the following meditation. Challenge your group to do the same sometime.

You're walking down a long corridor. At the end of the hall stands a person. As you approach, you see that the person is someone with whom you've had a rough or broken relationship. Visualize yourself asking the person, "Is there any way that I've wronged you?" Wait quietly for any response—it's a prime time for God's Spirit to remind you of any relational wrong-doing. If you imagine the person stating something, plan now to right the wrong, to ask that person in reality for forgiveness, to confess to him and to God your faults in the relationship. If you're clean in the broken relationship, great. Stop and ask God to give you the ability to keep caring, to keep loving that person regardless of how he relates to you.

Wild Thought #4: A youth leader is supposed to be popular.

Q. Describe society's Joe Popular.

A. Joe is, of course, fun. He's athletic. He's attractive. He's talented musically. He's had lots of exciting experiences. And he's outgoing. He's one sharp banana.

Q. Describe Christendom's ideal Joe Youth Leader.

A. Joe is, of course, fun. He's athletic. He's attractive. He's talented musically. He's had lots of exciting experiences. And he's outgoing. He's one sharp banana.

Society's Joe Popular is the model selected by many churches as Most Likely to Succeed in Youth Ministry. He's the favorite youth speaker. He's the popular youth leader. Joe is sharp, and sharpies are popular.

But here's the real question: Do youth leaders have to be sharp bananas?

One of the most successful youth ministers I've known is hardly athletic. He's blind. Another is bald and old and basically unattractive. Another successful youth leader is an overweight girl who has no—and I mean no—musical talent.

A well-known pastor in a San Diego church says that the best youth leader he ever worked with was incredibly quiet. He didn't like to be in front of a group. He didn't want to do everything himself but asked for help from other adults. He wasn't a step-back-folks-let-me-be-the-center-of-everything. But he was successful.

So when the popularity myth is exposed to a little reality, it gets shaky. And ugly.

The call of the sharpies

Christ didn't call many sharpies. Sharpness and its sidekick popularity aren't the essential elements of Christianity.

The essential elements of real Christianity are inner, Christlike qualities of love, joy, tranquility, patience, kindness, goodness, faithfulness, gentleness, self-control. These qualities should characterize the ideal Joe Youth Leader.

So society wants you to be sharp and popular; Jesus wants you to be like him. And Jesus, the perfect leader, wasn't and isn't the epitome of popularity. It really doesn't matter that you may not be wildly popular, that some of your kids just flat don't like you.

Plan, as part of your youth ministry "modeling career," to defuse the pressure on your kids to be "sharp." Regularly ask questions about what makes people valuable—good looks, brains, talent or inner qualities of love, tranquility, faithfulness.

Popularity as a youth leader can be a pain. The youth leader who believes he can fulfill the relational needs of every teenager in his or her group is an ego-freak. Being all things to all kids is dangerous in at least four ways.

Popularity vs. unity. Jews, Greeks, males, females, bondmen and sophomores (even freshmen) can live together in Christian unity, not as their differences are dissolved, but as they learn to relate in spite of differences. If your group sticks together because of the kids' attraction to you, it's a sure sign they're all like you. Having great differences to overcome in your group gives everyone chances to learn real unity!

Popularity vs. balance. If all the kids adore you, there'll be no dissent, no differing ideas, no viewpoints other than yours. You'll have a lopsided ministry. If everyone likes you too well, you might even pick up the idea that it's unspiritual to be criticized, or that you should feel guilty when you're disliked. (Jesus demonstrated that neither is true.)

Popularity vs. delegation. Kids who need a father figure might best be discipled by a fatherly man. Quiet youth might best see real Christianity in a quiet adult. Lots of kids need a mother figure. And you're not all those people. You don't have to be. Many of your interaction opportunities should be delegated to adults who'll work with you. The one-man-show youth leader who excels at keeping all the plates—all the kids relational needs—spinning by himself belongs in the carnival.

Popularity vs. continuity. You probably know a youth leader who thinks every kid should relate closely to him alone. And you know what happens when he leaves that ministry—the bottom drops out. The average youth leader works at a youth ministry for an average of 18 months, so the relationships kids develop with him are routinely ripped to shreds. But if kids build relationships with adults other than the youth leader, the intimate discipling process continues well beyond 18 months. Being admired too much by too many makes the typical "transient" youth leader dangerous to the continuity of kids' relational growth.

Let's review some realities.

1. You don't have to pretend to have positive feelings about every kid in your group.

2. You can, however, care about any kid. You can remove barriers to his caring about you by developing your social and relational skills.

3. Regardless of how hard you try, all youth won't have positive feelings about you. So expect it—you can't make them relate to you.

4. Don't expect to be popular. Don't drool for popularity; because relating to kids who don't relate to you will force you and your group to learn unity, to enjoy a balanced ministry, to delegate and to see continuity in kids' growth.

Now when your group enters your name in the Youth Worker Popularity Contest, you can relax, right? You know it's no big deal. Even if you lose.

"The biggest pain of my high school life is having to deal with all the cliques," says Joe M., a senior at Glenbard West High School near Chicago.

"I keep wondering how I can be more popular and how I can fit in with the group I want," admitted Heidi E., of Boston. She looked scared. "I keep remembering last year—when I tried to get Lori's friendship, you know, be perfect, say the right things. I'm tired of trying so hard."

Most of us have heard comments like these from our young people, probably even said something like that ourselves. And most of us have either given or received the advice, "Be yourself."

But as you may have discovered, dealing with cliques—small, exclusive groups of close friends—isn't as simple as the two-word piece of advice implies. Although accepting yourself is an important part of belonging to groups and making friends, it's not the definitive answer for handling cliques in youth groups.

Where do you start? Do you try an end run around the clique? Do you ignore it? Or do you hit it head-on and try to crush it? In any case, the stakes are extremely high.

The Use and Abuse of Youth Group Cliques

by Gary Richardson

Cliques aren't always bad news

The first step in dealing with cliques in your youth group is to realize that they aren't always bad news.

"I don't know what I would have done without the three guys I used to run around with," writes Rich Franklin, a part-time youth worker. "Those guys were my only source of support and attention. I probably would have faded out of existence had they not been around when I needed them."

Sometimes we forget how crucial that one-for-all-and-all-for-everybody group of three or four people is to their development as normal, healthy young adults. Roland Martinson, dean of students at Luther-Northwestern Seminary and consultant for Youth Research Center, puts it this way: "Cliques have to do with loneliness, of being liked, of counting for something, of having a context within which to relate to people.

"At the age of 12 or 13 most young people begin to move from the 'me' world—the small, secure world of parents and brothers and sisters—to the 'I' world, a world where the 'family' is made of close friends. This second family isn't made up of big people and snotty little brothers or sisters, but a family of pure people:

guys and gals who walk, talk, eat and say the same things, have the same interests and even chew their gum the same way."

Mark Cline found his second family at church. He was one of the "rejects" when it came to being included in "the" groups at his high school. He was a wild driver, had sometimes abusive behavior and never knew when to act crazy or sophisticated.

But for Mark the "in" group at church was different. The members of the church clique he wanted to join went to different schools and weren't aware of his rough edges.

Over the months of spending more and more time with the clique at church, Mark felt a great deal of unspoken pressure to cool his driving habits and watch his behavior and language. His desire to please the members of the clique changed his behavior and attitude faster than strict rules and constant discipline.

Sometimes members of cliques can even help each other overcome tremendous personal problems. The clique's sensitive guidance and authentic sympathy can often help a girl deal with the pressures of living with a critical, perfectionist father or help a guy break away from the tenacles of an overprotective mother.

The Use and Abuse of Youth Group Cliques CONT.

GROUP ANALYSIS FORM
1. Why do you think people want to join groups?
2. When I'm accepted by my group, I feel. . .
3. When I'm rejected by a group I want to join, I feel. . .
4. Think about a group you belong to and feel comfortable with. If your group were a person, what would its personality be like?
5. Describe what cliques are like. Write as many one-word descriptions as you can [positive and negative].
6. What are some rules, unspoken or spoken, that cliques have?
   A. Rules about how people in the group relate to other people.
   B. Rules concerning individuals in the group.
   C. Rules toward attitudes and opinions of group members.
7. Cliques are helpful when they. . .
8. Cliques are harmful when they. . .
9. Some people aren't included in cliques at school or in our youth group because. . .
10. Three things I can do to make people feel more a part of our group are. . .

Cliques aren't all good news either

If you've worked much with young people, you know that not all one-for-all-and-all-for-everybody groups are open and affirming in their treatment of outsiders.

Cliques hurt "outside" youth because of their exclusiveness. Curses on the poor guy or gal who somehow finds himself or herself slipping between the cracks of the different cliques in the youth group. The kid's youth leaders won't have to look far for reasons when he eventually drops out.

Linda McKay of Chicago summed up one of the most negative sides of cliques when she wrote, "A close friend of mine could have excelled at field hockey, but because it wasn't a 'cool' sport, she decided not to try out, a decision she now regrets." Close-knit groups exert great pressure to conform, no matter if what they're conforming to is fantastic or rotten. This safe, secure and narrow way of thinking restricts personal growth and shrinks the freedom to choose friends and build relationships with people outside the group. And these skills are essential in later life.

So how do we deal with cliques when on the one hand they're a normal part of the growing up process, yet their exclusiveness and pressure to conform can keep their members from maturing personally and spiritually?

Since cliques won't go away if ignored, how can we learn to live with them? How can we deal with cliques when they threaten to divide our youth group?

Roland Martinson gives five basic strategies for youth leaders.

1. Emphasize that each person in your group is a free and responsible person. God has made each person absolutely unique—one of a kind. Over half the kids in America wish they were someone else. And an even greater number think they're too fat, too skinny, too short, too tall, too ugly, and on and on. Point out that God doesn't make junk, that the Creator is inside each

person, that each person in the group is so valuable that Jesus died especially for him or her.

Consider developing a unit of study where your group clarifies what's really important in life. Study the different ways the world tries to force us into its way of comparing and evaluating people on the basis of looks, interests or abilities.

2. Work on developing an atmosphere in your group where caring is a top priority. Create a series of experiences where you and your group work through what it means to care about each other. Evaluate yourself and your group as a caring community where people can be affirmed and learn how to be affirming. What are the elements you need to work on? Where can you start?

3. In almost every group there are some people who have a way of helping others to get together. Brainstorm with these young people ways of getting everyone to know each other better.

Consider planning a retreat to build more unity in your group. See the retreat described in Chapter 26. It'll help you plan a retreat for the specific purpose of developing group unity.

Conduct a series of sessions on what the Bible says about relationships and how Christians should treat each other.

4. Cliques have wounded most people at one time or another. Help those "wounded" people in your group to use that sensitivity to reach out to others who are also wounded. Encourage them to analyze their hurt feelings and to discover ways of using those rotten times for positive personal and spiritual growth.

5. Kids need to be in bunches. Provide unique situations for kids who don't normally hang around with each other. Program ways for kids to start developing relationships with each other. **The New Games Book**, edited by Andrew Fluegelman (Doubleday) is a good resource for getting your group members to interact with each other in non-threatening situations.

A clique think session

Explore with your group the need people have for intimate relationships as well as the dangers involved in blindly conforming to group standards.

Either print the questionnaire form on page 214 and have people jot down their thoughts and feelings or divide into groups of four or five and discuss the questions in small groups.

A clique simulation game

Try this "Go Away" game to help your group experience how cliques operate.

Preparation: You'll need toothpicks, glue, old magazines, clay and posterboard for each team.

Divide your group into teams of six to eight. Tell each team that it is to use the supplies and work together to construct a symbol of what "community" or "togetherness" means to them. Tell each group to be prepared to explain its completed symbol. Set a time limit.

The sting: Before this session, pick one person to be in each team who is to argue, refuse to cooperate, hinder progress and otherwise be a headache. Caution the "plants" not to make their behavior too obvious. Explain that their purpose is to test the team's reactions to negative behavior. Locate the teams far enough apart so they can't see each other.

After the teams have worked on the project long enough for the "plant" to cause some problems, stop the activity temporarily.

Explain that you're trying an experiment to see if a new team can catch up with the existing teams. Explain that you'll form the new team by taking one person from each existing team. Tell each team to send one person from their membership to the new team. Normally, each team will send the troublemaker, but even if someone else is sent, it doesn't change the experience.

Under the guise of giving the new team "catch-up" instructions, explain that in a minute or two each person is to return to his original team and ask to be readmitted, saying he doesn't like the new group.

When each team has had enough time to react, either by accepting the person back or by refusing readmittance, stop the activity and call all the groups back together. It's a good idea to confess that each group had a "plant."

Use some or all of the following questions.

1. How did you feel about the "plant" in your team?
2. How did you feel about having to tell one person to leave?
3. Why did you reject the person you did?
4. How did you feel when he returned and asked to be readmitted?
5. If you didn't accept him, what was your reason?
6. If you accepted him back, why? Did you place any conditions for accepting him back?
7. How did you show him you really accepted him back?
8. To the "plants": How did you feel about the whole process?
9. In what ways was this experience similar to the way groups treat some people at school or at church?
10. How do most "real" groups deal with someone who's different?

You could end this experience by having everyone help plan a session where the emphasis is on learning how to accept people who are new to the group.

In the end

All of us have a burning need to be liked, to have close friends and to feel accepted. Don't forget that your young people have the same needs. When you have cliques in your group, evaluate what needs the clique is meeting and try to meet those needs.

When someone in your group confides, "It's so hard for me. . .I just want to be included. I want to feel close to someone." You can say, "I know how you feel. I've been there too. Let's talk."

How to Love Obnoxious Members

by John Shaw

"**I**'m not going on the trip if Joe is going. He's so obnoxious in public it makes me sick!"

Sometimes a group faces a problem with one or two members who are constantly way out of line and a source of embarrassment to most of the group. Often, other members react by withdrawing. When someone quits a group that has an obnoxious member, it doesn't take long to discover the negative feelings involved. "Why should I spend my time with the group when Joe ruins so many of the meetings?" "We can't get anything done because he's too gross." Complaints like

this reflect a lot of frustration. It's hard to know what to do.

If the group gripes at Joe for his behavior, he could be getting rewarded by their attention. Then he learns to get attention by being obnoxious. And, usually, he doesn't know any better way to be the center of attention. So, the process can become a self-feeding circle.

Every response from the group builds more motivation to continue the behavior that is causing the problems in the group. For Joe, negative responses feel better than being ignored.

Then, too, the complaints of the group could be providing punishment that tends to relieve guilt feelings or reinforcement of the feeling "I'm no good." Again, the responses of the group tend to keep the obnoxious behavior going. By giving the expected negative response, the group unwittingly helps Joe maintain his pattern of behavior. The group confirms Joe's bad feelings about himself and provides the punishment he expects because he feels he is a bad person. And if the process goes too far, Joe could get kicked out of the group and further entrench his low self-image. His self-judgment is confirmed, and he can keep feeling about himself, "Nobody cares about a guy like me."

Obviously, the authoritative, judgmental approach works better in the Marines than in a church youth group. Most everyone feels a sense of failure when meetings go sour or someone gets booted out.

How can a Christian group deal with Joe? Jesus advocated the direct, personal approach in a situation where there was interpersonal conflict. He said, in effect, try to talk it out—have a group discussion about the problem. He suggested that several people go talk with the offender. Many groups will have to work hard to develop the skill to handle direct interpersonal discussions. It will take time and possibly some painful experiences, but it will be worth it if the group can learn to talk out its problems.

A helpful approach would be to enlist the support of each member for the development of personal discussions. Talk about possible goals or advantages of open communication. What could be gained? How would it help individuals or the total group? Then, what would be the cost of that kind of involvement? How much time would it take?

1. Go and talk.

2. Give positive messages on own initiative.

3. Matter of factly point out inappropriateness— don't respond emotionally—provide for successes.

Would it be too threatening to anyone? Would it be worth the effort? Let everyone gradually identify and express their feelings about personally discussing problems in a total group setting. You will be developing your skill in communication by carefully sharing your concerns and feelings. The group will feel closer and more capable of dealing with problems directly. Once you have reached a group decision to face the problem, you will have developed a lot of ability for group discussion.

It is important to let each other know that you care enough to work through a problem rather than ignoring it or judging it. The obnoxious member will have to be personally reassured that you are on his side. He will have to be reminded again and again that you support his efforts to face the problem and that you share the responsibility for working it out. Then you can talk about his behavior as a problem. You can talk about your judgmental responses and your withdrawing from him as problems. You can look for other more appropriate ways of relating to each other.

When approaching a specific problem like Joe's, try to discover what the obnoxious behavior has accomplished for him. Attention? Punishment? Confirming bad feelings? Once you have identified what he was attempting to get, you can explore other ways of getting the same result. Or, in the case of punishment, you can consider whether the result is really desirable or not. Maybe he could decide he did not really need punishment and begin to work for other results that are more possible. With the support and understanding of the group, Joe may feel free to try some new approaches to other people.

The group can offer support in many ways. Importantly, your personal acceptance of Joe while he tries new behavior will be the undergirding feeling that can keep him going. This support is the love that can accomplish all things. If Joe feels accepted while he faces the uncomfortable and often frightening experience of trying to change, he will be more apt to succeed.

If you discover that Joe was trying to get attention by creating problems, the group can consider ways of giving attention without waiting for Joe to cause a problem. Take the initiative and give Joe attention on your own terms. Give him an important job and let him know what it means to the group. Pick out some of the things you like about him and let him know how you admire and appreciate those things. Encourage his positive efforts by rewarding them. Jesus often used this same approach by rewarding the behavior he liked. When he saw Zacchaeus making a special effort to see him by climbing a tree, he rewarded the little man by spending the evening at his house. Similarly, he rewarded behavior when the man was let down through the roof to be healed and when the centurion showed faith in Jesus' authority to command the healing of his daughter.

If Joe falls back into his old habits at times (as can be expected), matter of factly point out that he has relapsed and then look for a behavior that would be more appropriate to achieve the results he wants. Don't respond emotionally by getting angry or upset at his falling back into old patterns. The emotional responses tend to encourage the old habit. Try to shift your attention and emotional investment to more positive behaviors that he is developing. Point to his successes and help him set several small, short-term goals that he can accomplish fairly quickly. Then he will feel success more frequently.

Working through the problems of obnoxious behavior can result in a warm and caring group that has arrived at mutual understanding. You will develop the courage and self-confidence to face conflict and deal with it effectively. It may be easier to quit the group or get rid of the problem person, but the expectation of being Christian can be fulfilled best by direct, personal involvement. You will show that you care enough to work out new and better experiences. Your patience and understanding will make the difference.

Welcome to my office! Look around and see how many principles of time management you observe in my 12 x 15 room. I have piles of papers on the floor. Each pile represents a project that must be completed this month. Working on more than one job at a time allows me to work the kinks out of my ideas. What sounded good on Monday when I had a great brainstorm, sometimes isn't quite as great when I begin to modify it on Thursday. Notice that some of the piles contain materials from other publishers. Even though I am employed by the Christian and Missionary Alliance, I save hundreds of hours each year by using resources other people have developed.

Stretching and Managing Your Time

by Daryl Dale

Bulletin board

Let's move from the project piles to my bulletin board. Yes, those pieces of paper are notes I have written to myself. I pin them at nose level so I won't miss them. When someone asks me for help I try to respond immediately. This saves time. If I can't help right away I make a note to myself so I will have that unfinished task in front of me constantly.

Beside the personal notes you see a half sheet of paper with DO penned across the top. That list tells me what I need to accomplish by the end of the week. This is the way I set personal goals for myself.

Oh yes, you see the calendar on the bulletin board displaying three months at a time. If you look at the calendar in my desk drawer, you see it has projects lined up for the entire year. The calendar keeps me on target because the do list doesn't warn me of projects I have before me in two or three weeks.

Looking at the calendar carefully, you see I attend one Christian education conference every three months. When I was working in a small church I attended two a year. As long as I have fresh input, new ideas keep coming to my attention.

On the bulletin board is a list of 20 very important people. Many of my projects depend on their work. They probably triple my effectiveness. They know I need them because I am always telling them how valuable they are to me. Every week two or three items come from these people because they believe I will use their ideas.

Secretarial help

Behind my desk is a table with a dictating machine.

It makes me look like a big time operator, but don't let that fool you. There is a principle of time management beside that machine. Yes, there you see it—that pile of wrinkled letters. Those came this morning, and they're already answered. Instead of reading a letter and setting it aside only to have to read it again another day, I answer it immediately. I handle all reports the same way. It takes extra time to wait until tomorrow to do a job I know I should do today.

You probably feel I have it made because I have a secretary. Well, you're right! A secretary surely helps my use of time. But I know several youth workers on tight budgets who've asked people in their church to give one or two mornings a week to type for them. If you don't get a lot of mail you probably need only a part-time secretary anyway.

Before we leave this matter of a secretary, let me share a problem. Not very many great ideas hit me while I am at work. There are just too many people around, including the secretary. I also drive myself very hard. I find that getting off by myself helps keep me productive and fresh. I sometimes drive my car on a long trip to a conference just so I can be by myself. These quiet, private times are valuable to me.

Bookcase tidbits

Let's go over to the bookcase. On the top you see a Bible. I don't often use it during work hours, but it serves as a visible reminder of whom I serve and that I must prove to you the importance of a quiet time with Christ each day by showing you it will increase your productivity.

My bookcase is full of magazines. They are like

having a half dozen youth experts in my office each month to give me more ideas. They are some of my best advisors. My productivity depends on this constant flow of ideas.

Well, that concludes the tour of my office. But let me add a few more time management principles that have been helpful to me.

1. Pray before starting work, acknowledging your partnership with Christ.

2. Keep a work schedule. Get into your office on time. Don't leave early unless fatigue has set in. If you don't have a full-time position, set aside an hour or two several days a week to plan and develop youth ministries for your young people. Guard that designated time and watch it increase your productivity.

3. Utilize what others have done. Don't plagiarize, but don't write off a program someone else has already written. Adapt other ideas to your own situation. Spend some money on youth resources.

4. Delegate work to others. Delegation takes time because you have to support delegation with praise, encouragement, and accountability. But a leader multiplies himself through delegation. Give people decision-making power and don't force them to do things your way. Meet with them regularly and give them all the assistance they need to assure them success in the task they undertake for you. It is important to remember we are in the business of building and equipping people, not just accomplishing projects.

5. Recyle your ideas and get as much mileage from them as possible. A devotional idea can be used with youth, in a staff meeting, during a training conference and written for a newsletter. Some projects and programs can be repeated fruitfully every two or three years. Don't hesitate to repeat a successful ministry.

6. Discipline yourself. Find one workable idea at every training conference and begin working on the idea when you return home. You either use it or lose it.

7. Build a team. People like to work when they are appreciated and their work is valued. Just a postcard with a three-sentence thank-you makes an impression. People are your most valuable resource. Treat them as such through frequent appreciative conversations.

8. Plan your day: Some people are morning people.

They get the most work accomplished in the morning and do their errands in the afternoon, because they think a little slower in the afternoon. Find your most productive time of day and use it to your best advantage.

9. Rest when you are tired. It is hard to be productive when you are fatigued. Take a day off when you find yourself going in circles or giving five hours to a one-hour project. Stay physically and mentally fresh.

10. Set long-range goals. Effective ministry has plan and purpose to it. It is not a bunch of unrelated ideas and programs. Decide your long-range objectives, and set goals that help you reach those objectives. Long-range plans also help you know what to look for when you read a magazine or attend a conference. Three-year plans are not difficult to develop. Both small and large churches can benefit equally from such plans.

11. Set priorities. Work on important things first. Don't get bogged down with details until you've accomplished the basics. Evaluate the items on your DO list and prioritize them. Make sure your list is related to your long-range goals as much as possible.

12. If you are a part-time youth worker, don't become bogged down with your secular job. I know many people who work long, hard hours in their business and then have little energy left to serve the Lord in the evenings or on weekends. Everyone needs time for himself. But too many people are overworking for money and underworking for the Lord. Lay up treasure in heaven by giving yourself to building people in Christ.

Your turn

These ideas have worked for me in a small church with fewer than 100 people, in an office of just three employees where I did almost everything for myself and in a large denominational office which doesn't even let me lick envelopes. I trust these ideas encourage you to make the most of your minutes.

As I look at churches, youth groups and people all around me, I am overwhelmed at times by the magnitude of the task before us in serving Christ. There is so much to do. Let us work and work hard. Let us spend time generously for the cause of Christ.

More Time Tips

• Force yourself to make decisions. Don't just stare at a blank sheet of paper. Set a deadline for a decision, if more thinking is needed.
• Learn to say "no" to others and to yourself. Don't get involved in activities you don't have time to do.
• Look for outdated or unneeded procedures.
• Use your time twice. Listen to tapes while doing mechanical work. Look for work that can be done if there are dead times in large meetings.
• Plan your activities during the evening hours.

• Be sensitive to how much time you spend talking with your friends. It's easy to waste valuable time discussing unimportant things.
• Allow from one to three hours of uninterrupted time for think work (preparing lessons, talks, etc.).
• Don't be afraid to take breaks if you need them.
• Schedule tough jobs for when you are most likely to be in the right frame of mind and have the energy to do them.
• Watch your eating habits. A huge lunch can really slow you down. As you work,

you need your blood to be working for you in your head, not in your stomach.
• Set specific objectives for all your meetings. Then work toward them. Be leary of the statement, "Since we are here, we probably ought to discuss. . ."
• Use a phone call when it would take several letters back and forth to communicate the same thing.

Adapted from **Managing Yourself**, by Stephen Douglass © 1978 by Here's Life Publishers, Inc. Used with permission.

Using the Summers Wisely for Youth Ministry

by Gary Richardson

While many youth leaders see summer as the official youth group hibernation season, other leaders are seeing summer as a prime time to joggle their ministries and increase their number.

Take Hope Church in St. Louis, for example. Don Miller, the church's youth minister says, "We bring in 11 or 12 summer interns, people who've been in college and are interested in spending their summer in ministry-type work. We ask them to help with both junior and senior high ministries by working in summer camps, running group meetings, helping set up the fall program—but mainly just being with the kids."

Don's group takes advantage of kids' erratic schedules by emphasizing activities in small groups. He also moves more of the activities away from the church and into the kids' homes. "We keep our regular Sunday school program, but we emphasize our 'Wednesday Night Live' program more. While these meetings aren't as intense spritually, we work on building close r⁰lationships and getting to know each other better."

Like Hope Church's group, the key word at Dubuque (Iowa) Church of the Nazarene is *flexibility*. "We get several new people in our group through the summer months," says Burnie Burnside.

"We hold most of our activities when the kids are free, usually in the mornings. Different small groups have morning tennis matches, small group swimming, camping, canoeing—special things." These "special things" also have special benefits: "Our kids pretty much plan the activities and follow through with them."

Additionally, the entire youth group plans one or two big events—mission trips to nearby states and recreational trips to Chicago.

Different strokes

There are probably as many types of summer ministries as there are churches. Some churches continue their regular youth programming, but expect fewer young people to be involved. Other churches continue their regular programming, but offer exciting sounding alternatives: weeklong bike trips, family camps, rafting trips, sandlot baseball games, Bible camps and so on. Still other churches cancel their regular programming and go with a relaxed and informal activity schedule. A surprising number of churches cancel everything, give their kids a summer break and try to start all over again in the fall.

"We certainly don't cash in our youth group during the summer months," says Bruce Lawson, youth minister at First Covenant Church, in St. Paul, MN. "Summer is the climax for much of our year's work— we plan all year for our summer mission projects."

Bruce's church often cancels Sunday school and Wednesday night youth meetings for the summer. "We are more relaxed during the summer," he adds. "We plan lots of different activities that are aimed at establishing solid relationships."

Perry Downs, youth ministry instructor at Trinity Evangelical Divinity School in Deerfield, Illinois, suggests a multilevel approach to summer ministry:

• Keep your regular program functioning for those who need the security of a consistent ministry.

• Add additional creative events, studies and activities for those who have more time and are available.

• During the fall and winter months, plan for an organized program for those who want to spend part of their summer in an in-depth ministry. The summertime is about the only time young Christians can get a taste of in-depth Christian service.

• Practice creative hanging around. That is, plan to be with your young people, even when there's nothing formally planned. Just "being there" to hang around with is an especially positive experience for younger kids, those who don't work and are bored with the unstructured summer hours.

More thoughts

1. Unless many of your group members work early shifts, you can plan longer and later activities, ones that begin around 7 p.m. and run to 10:30 or 11 p.m. The extra time allows all sorts of flexibility for activities and program ideas.

2. Use the summer months for leadership training labs for volunteer leaders and for interested young people in your group.

3. Plan one or two creative and "different" retreats.

4. Spend quality, in-depth time with young people when nothing special is planned.

5. Provide alternatives and experiences that are new to your young people.

6. Adjust your group's activities to the pattern of your church and community.

7. Maybe some of your group members need an activity break. Allow them to take a vacation from the group for a while. But never go without having activities and studies for your people to tie into if they wish.

8. Think flexible!

9. Think small groups!

10. Plan activities with other youth groups in your area.

11. Travel.

12. Use recreational and creative activities to get kids who have free time to visit your group.

13. Summer is a great time to move your style of ministry closer to the style Jesus used. Spend quality time with a few young people. Develop them to be leaders.

Summer doesn't mean your ministry has to sweat it out. Be flexible, think creatively and go where the kids are. Your group will benefit from it.

BURN-OUT:

Preventing and Dealing with a Common Malady

by John Shaw

If you are a typical youth worker, you are a prime candidate for burn-out. In fact, you're probably suffering right now from symptoms associated with burn-out's early stages.

Youth ministry takes energy, imagination and motivation. And few, if any, people in the church are willing to give as much time as the youth need. So you, and maybe a few others, try to carry the entire load. But the expanding needs of a growing group and the beautiful potential of blossoming young Christians force you into doing more and more. Before you know it, your energy, imagination and motivation levels are in disastrously short supply.

What is burn-out?

Burn-out is a deep-seated feeling that makes us believe that vital strengths and energies can't be replenished. People experiencing burn-out have a vague sense of being trapped. They feel drained emotionally, mentally, physically and spiritually, with nothing to show for their efforts. Personal rewards and satisfaction from work are dwarfed by the mountain of energy needed to get the job done.

Burn-out symptoms

The signs of burn-out become clearer as they multiply. The more signs that are present and the stronger they are, the closer you are to becoming a cinder of your former self.

Some of the most common signs of burn-out include:

• Procrastination. Standard operating procedure becomes, "Put it off till tomorrow." Soon, everything needs to be done at the last minute. Planning ahead gives way to crisis management.

• Grouchitis. You become a grouch at home. Your family, spouse or close friends become sparring partners. You notice that you are slowly becoming a tense and irritable monster.

• Mind fatigue. You daydream too much, wake up tired in the mornings, feel listless, forget meetings and take important responsibilities lightly.

• A loss of vitality, energy and keen interest in what you are doing.

• Disillusionment. A feeling that what you are doing has lost its purpose or meaning.

• Loss of motivation—can't get started or excited about anything.

• A feeling that others don't appreciate what you are doing.

• A feeling that no one cares about you and your feelings.

• An intolerance for mistakes, problems or surprises.

• Loss of empathy, sensitivity, capacity to go the second mile.

• Inability to renew personal strengths.

The causes of burn-out are as varied as the types of people who are active in youth ministry. But most of the different factors fit into one of two broad areas: job-related stress and personal stress.

Job-related stress

Jobs that have unlimited or increasing demands create a potential burn-out situation. Failure to set limits on job demands opens the fiery doors of burn-out. (Isn't it interesting that pictures of hell as a blazing furnace reflect the image of burn-out?)

Unrealistic expectations of job performance also do their bit for burn-out. Pushing yourself to meet unreasonable expectations betrays a tendency toward trying to be god. A feverish effort to do perfect work reflects a resentment that only God is perfect. If you can't risk the possibility of mistakes, you risk losing sight of the person who can lend a helping hand when things go wrong.

Many work-related forms of stress grow out of the mistaken idea that self-value is a by-product of productivity or success. Even though there is value in effective work, self-value is a gift from God that we can't create on our own. Good works grow from that gift. But doing great things will never create the gift of self-value.

Many youth workers also suffer burn-out on the job because they expect instant success in their ministries. But most youth ministry "successes" take years to appear. Kids in the youth group won't usually recognize their youth worker's value until years later. In the meantime, many youth workers burn themselves out by skipping the planting, watering and growing stages and forcing a quick harvest (or else move on to where the soil and the seeds look better).

223

BURNOUT CONT.

Personal stress producers

Choices about how you manage yourself also add up to potential no-win situations. A person who always accepts requests to speak or help a good cause is dangling from a thin rope. Failure to limit responsibilities unravels another strand in the lifeline. Without a clear understanding of yourself, it's easy to go beyond personal limits. This lack of self-understanding prevents you from accepting yourself as you really are—a finite creature who can't save the world alone.

Another sure-fire burn-out situation comes disguised as busyness. The rush of activities insulates you from people. Others around you see you as a hard worker who's too busy to listen carefully and completely to anyone else. Isolation slowly shrinks your spirit as you totter alone on the brink of burn-out.

A burn-out inventory

Now you know a little about burn-out and what produces it. But how do you know if you're in real danger? Taking a careful look at yourself—your choices and patterns in life—can help you detect various burn-out symptoms. Use the inventory (bottom-right) as a window looking into yourself. Identify how you feel as you answer the questions. Pray for insight into yourself.

What to do

A first step in combatting burn-out is to set priorities and limits in your work situation. Then stick to your decisions. Having your priorities in writing will help you see if you have been respecting your priorities and limitations. It's easier to make small adjustments than it is to change a full-blown habit.

Provide time and money for relaxation. Develop ways to create a change of pace in your work schedule. Plan various responsibilities so you will have a variety of things to do each day. For instance, plan your phone calling for a portion of each day, rather than doing all your calling on one day of the week.

Make a clear transition from your job to your home life. Devise "bridge" players that let your mind and spirit know you are fully at home. You could take a shower, go jogging, spend 20 minutes in complete quiet, listen to music, hold hands with your honey. Do the same thing every day so you can condition your mind and body to believe that you have quit work for the day.

Develop some ways to replenish your energy level. Do anything that will help you feel that your unique needs are being met. You could create a support system of friends, or find a place to do some uninterrupted planning or meditation. Try some type of activity that allows you to "let go" and do something totally unserious.

Use your imagination. You are the best expert on what you need to do to renew yourself. You may need simply to tell yourself that you did a fantastic job for that day after looking back over what you have done. God used that approach when he started the work of creation. Regularly, he would look over what he had done and tell himself that it was good (Genesis 1:1-31).

Remind yourself that God is working too—you don't have to do it all. Allow God to be himself with you: forgiving, patient, accepting of your limitation, helping you renew your strength. Let God help you see your place in his plan. Spend some time each day in quiet prayer, tuning in to God's viewpoint of your life. If you can see yourself from his perspective, you won't need to burn yourself out trying to prove your own value.

Convince yourself that God expects you to spend at least one-seventh of your time resting and renewing yourself. God rested one day out of seven. Are you any stronger than God?

Love yourself as much as you love others. Then you will take better care of yourself as you work and live in Christ's spirit.

Am I working at a job that I enjoy and want to continue?
- ☐ How do I feel about my role in the job?
- ☐ How do I feel about my activities and responsibilities?
- ☐ How you I feel about the people who have an impact on my responsibilities?

Am I sure God wants me to do what I'm doing?
- ☐ What is God's purpose for me in this job?
- ☐ How did I decide to take up this work?
- ☐ Did I pray carefully to discover God's will?
- ☐ Did I react to pressure from others?
- ☐ Did I consider my own needs, likes and dislikes?

Does my present responsibility fit into my long-range vocational plan?
- ☐ Do I see my present activities as a meaningful ministry?
- ☐ Do I feel that my activities are temporary and are preparing me for a larger ministry?

Have I ever felt excited and fully committed to my work?
- ☐ When have I felt best about my work? At the beginning? Recently? At certain times of the year?

- ☐ Have my feelings been negative at any certain times? When? Why?
- ☐ Will I feel more excited and committed next year than this year? Why or why not?

Do my friends and family fully appreciate what I am doing?
- ☐ Do they support my efforts?
- ☐ Do they praise my achievements?
- ☐ Do they accept the problems and tensions associated with my job?
- ☐ Do they believe I am doing valuable work?

Does my work allow for growing relationships with family and friends?
- ☐ How much time do I feel is essential for meaningful relationship with family and friends?
- ☐ Does my job allow me to choose to be with family and friends?
- ☐ Am I spending enough meaningful time with family and friends?

Can I give and take with others on a feeling level?
- ☐ Is there anything about my lifestyle that prevents my feelings with others?
- ☐ Do I spend as much time as I need sharing thoughts and feelings with my friends?